GREAT
Cakes & Pastries

GREAT

Cakes &

Pastries

Christian Teubner

Jacques Charrette

Hannelore Blohm

HAMLYN

This edition published in 1989 by the Hamlyn Publishing Group Limited,
a division of the Octopus Publishing Group,
Michelin House, 81 Fulham Road, London SW3 6RB

ISBN 0 600 32428 1

Set in $9\frac{1}{2}$ on $10\frac{1}{2}$ pt Monophoto Times
by Tameside Filmsetting Limited, Lancashire

Produced by Mandarin Offset.
Printed and bound in Hong Kong.

Contents

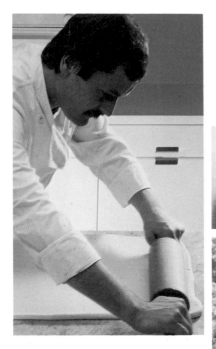

Foreword

Great Cakes and Pastries is the latest volume in a splendid series of which the first two – *Great Desserts* and *Pâtés and Terrines* – are currently available. This book is the ideal manual for both the amateur home cook and the professional. The first chapter describes the major ingredients used in patisserie, briefly covering their history and useful facts about their use in baking. The next section is devoted to the basic recipes which are the foundations upon which everything else is structured. Each basic method is illustrated by clear step-by-step photographs and numbered instructions. Sponges, meringues, shortcrust, puff and choux pastry as well as yeast dough are all covered. Their accompaniments in the form of creams, custards, butter creams and icings are all described in mouthwatering detail. There is also a section on chocolate and its use in decorating gâteaux as well as a piece on cake decorations that can be bought ready-made.

'Cakes and Company' encompasses plain cakes of the loaf or cylindrical type and also a small section on British traditional cooking. Baking with fruit of all kinds – either in a pie, tart, small tartlet or on a baking sheet – shows how they can be used to provide delectable desserts using whatever fruit is in season at the time.

The chapter on cheesecakes also has recipes which use yogurt as a

delicious alternative to the slightly heavier curd or cream cheese that is used elsewhere. 'Baking with Yeast' and 'Baking for the Morning' contain a large selection of sweet bread, brioche, croissant and Danish pastry recipes. Also included is the well-known Gugelhupf cake – originally a German favourite whose popularity has spread throughout the world.

Large cakes and gâteaux from several European countries, among them the famous Sachertorte, the Black Forest Gâteau, Dobostorte, Millefeuille and many more, are next in line. For morning coffee or afternoon tea the 'Small Cakes' chapter is particularly appropriate as quantities can be adapted to fit the occasion. A selection of two or three kinds of small cakes, cream slices or Swiss rolls would form the focal point of any gathering.

The recipes in the final chapter are specifically designed for the time around Christmas, Easter and other traditional festive celebrations. These recipes are gathered together from all over Europe: from as far afield as Russia through Italy, Germany, France and thus to Britain.

The book ends with a useful glossary, an illustrated description of how to divide a large cake into a number of portions and finally a helpful guide to equipment and utensils.

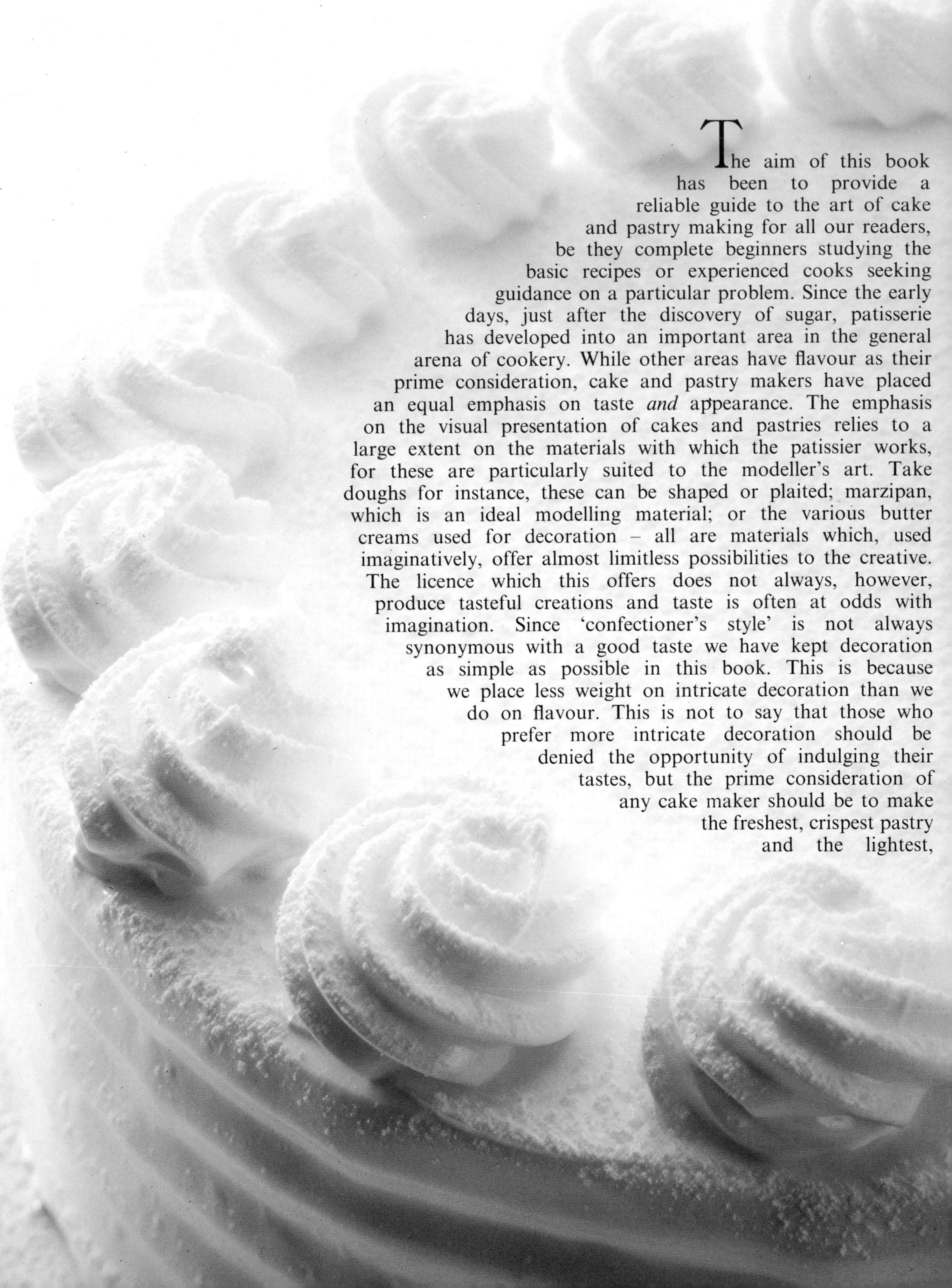

The aim of this book has been to provide a reliable guide to the art of cake and pastry making for all our readers, be they complete beginners studying the basic recipes or experienced cooks seeking guidance on a particular problem. Since the early days, just after the discovery of sugar, patisserie has developed into an important area in the general arena of cookery. While other areas have flavour as their prime consideration, cake and pastry makers have placed an equal emphasis on taste *and* appearance. The emphasis on the visual presentation of cakes and pastries relies to a large extent on the materials with which the patissier works, for these are particularly suited to the modeller's art. Take doughs for instance, these can be shaped or plaited; marzipan, which is an ideal modelling material; or the various butter creams used for decoration – all are materials which, used imaginatively, offer almost limitless possibilities to the creative. The licence which this offers does not always, however, produce tasteful creations and taste is often at odds with imagination. Since 'confectioner's style' is not always synonymous with a good taste we have kept decoration as simple as possible in this book. This is because we place less weight on intricate decoration than we do on flavour. This is not to say that those who prefer more intricate decoration should be denied the opportunity of indulging their tastes, but the prime consideration of any cake maker should be to make the freshest, crispest pastry and the lightest,

most delicious fillings.
  As in the previous books
in this series – *Great Desserts*
and *Pâtés and Terrines* – we have
tried to follow the basic guidelines of
providing reliable and relevant technical
information, and in this we have been helped
by a number of international experts. Once again
we have used the basic recipes as a starting point
and these have been presented as clearly as possible
in a series of photographs. Building on these basic recipes,
it is a short step to successfully making much more complicated
cakes or even producing one's own original creations.

We wish you every success.

Christian Teubner · Jacques Charrette

Nothing But The Best

Cake and pastry making has been raised to the level of a sophisticated art in many countries, especially in Europe with its history of making use of dairy produce. To obtain the best results you must use the very best ingredients.

Over the last two hundred years the area of baking and patisserie has made great advances, seen principally in efforts to better quality by improving the rather coarse and primitive ingredients of the past. Better methods of milling, for instance, allowed millers to provide finer flour. This alone improved the results of both professional bakers and housewives. In addition advances in world trade provided the confectioner with the finest ingredients from all parts of the world. But difficulties still remained with regard to quality and those who wanted first-class products required more than a little experience. One egg could be very different from another, milk had no standardised fat content and in dealing with millers you not only needed to know something about flour, you also had to be able to trust the miller.

Changes wrought by the industrial revolution were not confined to iron or textile production. Agricultural producers were not slow to take advantage of new methods in marketing their products. Acceptance of the new industrially produced goods was a gradual process, with the self-sufficient country areas clinging longest to old traditions. But it was only a matter of time before the standardised food products captured the market, rationalising the job of the professional cook and making life much easier for the housewife who now had such products as baking powder at her disposal. There is no doubt that in recent years the food industry has developed high quality products, but care is still needed when shopping. It is up to the individual to decide which semi-manufactured products can be used without affecting quality or which may even improve quality.

Baking is no different from any other area of cooking, and as in other sectors only the best and freshest products can guarantee good results. This does not mean, however, that in cake and pastry making one has to ignore the aids offered by the food industry as a matter of course. Take marzipan, nougat or fondant icing. These are examples of manufactured products which not only make the job considerably easier, but where it is often difficult to achieve the same quality in the kitchen. So it is a matter of knowing how to successfully combine natural products and modern time-saving aids. If a sound knowledge of methods is combined with this then success is ensured.

Flour – the basis of baking

Dictionaries define flour as 'a foodstuff obtained by grinding grain cereals'. Any type of grain, wheat, rye, barley, rice or maize, can be milled to produce flour. Different grades of milling produce either coarse or superfine flour. For cakes and pastries we are mainly interested in wheat flour, with rye flour being used for a few specialised recipes such as gingerbread.

The role of wheat as the main foodstuff of the world is not confined to the present day. It has been closely linked with the history of mankind since the earliest times when man the hunter began to form settlements and to take up agriculture. The various methods of grinding grain into flour had their origins in these early days and have gradually evolved to produce the very latest techniques of flour production.

To understand flour properly you must know something about wheat grain and its internal structure. A cross-section through the grain shows the large kernel (endosperm) in the centre, then the honey-comb aleuron layer which is rich in minerals and lies just below the skin of the grain. The grain itself is enclosed by a fibrous layer known as bran. At the bottom of the grain is found the germ-bud which is rich in vitamins and fat. All the goodness in the grain, its protein, vitamins, phosphorus and minerals are found within the endosperm.

How is wheat flour produced from grain? In answering this question we will attempt to avoid becoming bogged down in technicalities and stick to a simplified explanation of the process used today. The grain is first cleaned and then crushed by rollers. In the milling of wheat there is considerable slack between the rollers for if the grain was crushed too finely much of the goodness in the outer layer would be lost. The grinding process which follows is known as 'groats' or 'wheat' milling, a technique which is marked by the distance separating the rollers which, as we have said, ensures the careful crushing of the grain, followed by a gradual process of grinding in several stages. The grain is first coarsely ground into groats and then the groats are ground into flour.

In order to keep the properties of the flour constant, and to achieve uniform quality, various types of wheat are combined for grinding. There are two basic kinds of wheat: hard and soft. Hard wheat when milled produces a strong flour that is mainly used for bread and doughs; soft-grained or weak wheat is suitable for cakes and general use. Wholewheat or wholemeal flour is made from the entire grain of wheat and bread made with this flour is quite dense, with a nutty taste. Wheatmeal flour contains between 80 and 90 per cent of the wheat with some of the bran and germ having been removed.

Strong plain white flour is usually a blend of soft and hard wheats. Unbleached plain flour has a better flavour than the bleached variety which has been whitened artificially. Plain flour is the refined and bleached product of soft wheat. It has a light, short texture in baking because soft wheat flours contain only a small amount of gluten. It is particularly good for cakes and shortcrust pastry.

These different types of flour are to be found in any shop. If more specialised flours, such as potato flour, were needed you could try buying from a health-food shop or delicatessen which should offer a wide range of high quality flours. This book however only requires the usual types of flour that are generally sold.

The gluten in wheatflour

Gluten is a sticky, rubber-like substance which is present to a larger or lesser degree in all types of flour. As previously mentioned, flours made from hard wheat produce the largest amount of gluten. Fine plain flour has the lowest gluten content.

The proteins that make up gluten are found in varying quantities in different types of wheat. In warm, dry climates the gluten content is increased and also it is higher in hard or strong wheats. In yeast dough, for instance, the gluten content of the flour is important. Since gluten can absorb water it binds the liquid in the pastry and gives it its elastic quality. In baking the liquids bound by the gluten evaporate into steam allowing the air in the pastry to expand. At around 70 c / 160 f, the gluten coagulates and combines with the starches in the flour to give pastry its crumbly texture. The pastry or cake mixture has risen and become firm and will not now fall.

A further factor determining the quality of flour is its feel. It is a sign of quality if you can feel the 'graininess' of the flour between your fingers for this shows that the flour is rich in gluten and that it has been properly milled. With modern grinding methods all flours should be of high quality in this respect, but you can also recognise quality flour by its colour – a bright creamy-white. Flour is sensitive to smells and will pick up other odours so it should be stored in a dry, ventilated cupboard. When flour is stored too long the fat in the flour goes bad giving the flour a rancid taste and smell.

Cornflour and other edible starch

The gluten content of the flour, and the extent to which the gluten is developed during preparation, determines to a certain extent the finished texture of baked goods. For example in a yeast dough a strong flour with a high gluten content is used and the gluten is developed during the kneading stages. This gives a tough dough lightened by the yeast working to produce gas which is then trapped within the mixture.

For sponges and light cakes a low-gluten flour is necessary for a more crumbly result. The addition of sugar, and the fact that the cake mixture must be handled lightly to prevent the gluten from toughening, goes to make a soft, crumbly mixture. To further reduce the effect of the gluten in wheat flour a proportion of cornflour or other starches can be introduced into the mixture.

Other edible starches which can be used for some cakes or light pastry doughs include rice flour, potato flour and arrowroot. The use of these ingredients is not particularly common in simple cakes, but they are required to give the fine texture expected of certain special sponges and pastries.

Yeast

Yeast consists of micro-organisms, tiny living creatures which centuries of research have revealed as a type of fungus. Under the right conditions the fungus cells increase by division and it is this process which makes yeast a useful ingredient in baking.

The conditions which yeast needs consist of air, moisture, warmth and nourishment (in the form of sugar for instance) and the fungus cells find everything they require in dough. In these conditions the cells divide very quickly, changing the sugar into alcohol and carbon dioxide. This in combination with the gluten in the flour causes fermentation. This produces many tiny, gas-filled bubbles in the dough which increase the volume of the dough considerably. To prevent the dough 'asphyxiating' air must be beaten into it. The more oxygen you can incorporate into the mixture the lighter the finished product will be.

Fresh yeast has a pleasant, rather sour smell and taste, is pale beige in colour and should be crumbly and not greasy. It should be stored in the refrigerator where it will keep for a couple of weeks or it can be frozen for several months. Dried yeast will keep for several months if stored in a cool, dry place. Half the quantity of dried yeast should be used to that of fresh as it is more concentrated.

Yeast is by no means a modern raising agent. It was used in baking as long ago as the sixteenth century. The bakers of Nuremburg are said to have discovered its effects by using the yeast provided by the town's brewers. It was the French chemist and biologist Louis Pasteur (1822–92) who discovered that yeast consisted of micro-organisms, but it was the Nobel Prize winner for chemistry, Eduard Buchner (1860–1917) who first separated yeast into its component parts and isolated the enzyme zymase which causes fermentation.

Besides yeast, which is a biological lightening and raising agent, there are also chemical raising agents.

Baking powder, carbonate of ammonia and potash

Baking powder is a mixture of sodium carbonate, cream of tartar (or tartaric acid) and a separator, usually rice or potato starch. Under the combined effect of air, moisture and warmth carbon dioxide is produced which again causes fermentation. It is the function of the separator to prevent the two other ingredients working prematurely – it therefore acts as a kind of insulator. It also absorbs moisture in the air when the baking powder is not in use. The inclusion of either cream of tartar or tartaric acid gives either fast or slower raising.

When baking in large quantities, in a patisserie for example, a raising agent known as ABC (ammonium bicarbonate) is often used. This works in the same way as baking powder. A much more traditional raising agent is carbonate of ammonia. This is a white salt which used to be obtained from horns and hooves (hence its alternative name, hartshorn). It is a mixture of substances formed by ammonia and carbonic acid. It decomposes in the air and must be stored in a tightly sealed tin, but it is soluble in water with no decomposition and is usually added to a cake mixture in dilute form. It acts in the same way as the above raising agents. With deep cakes some ammonia may remain at the end of the baking process and this gives a highly unpleasant taste. This is the reason why carbonate of ammonia is usually recommended only for thin spicy cakes (gingerbread). Potash (potassium carbonate) is another long-established raising agent. This white powder has no smell, but tastes rather caustic and is again recommended only for thin cakes.

Milk

The land of milk and honey . . . this phrase tells us much of the importance of milk which forms the basis of a range of dairy products such as cream, curds, yogurt and butter. Milk has always existed, and it became important to mankind from the time when he first learnt to milk a nursing animal, be it a cow, goat, sheep, ass, camel, horse or buffalo. We know that in Babylon, the rich land between the Euphrates and the Tigris, milk was used for human consumption five thousand years before the birth of Christ. Excavations in the Babylonian city of Ur produced clay tablets which record the raising of milk cattle in 3,000 BC. Relief sculptures depict the separate stages in the treatment of milk. Other races too – Egyptians, Greeks, Romans, Germans and the nomadic horsemen of central Asia – were all heavily involved in milk production and the production of dairy products. Curds flavoured with honey or herbs was a delicacy of the German tribes and the forefathers of Genghis Khan made kefir (a soured milk) and dried milk. For the latter the cream was skimmed off and dried in flat bowls in the sun: it was as simple as that in those days.

Modern dairy science is the result of technical developments over many centuries but most particularly in the nineteenth century. As early as 812 the Emperor Charlemagne gave his court precise instructions on milk, butter and cheese production. In 1679 the Dutchman Leeuwenhoek, who also discovered the microscope, identified the fat globules in milk. The invention of the steam engine and the subsequent development of railways was of considerable importance to the dairy industry as milk could be transported quickly and efficiently from the country to the city. The introduction of condensed milk took place in 1849, 1853 brought the invention of condensed milk by evaporation at low temperatures and in 1859 the protein content of milk was discovered.

Milk of constant quality

Progress in food technology, the desire for the most constant quality possible and the need for health control resulted in stringent regulations for the production of milk for the general public. Anyone who has ever drunk a glass of milk direct from the farm will have found that it is different from treated milk. In the case of milk this has little adverse effect in cake-making where it has to be heated anyway, but in the case of cream which is normally used fresh as a filling or accompaniment to cakes, modern production methods have brought a considerable diminution of flavour.

A nutritious product

Cow's milk – the only type of milk that need concern us in baking – consists of 87 per cent water. The remaining 13 per cent consists of highly nutritious substances such as fat, milk sugar (lactose), casein, globulin, albumen (which coagulates to form a skin when milk is boiled), a number of important minerals and vitamins as well as enzymes and hormones. Thus milk contains all the main substances which the human body requires combined with a high nutritious value.

It is milk fat which gives milk its creamy colour. It consists of tiny globules each enclosed by a skin of protein which are dispersed in the liquid. Milk sugar gives milk its sweet taste and when bacteria are present produces lactic acid. This in turn combines with the calcium in the milk which was previously combined with protein. The protein is thus freed and rises to the top and the milk becomes thick and sour. Proteins in milk which are important to the human organism can be roughly divided into casein, globulin and albumen. Of all the minerals and trace elements found in milk calcium and phosphorus are the most important to man, however its potassium, sodium, magnesium, iron and iodine are also needed by the human body. Milk is particularly rich in vitamins and its high content of the vitamins C, B_2, B_6, B_{12} is extremely important to growth.

Cow's milk, as it comes from the farm, is tested in the dairy for purity, quality and presence of antibiotics or other chemical impurities. When it has passed these tests it is cooled to 4 C/39 F, before being separated by centrifuges into skimmed milk and cream. Depending on whether the end product is to be full-fat, low-fat or skimmed milk, the correct amount of fat is then replaced. The milk is then pasteurised in a process, invented by and named after Louis Pasteur, for heating the milk sufficiently to kill off potentially dangerous bacilli but not so much as to destroy its nutritious qualities. Some milk is also homogenised, a process which makes the tiny fat globules even smaller so that they do not rise to the top when the milk is left to stand – i.e. no cream forms on the top of the milk. This milk is no lower in fat content, the fat is merely more finely distributed. Alongside methods of making milk keep better (sterilisation for example), various methods of milk conservation have been developed. This has produced the familiar condensed milk, both sweetened and unsweetened, as well as low-fat condensed milk. As the name indicates this type of milk has been condensed to make it thicker.

Another type of condensed milk is obtained by evaporation; this is dried milk. Here again various fat contents are available in the form of dried full-fat milk, dried cream or dried skimmed milk. If you have to use dried milk in baking it should be mixed dry with the flour or diluted and used in the normal way, it is better to use fresh milk if possible. Fresh milk soon goes off and must be stored in a cool place, preferably a refrigerator.

Cream – something special

The very word 'cream' has a special festive sound. It has always been used for entertaining, as a special treat at such times as birthdays, when cakes or desserts would be topped with whipped cream and even today cream has lost none of its specialness. Anything made with cream or served with whipped cream has added goodness and flavour. Cream makes anything special. Rich Egyptians even took cream with them on their travels and the Greeks prized it highly. To come back to modern times, as we have said in the section on milk, the separation of the milk in a centrifuge produces large quantities of cream, for untreated milk usually contains more fat than is put back into the skimmed milk. Cream is thus the 'skimmed' milk fat. Regretably real 'fresh cream' (untreated) is no longer generally available and its excellent flavour remains only a memory.

Pasteurisation unfortunately does take away the natural fresh taste of the cream and sacrifices flavour in favour of a purer product which will keep better. Creams vary in thickness and richness and there are laws governing the minimum butterfat content of creams: single cream 18 per cent, whipping cream 35 per cent, soured cream (soured with lactic acid) again 35 per cent and double cream 55 per cent. The higher the butterfat content the less likely cream is to fall and only whipping or double cream will whip successfully. Whipped in a chilled bowl and preferably in a cool room, cream should be of the right consistency and double or triple in volume after whipping. Take care not to overwhip or the cream will become granular in appearance and this cannot be rectified once it has occurred. As with milk, cream needs to be stored in a cool place or in the refrigerator.

For and against butter

It is not necessary here to go into the arguments between the medical profession and the butter producers about the merits and otherwise of fat, but it is an incontrovertible fact that butter improves both the flavour and consistency of patisserie. Many housewives prefer to replace butter with other fats, not only for economic or health reasons, but also because, with improved ingredients and production techniques, they can now give similar or in some cases better results. They are usually easier to work with and keep longer. Every cook will have to make up his or her own mind whether to use butter exclusively or whether to turn to other fats where possible. The argument concerns not only butter and margarine but other traditional fats too, such as oil, lard and suet, each of which still has a place in some areas of cooking.

Butter has existed almost as long as the milk from which it is made. In the Bible Proverbs XXX, verse 33 reads 'for pressing milk produces butter'. In the Near East and Mediterranean it was long used as an ointment rather than a foodstuff, for with their olives and other oil-producing fruit the people of these regions had no shortage of fats. In cooler climes such as Europe, and Scandinavia in particular, butter was used much earlier as an edible fat. Butter was used as a food in western Europe around AD 600. In the Middle Ages butter was prohibited on fast days because it was considered a luxury. Butter has the longest list of ingredients of all fats: it contains all the fatty acids which the body needs but cannot produce itself, together with proteins, minerals (particularly calcium and phosphorus), trace elements and vitamins A, D and E. Of all the fats butter is the most

nourishing and the most easily digestible: since its melting point is below body temperature butter fat is quickly absorbed by the body.

For centuries butter was made in a churn with either a rotating beater or a wooden disc on a handle which was pushed up and down. In this way cream was beaten and 'pressed' until the globules of cream fat come together to form butter and separated from the 'butter milk'. The ball of butter was then kneaded and shaped. Many of the old moulds are still around today and show the artistry with which the butter was presented. Today butter is still churned but in automatic, continuous machines.

Modern butter production guarantees absolutely constant quality. Today the various types of butter are produced by a process of pasteurisation and are differentiated by the amount of salt added. Lightly salted butter is often ideal for shortcrust or yeast pastry which, in fruit flans for example, can take a little salt. A variation on butter which keeps well is butter fat. You can make it yourself by 'rendering the butter down'. The butter is melted so that the water it contains is evaporated off and any bacteria are killed by heating, but the process also lowers the butter's protein, lactose and salt content. Stored in a cool place in earthenware containers butter fat will keep for up to a year. Butter itself is extremely susceptible to heat, light and smell and is best stored in an airtight container in a cool, dark place.

Butter makes light pastry and much more besides, but other fats are just as necessary in baking. After butter comes margarine which is available in three types. Block margarine is firmer and more elastic than butter and withstands kneading and beating better. It is excellent for shortcrust and flan pastry, for it gives a less crumbly pastry that keeps better. Creamed margarine is excellent for making custards and cream desserts for it whips well, has no taste of its own and has good binding qualities. It whips easily with eggs, sugar or *crème patissière*. Spreading margarine should be elastic but of spreading texture. These qualities, which are especially desirable for puff pastry or croissant dough, are also present in suet or suet-like fats. Although these fats are easier to use than butter they cannot give the delicate butter flavour we associate with, for example, puff pastry (and this becomes more noticeable if the pastry is not completely fresh). A large number of vegetable fats and oils have their uses in pastry-making. They are particularly useful for deep-frying cakes like doughnuts, for they can reach relatively high temperatures without burning. Lard is excellent for deep-frying too. High quality lard can also be used in shortcrust pastry to make fruit flan cases.

Eggs

For thousands of years the egg has been a fertility symbol, the source of life, in every culture imaginable. In the myths of India or Ancient Egypt, in the religious ceremonies of Central America or Europe, people regarded the egg as a sign of fertility, of renewed life for nature and for themselves. And these associations have some truth in them for the egg provides one of the best possible sources of nourishment. An egg contains everything the body needs: protein, fat, carbohydrate, vitamins, minerals and trace elements. The best in terms of nourishment and digestibility is the hen's egg, and it is this type alone which is discussed in this book. Eggs are an indispensable part of cake-making. They are fundamentally very simple things with few component parts: shell, white and yolk, but the essential differences between the yolk and the white and the ease with which they can be separated are important factors in their uses in the kitchen.

An average egg weighs around 50 g / 2 oz. The energy value of an average egg is between 75 and 90 calories. Egg white whisks easily and makes cakes lighter. During baking it solidifies to lock in the air. The effect of heat also produces several proteins. Egg yolk can be used as a glaze to improve the look of your baking. Because of its high lezithin content egg yolk emulsifies well, especially in mixtures rich in fat or sugar, in cream desserts and, naturally, ice cream. Adding egg yolks to cakes not only provides extra nourishment but also improves the texture, flavour and colour.

Because of their high nutritional value and moisture content eggs will not keep long. For a long time attempts have been made to conserve eggs. At one time they were stored in a chalk and water solution, and lasted through the winter. Alternatively they were coated with wax and stored in a cool place. Today eggs can be kept for relatively short periods in cold stores. For longer periods there are two main methods of conserving eggs: by removing liquid to make dried eggs, or by freezing. Today when the supply of fresh eggs is guaranteed all year round and when there are no seasonal price fluctuations the need for these conserved products should be extremely rare. Occasionally it may make sense economically to use frozen egg white where large quantities are involved, for meringues for instance. Thaw frozen egg or egg white slowly (preferably under cold running water) and use them immediately. Since 1 July 1969 eggs have been standardised throughout the EEC and are differentiated by quality and weight. The colour of the shell, brown or white, is quite irrelevant and has nothing to do with quality or taste. The eggs are assessed for size from 1 to 7 and graded A, B or C for quality according to strength and shape of shell and size of air cavity. The air cavity increases in size as the egg becomes older so it is one way of telling how fresh an egg is. In a fresh egg the white consists of a thicker layer around the yolk and a slightly more runny part. If the egg white is completely runny it is a sign that the egg has been stored too long. The white should also be free from all impurities as should the yolk be free from flecks or impurities, but the colour, pale or dark yellow, is not a sign of quality nor of the nutritional value of the yolk. Fresh eggs are first checked for external irregularities, illuminated to show up any internal impurities, and then weighed, sorted and packed. Only Class A are sold fresh in the shops. For best-quality home cooking – and this certainly includes cakes and pastries – only the best fresh eggs should be used. Size 3 eggs have been used for the recipes in this book.

Honey

Long before the birth of Christ honey was considered the food of the gods, especially amongst the Indo-germanic peoples. One of the earliest of man's artistic creations, a famous cave painting in Eastern Spain, shows a figure searching for honey, climbing up to a cleft in the rock face where the bees had made their honeycomb. From the same period there is also evidence of beekeeping in Ancient Egypt where clay pots were stacked to form the first bee-hives. We also know that later the Germanic tribes made a delicious drink, mead, from honey. In the Carolingian period, around the tenth century, the 'Lorscher Bees Blessing' – an exhortation to the bees to produce lots of honey in honour of the Virgin – was recorded in Old High German at a monastery in the Rhineland. As early as the time of Charlemagne, German emperor from AD 800 to 814, the Emperor himself kept fifty swarms of bees and ordered the peasants to increase stocks of plants and flowers whose nectar was specially attractive to bees. Monasteries were forced to employ bee-keepers since honey was used to sweeten foods and drinks and the wax was necessary for candles for both religious and secular purposes. Most medieval farms included a few beehives and honey remained the most widely used sweetener until well into the seventeenth century – for cane sugar was expensive and was available only for special occasions, even for the better-off families. Anton Tucher of Nuremburg who wrote a highly detailed book of household management between 1507 and 1517 revealed that he used very little cane sugar, but huge quantities of spices such as saffron, cloves, nutmeg, cinnamon, ginger, cardamom, almonds, and figs and honey. This book describes the great feastdays in Tucher's household and reveals that it was only at the great New Year festival that 'fine sugar' was used. For daily use honey was to remain the most common sweetener for a long time to come.

Honey is a sweet substance produced by bees as they take in nectar from flowers, transform it inside their bodies by enriching it with secretions, then emit it from their bodies into honeycombs where it is left to mature. Honey varies in smell, flavour, colour and texture according to where it is produced, so to some experts the range of honeys is boundless. First honey is differentiated by the type of plant from which it is produced so that there is clover, lime-tree, wood or heather honey, to name but a few, and then by its geographical source. The choice of which honey to use depends on the individual's own taste. Blended honey, as well as the more exotic varieties, is readily obtainable and is reliable and consistent.

Fresh honey is clear and fluid, but with time it becomes slightly grainy, cloudy and thick. This has nothing to do with quality, however. Honey can be returned to its liquid state by slowly warming over hot water (not higher than 50 C/122 F). Sunlight encourages crystalisation so honey should be stored in a well ventilated, dark cupboard.

Sugar – cane and beet

It is difficult for us to imagine a world without sugar, and yet until quite recently honey and sweet fruits were the only sweeteners available to the average man. Cane sugar is thought to have originated from New Guinea. Cane sugar was being cultivated thousands of years before the birth of Christ as Indian texts dating from 1400 BC reveal. From India the plant spread in every direction. Alexander the Great came across it in the Indus Valley in 327 BC and between AD 700 and 900 the Arabs brought cane sugar to the Mediterranean. Marco Polo also came across sugar cane in 1280 during one of his journeys to China. Later sugar cane, which really only grows well in a hot, damp climate, was taken by the Spanish and Portuguese to the West Indies and Central and Southern America, while the Dutch established plantations in Indonesia. Eventually sugar was imported to Europe but for centuries it remained a luxury item for royalty and rich merchants.

The great revolution in cooking and baking came with the discovery of sugar beet. In 1747 A. S. Marggraf, a chemist in Berlin, discovered that the sugar obtained from beet was chemically identical with cane sugar, and his findings were later taken up by his pupil, F. G. Achard in 1786. With financial help from King Friedrich Wilhelm III of Prussia the first sugar beet factory was set up in Cunern in Silesia in 1802. By 1830 the cost of beet sugar was similar to that of cane sugar. Today sugar beet is grown throughout the world wherever sugar cane will not grow, even in the sub-tropics. Today around 55 per cent of world sugar production consists of cane sugar and 45 per cent beet sugar.

Regardless of whether it comes from cane or beet, all sugar consists of 99 per cent water-soluble carbohydrates and 1 per cent water. The various types of sugar are divided into refined, white sugar and the less fully refined brown sugar. The main types of white sugar are granulated sugar – the most common type of sugar to be found in the kitchen; lump or cube sugar is granulated sugar pressed together and used for hot drinks; caster sugar is a finer form of granulated sugar; icing sugar is very finely powdered white sugar which is the fastest dissolving form of sugar; and finally preserving sugar which is used for making jams and jellies and has large, clear crystals.

Brown sugar can be subdivided into muscovado, molasses, and demerara. Many of the other brown sugars – often labelled light brown or soft dark brown – are actually fully refined white sugar tossed in syrup or molasses.

There is one other important type of sugar which is starch sugar, otherwise known as glucose syrup. This is obtained from potato or corn starch and is a highly concentrated, refined syrup with a high glucose content. It is much used by the food industry in sweets, liqueurs and jams. It is very elastic and binds excellently in marzipan or icings. This must not be confused with sugar syrup which is sugar boiled in water to various concentrations and which you make yourself.

Sugar is of course an important constituent of home baking and patisserie. Sugar as an ingredient makes cakes and pastries cook quicker; it browns, improves flavour and nutritional value and helps food keep longer. It can be used for decoration in various ways, sprinkled onto cakes in the form of sugar crystals or hundreds and thousands, or dusted on as icing sugar, or to cover cakes in the form of icing. But sugar has one more outstanding quality, it conserves and gives rise to a whole range of products, jams, marmalades, jellies, candied fruit and many more besides. Sugar is susceptible to damp and smells, so it must be stored in a dry place away from any contaminating odours.

There are also various types of syrup which can be used in baking. Golden syrup is a by-product of sugar refining. Molasses or dark treacle is the natural syrup drained from sugar cane. There also exist more basic syrups of which the most popular is maple syurp, which was used by the North American and Canadian Indians for hundreds of years. It is still used, today, especially in the English-speaking world. The trees are tapped between February and late March and the sap is made into syrup. Maple syrup is used in sweets such as candy and caramels and also in cream desserts and highly spiced cakes. It is also very popular in North America for serving with waffles at breakfast time, with pancakes and with ice cream.

Dried fruit

Since earliest times dried fruits have featured amongst winter provisions, particularly in temperate or cool climates where fresh fruit is available for only a relatively minor part of the year. Today, in the age of tinned and bottled fruit, freezers and year-round supplies of fresh fruit, dried fruit has rather a hard time of it, and wrongly so, for they contain vitamins and minerals in concentrated form as well as high levels of fructose. Ripe fruit is carefully sorted and cleaned before being slowly dried in the air or, principally in California and Australia, in drying cabinets. Before drying apples, pears, apricots and peaches are cut into slices, rings or halves. Plums, dates, figs and bananas are dried whole. Fruits, like apples and apricots, which quickly turn brown are dipped in sulphur dioxide, and must be labelled 'sulphurised'.

For baking purposes dried fruit is used as fillings and toppings for pies and cakes, and is particularly associated with the fruit loaves baked for Advent and Christmas. Before use dried fruit should be washed thoroughly and sulphurised fruit pre-boiled, and the water thrown away. Before stewing dried fruit it is usual to steep it overnight in water, as this brings out the flavour and makes the fruit swell.

We have not yet mentioned the main group of dried fruit: raisins, sultanas and currants. These grow best in Greece, Crete and Cyprus, in Iran, Turkey and Spain, and in large quantities in the favourable climate of California.

Raisins are quite large fruits which can have seeds but are more usually seedless with a beautiful purplish-black colour and are usually eaten uncooked. Vine raisins (with stems) come in several varieties, 'Muscatel' from Spain and California, 'Malagas' also from Spain, 'Eleme' raisins from Greece, and 'Rozaki' from Turkey. Raisins are also used for wine-making, producing the popular Hungarian dessert wines.

Sultanas are also quite large and are always seedless, being golden yellow to light brown in colour. They are the dried fruit of the extremely sweet, seedless 'Sultana' grape. The finest sultanas come from Turkey and used to be known as 'Smyrna raisins' as that was the part from which they were exported. Nowadays sultanas come from Greece, Crete, the Peloponnese and of course Australia.

Currants are small, black seedless fruits with a very tender skin. The small-berried grapes from which they are made have been grown in the Greek Peloponnese since earliest times. Their name is a derivation from the town of Corinth, a port and trading town even for the Ancient Greeks.

How are these different grapes treated and dried? First the grapes are left on the vine until over-ripe. Once picked they are left to dry in the open air (only a very small percentage is treated in drying cabinets). Drying takes from three to four weeks, during which time their water content is reduced to about 15 per cent while the starches in the grape turn into fructose which by the end of the process makes up around 70 per cent of the dried fruit. After drying the fruit is automatically sorted by size, destalked and washed.

Candied fruit

Everyone remembers grandmother's cooking with great pleasure. Candied orange and lemon peel and the bright colours provided by other candied fruit were a permanent feature of the cooking of our grandmothers' day.

Orange rind is not made from ordinary oranges but from Spanish bitter oranges commonly known as 'Seville' oranges. The Seville orange tree (botanical name *Citrus aurantium*) used to be grown in the Orangeries of noble houses. It has small, deep-orange fruit with thick skins, the type used to make orange marmalade. Oil from the rind is also used in the making of liqueurs. These oranges are grown principally in Spain, Sicily, southern France, South Africa and India.

Lemon rind comes from the mother of all citrus fruit, the lemon tree *Citrus medica*. This tree comes originally from the Far East, and is now grown in Greece, Corsica, Sicily, Brazil and California.

Candied orange and lemon peel are both made by the same process. The skins of unripe fruit are halved and steeped in brine until transparent. Then they are soaked to remove the salt and placed in a concentrated sugar solution. The concentration is increased every day over a two-week period until the rind can soak up no more sugar or until the sugar content reaches at least 65 per cent. If the peel is to be sold in whole pieces they are covered with a glaze of sugar, but there are also unglazed, chopped rinds available, which save the housewife a lot of time. If you buy peel in large pieces to chop yourself, however, the oils do not evaporate so quickly and the flavour and smell is better retained.

Nuts

It is difficult to imagine cakes and pastries without nuts in one form or another. We should remember that nuts are of great nutrional value and have formed part of man's basic diet for thousands of years.

Hazelnuts, botanical name *Corylus avellana*, are usually heart-shaped and medium-brown in colour. They are widespread throughout the whole northern temperate zone, although cultivation for commercial purposes is mainly restricted to the Mediterranean countries, Turkey, Italy and Spain. From Italy, with extensive growing areas in Campania, Sicily and Piedmont, we import mainly hazelnuts in shells. Spain supplies mostly shelled nuts. Spanish hazelnuts do not go bad as quickly as other varieties for they contain only 50 per cent fat (compared with 68 per cent in Turkish nuts). Nuts in their shells naturally keep much longer than shelled nuts.

Walnuts (*Juglans regia*) grow in southern Europe, through central Asia to China. In Europe they are grown commercially in mild, warm areas. The main exporting countries are Italy, France, Spain, Turkey, Romania and California, the latter being the largest grower in the world. French walnuts are one of the most popular types and there are also 'Welsh nuts' from west Wales.

Pecan nuts grow in the United States, usually in cotton-growing areas. The hickory tree from which they come (*Carya illinoinensis*) also gives excellent wood. Its nuts, which are sandy-red in colour and an elongated oval in shape, are closely related to the walnut.

Pistachio nuts (*Pistacia vera*) flourish from the Mediterranean to central Asia. The trees produce nuts only in alternate years and many live to over a hundred years of age. The nuts contain around 22 per cent protein and 60 per cent fat. Depending on variety the kernel may be pale green, yellow or pink. The best nuts come from Turkey and Sicily.

Pine nut or kernel, the edible nut of the pine tree *Pinus pinea*, which grows principally in the Mediterranean region. The white nuts have an almond-like taste and are sometimes used as an almond substitute.

Coconut, large fruit of the coconut palm (*Cocos nucifera*). The nut floats excellently in water and this accounts for its presence on all tropical beaches and river banks throughout the world. The coconut as we know it, with its hard shell and tuft of fibres is merely the ripe or unripe kernel of the fruit. The outer shell with its thick layer of fibre is removed at source. If the nut produces gurgling noises when shaken it still contains liquid (not to be confused with coconut milk) and is not yet ripe. In ripe nuts the liquid has completely evaporated. For home-baking dessicated coconut (made by grating the fresh nut) is generally used. Coconut milk is sometimes used in special foreign dishes.

Peanut or groundnut (*Arachis hypogaea*) derives its name from the strange behaviour of the parent plant: after pollination the flower stem droops to the ground, burrows into the ground for protection against the heat and develops its fruit underground. In baking and sweet-making peanuts are used in the same way as other nuts, but they are processed commercially to produce oil.

Chestnut (*Castanea sativa*) prefers a warm climate and thrives in the Mediterranean region, Japan, China, India, Australia and the United States. They are related to the horse chestnut but should not be confused with them as the latter are not edible. Chestnuts are sold either fresh or roasted, they are also available in cans and in puree form, either plain or sweetened.

Cashews look like an appendage to the Cashew apple (*Anacardium occidentale*), but are in fact the fruit while the 'apple' is merely the stem! Cashews contain around 45 per cent oil, 20 per cent protein and a high level of vitamin E. They come originally from Brazil, although today they are grown mainly in India and Africa. Since the oil has a rather sharp flavour they are usually shelled and then roasted in shallow trays. This is still done mainly by hand since mechanised shelling and roasting plants have only begun to be introduced in recent years.

Macadamia nut, botanical names *Macadamia tetraphylla* (rough shell) and *Macadamia integrifolia* (smooth shell), is quite an unfamiliar nut. It was discovered in Australia by John McAdam (hence its name). Trees over 15 years of age produce up to 50 kg/112 lb per tree per year. The nuts contain around 76 per cent oil, 16 per cent carbohydrate and 9 per cent protein. The kernels are tender and extremely flavoursome. They are usually sold shelled and roasted, either salted or unsalted.

Brazilian or Para nuts get their name from the Brazilian province of Para which exports to every corner of the world. The Paranut tree (*Bertholletia excelsa*), one of the largest trees of the primeval forest, has made its home throughout the tropical forests of South America. From ten years of age the tree produces enormous pods of around 30-cm/12-in diameter and 3 kg/6¾ lb in weight. Inside the pod may be as many as thirty nuts with extremely hard shells arranged like the segments of an orange. When the pods are ripe they fall to the ground, from where natives take them to collecting stations before they make their way to dealers or shelling plants. The nut kernel contains around 14 per cent protein, 66 per cent fat, essential minerals and vitamins B_1, B_2 and C. Although they can be obtained all through the year the nuts in their shell are most commonly seen at Christmas time.

Almonds and marzipan

Sweet almonds are the fruit of a tree (*Prunus dulcis*) which originally came from western and central Asia. Today almond trees are grown in all temperate climates. The tree itself is quite hardy against frost but the blossoms are not however, so this imposes a limit on its geographical distribution. Besides sweet almonds there are also bitter almonds from the almond tree *Prunus var. amara*, which produces pink rather than white flowers. Often, however, both bitter and sweet almonds are produced by the same tree and outside appearance gives no indication of what type of fruit you have. Bitter almonds are usually smaller, more pointed, more concave than sweet ones, but this is not always the case. The bitter flavour is given by the carbohydrate amygdalin that easily separates into prussic acid. During baking the effect of heat kills off the prussic acid in the bitter almonds and they are quite safe to use in cooking.

Almond blossom in Sicily. In this region trees flower in February or March depending on altitude. The fresh green of the delightful spring landscape is then dotted with the white or pale pink blossom of the almond trees.

The almonds are ripe when the velvety outer shell splits to expose the hard shell of the nut. Almonds are usually shelled prior to export and come to our shops as shelled almonds in their cinnamon-coloured skins. This thin skin is edible and in recipes which require 'brown almonds' is grated with the nut to give additional flavour.

anything else could be induced to eat his delicious little marzipan cakes. Ryff even provides us with a recipe which has not really changed even today.

Anyone who feels so inclined can still make their own marzipan. The almonds are blanched, peeled (if they are in the skin) and crushed with icing sugar. Grated lemon peel and a little rose-water is then worked in. When the mixture is smooth and glossy leave it to stand in a cool place for twelve hours. Then shape, decorate and dry in a warm oven. But most people prefer not to have to go to so much trouble. Best quality marzipan is produced commercially and most professional pastry-cooks use it. It is best to use the white marzipan rather than the yellow as this produces a more professional-looking result, but if you want a golden brown marzipan use natural colourings such as saffron or sugar colouring. Fruit extracts are not recommended as colouring agents as they can make the marzipan ferment when it is stored.

Harvesting almonds is still done by hand, at least by farmers in Mediterranean countries who have yet to introduce the mechanised methods of the large producers in California or Australia. The outer velvety husks are removed at the farm, often by children, before the almonds are dried in the warm autumn sun. Without drying almonds would not keep, nor would they be accepted by the exporters as they would weigh heavier than dried almonds.

Almonds from Portugal, California and Australia (from left to right). The latter two types have almost cornered the world market although they do not compare in quality with the traditional Italian varieties such as Ambrosia, Bari or Sicilian almonds. Spain too produces excellent almonds in Valencia, Alicante, Malaga and Mallorca.

Marzipan

is a delicacy that came to us from the Orient. We know that as early as AD 900 confectioners were making a sweetmeat from almonds and sugar and that it enjoyed great popularity. In later centuries the making of marzipan or almond paste was a province of the apothecary, particularly in northern Europe. It is listed in apothecaries' books of the sixteenth century, together with sugared almonds, as a cure for sleeplessness.

Anton Tucher, a rich burger of Nuremberg wrote in his household book of 1510 that he gave the provost of Wurzburg Cathedral two genuine crystal glasses and two marzipan cakes as a Christmas gift. Marzipan was a luxury that everyone wanted. This led to a ban in 1661 in Leipzig on giving marzipan as a christening present. Walther Ryff, who was first a doctor and surgeon in Strasburg and later court apothecary in Schwerin, published a book entitled *The Mirror and Government of Health* (published with beautiful woodcuts in 1571 in Frankfurt). Here he described how patients who could not eat

Almonds in everyday use. These prepared almonds make life much easier as shelling, chopping, etc. is extremely time-consuming. There is no noticeable difference in quality between prepared and fresh almonds although ready-prepared almonds are chopped or flaked much more uniformly than would be possible for the housewife, with the possible exception of ground almonds which can be easily ground in an electric grinder.

Cocoa and chocolate

Cocoa has been a highly prized commodity since earliest times and its importance is reflected in myths and legends. The chocolate drink of which it is the source played an important part in the lives of the upper classes amongst the Mayas, Incas and Aztecs: only the chosen few close to the king were allowed this drink which was flavoured with vanilla, ginger and other spices. It was known as theobroma, the food of the gods. Cocoa beans were in themselves a valuable means of currency. When Cortez conquered part of Mexico in 1519 he found extensive plantations of cocoa trees which he described to the Emperor Charles V in a letter dated 30 October 1520. He also described the drink made from cocoa beans as stimulating and extremely nutritious, having savoured it at the court of Montezuma, the Mexican emperor. Besides the stimulant theobromine, a caffeine-like alkaloid, the cocoa bean contains around 54 per cent fat, 14 per cent protein and 7 per cent starch. Cocoa is more a food than a drink.

In 1528 Cortez brought the first cocoa beans and the utensils needed for their presentation back to Spain, and the drink was found to be delicious with the addition of cane sugar. When the princess Anne of Austria married into the French royal family the drink passed to France and in 1657 the first chocolate shop was opened in London. Chocolate made its way to Germany in 1640, but as a medicine supplied by apothecaries.

The cocoa tree (*Theobroma cacao*) is a tree of the tropical rain forest which needs protection from sun and wind together with a lot of moisture and warmth. The main areas of production all lie along the equator: Mexico, Venezuela, Ecuador, Brazil and equatorial West Africa.

The flowers and fruit of the tree are not carried on the branches but grow on short stalks directly out of the trunk. Throughout the year any one tree will display a combination of both flowers and unripe or ripe cocoa pods. The fruits take four to six months to ripen, growing into fat cucumbers around 20-cm/8-in. in length. They are chopped off the tree with a large, curved knife and taken to a collection point where they are cut open and the beans and fruit pulp removed. This is piled into large heaps in the open air or fermented in large boxes, during which time the beans lose their bitterness, increase in flavour and turn brown. After six days the beans are washed and left in the sun for a few more days to dry before being sorted, sacked up and transported. All cleaning, roasting and shelling is done at source. The high fat content produces a thick paste when the beans are ground and in order to turn this into cocoa powder half the fat content, cocoa butter, must be pressed out before the mixture will dry. Drying leaves a low-fat 'cocoa cake' which is again ground to give the familiar cocoa powder.

A secret recipe is used to make chocolate, in which varying quantities of sugar, extra cocoa butter (which looks like cream-coloured butter), spices and milk are added to the cocoa powder. Of course quality depends to a great extent on the proportion of high and low quality cocoa beans (Criollo and Forastero beans) used in the original cocoa powder. After several processes in which the mixture is rolled and compressed, the mixture becomes smooth and creamy and is ready to be turned into the many forms which chocolate takes – chocolate bars or chocolates filled with nuts, fruit, cream, etc. This basic chocolate mixture also finds its way to bakers and confectioners in block form and should not be confused with its substitute cooking chocolate. The chocolate we are talking about is pure chocolate of top quality whereas cooking chocolate, although cheaper in price and easier to use, is mainly vegetable fat with a low cocoa content. Pure chocolate is unbeatable for both flavour and smell.

Alcohol, flavouring with spirit

Is there anyone who has not experienced the wonderful smell that fills the room as cakes and pastries are set upon the table? This often includes the tempting aroma of rum, brandy or other spirit with which the filling has been flavoured or the sponge soaked. *Rum* is an ideal alcoholic flavouring for cakes and pastries. It blends well with almost any other ingredient and emphasises the special quality of many cakes. But the rum itself must be of top quality. *Arrak* is a spirit made from rice, palm-wine or molasses. It is good for flavouring icings and also to pour over dry cakes. *Cognac*, like all brandies, is excellent for flavouring a wide variety of cakes. A large number of *liqueurs* are excellent as food flavourings, particular for light cream desserts and whipped cream. Fruit liqueurs especially can help bring out a particular flavour; try adding a dash of orange liqueur to an orange cream. The same applies to *fruit brandies*, the most obvious example being the combination of cherries and Kirsch in Black Forest Gâteau. Raspberries with raspberry brandy produces equally good results, but it is important to use a good quality brandy, mild but full of flavour. *Wines* too are an excellent source of flavour, especially as the basis of cream desserts, but here again high quality is paramount.

Aromatics and spices

Some of the best natural aromatics are provided by the ethereal oils in the skins of citrus fruit. These were used to flavour food in the Mediterranean region for many centuries. Today it is important to scrub the fruit before use to remove the waxy coating. The peel of oranges, lemons and limes make ideal seasoners, either grated with a fine grater or sugar cube or peeled into paper-thin strips.

Orange-flower water is obtained by distilling fresh, unopened blossoms, whereas oil, which is mainly used in the manufacture of liqueurs, is a distillation of the opened, dried blossoms. Orange-flower water is used for flavouring sponge cakes, creams and icing.

Rose-water is a mixture of rose oil and water, with only 1 drop of oil per 250 ml/8 fl oz water. It is a by-product of rose oil production. Since rose-water has a very short life-span most bakers tend to make their own from rose oil, water and a little alcohol. Rose-water's main use is in the making of marzipan, but it is also used for flavouring sponges and icings.

Allspice, *Pimenta officinalis*, is related to the clove but comes from the New World, hence its alternative name of Jamaican pepper. It combines the flavours of cloves, pepper and nutmeg and is used in baking mainly in spice cake and at Christmas time.

Aniseed is the dried seed of *Pimpinella anisum*, a member of the *umbelliferae* family. It is one of the most ancient spices in the world and is thought to have originated in Egypt. As well as its use in liqueurs, cough mixtures and liquorice, aniseed is used in straws, biscuits, bread and extensively in Continental Christmas baking.

Star aniseed, botanical name *Illicium verum*, has been used as a spice in China for a thousand years. Because of its ethereal oils it should be used sparingly as it is stronger than aniseed. Star aniseed is usually sold in powder form.

Bitter almonds come from the pink-flowered cherry tree, *Prunus amara*, but they can also appear on white trees too. Bitter almonds are used in combination with sweet almonds in any cake which requires a strong almond flavour, and of course the same applies to creams and fillings.

Cardamom, botanical name *Elettaria cardamomum*, the seed of an Indian shrub which was a popular spice in Roman times. For baking it is included in the spices for gingerbread and can be used occasionally for flavouring yeast or croissant dough.

Cinnamon is a spice that comes from two types of evergreen cinnamon tree. Ceylon cinnamon, *Cinnamomum zeylanicum*, has a thin, pale-brown bark which has a sweet, mild taste. Its excellent flavour is preferable whenever you want to use cinnamon in isolation. Cassia cinnamon, *Cinnamomum aromaticum* or *C. cassia*, the best of which is grown in Sumatra, is darker in colour and stronger in flavour. This type is ideal for mixed spice, for spice cake, gingerbread or honey cake.

Cloves are the dried flower buds of the East Asian clove tree, *Syzygium aromaticum*, which has been known in Western Europe since the Middle Ages. In baking ground cloves are used, generally in gingerbread and Christmas specialities. Whole cloves are employed when bottling fruit and in pies, most notably in apple pie.

Coffee is an excellent flavouring for creams, fillings and icings (especially combined with vanilla). To keep down the liquid content instant coffee is often used. Mocha is a type of coffee bean and the term mocha technically means flavoured with coffee but is more often used to denote a coffee and chocolate flavoured mixture.

Coriander, botanical name *Coriandrum sativum*, the dried seeds are similar in taste to aniseed. In baking it is used mainly for Christmas specialities and bread.

Fennel, botanical name *Foeniculum vulgare*, was regarded as a herb to cure all ills for centuries. Like aniseed, its seeds contain ethereal oils. In baking fennel is used to season a variety of cakes and loaves.

Ginger, botanical name *Zingiber officinale*, comes from the root of a tropical reed. Fresh or dried, preserved or ground, in any of its forms it gives baking a unique flavour. Excellent in a variety of fruit flans and essential for gingerbread.

Mace and nutmeg, *Myristica fragans*, grows in the tropical rain forests of Asia. The pretty outer coating is used to make mace while the nutmeg or seed is dried slowly. Today they are widely used in baking and desserts in the English-speaking world, although in some countries their use is restricted mainly to spice cake and Christmas baking.

Pepper, *Piper nigrum* is one of the oldest tropical seasonings. In baking only white pepper is utilised, in pepper cake and in the spices that go into gingerbread.

Poppy seed, *Papaver somniferum*, comes from Asia Minor. Its main role today is a source of oil. In baking the seeds are used whole for decoration or ground in flan fillings.

Saffron, *Crocus sativus*, is an ancient Asiatic plant which provides both a spice and a colourant. The spice itself comes from the stamens of the flower. Small cakes, especially sponges, are often coloured with saffron.

Vanilla, *Vanilla planifolia*, is an orchid from the tropical forests of Mexico. The best vanilla now comes from the islands of Madagascar, Reunion and Mauritius. To produce the spice the unripe fruit pods are gathered and fermented. Vanilla is widely used in cake mixes, cream fillings and is delicious with chocolate.

Basic Recipes

The ingredients and methods used to make basic cakes and pastries are described in this chapter. Many of them are sufficient in themselves and are delicious just as they are. Others greatly benefit by the addition of fillings, icings and decorations. It is the finishing touches that this involves which provides one of the most interesting aspects of home baking, and also help to raise the standard of home cooking to a professional level.

In this chapter you will find easy-to-follow, step-by-step instructions for making the basic pastries and sponges. These are the methods which will be referred to in later chapters of this book. It is no good buying the best ingredients unless you know how to use them properly so these first recipes should be tried and mastered then success is guaranteed.

Traditional cooking methods and fresh ingredients are used and this chapter does not refer to any of those convenience products which can be readily bought from the shelves of the local supermarket or grocer's shop. This does not, of course, rule out the use of kitchen machines such as electric whisks or food processors but it should be emphasised that all cooks should have an idea of how a particular mixture or dough should look and feel – and this is best gained by literally trying your hand at it first.

It is useful to remember to get out all the necessary equipment before you begin to bake. Look through the recipe before starting to make it up so that you can check that you have all the required equipment and ingredients. If the tin or baking tray is to be lined with greaseproof paper or greased and floured do this first. Then there will be no delay before baking when the mixture is ready – that can be important with a whisked mixture which could fall if left for too long before cooking.

The oven should always be preheated in good time; it will generally take from 15–20 minutes to reach the required temperature. Remember that the shelves should be placed at the right position in the oven before switching it on. As a general rule yeast and pastry mixtures should be cooked towards the top of the oven, cakes and biscuits should be placed towards the centre, while meringues should be cooked as low down in the oven as possible to prevent browning during the long cooking time. Do not open the oven door during the early cooking stage and avoid opening it too frequently during the course of baking.

Baking is an exact science

Successful baking depends primarily on following the instructions provided and above all on the correct proportions of the separate ingredients. Never try to rely on the judgement of your eye or hand. Accurate weighing scales are an essential for good results. It is helpful to buy a pair which shows both metric and Imperial measures. The same accuracy is necessary with liquids. For larger quantities you will need a graduated measuring jug or a millilitre/pint measure. A glass jug will enable you to see clearly that the right amount of liquid is reached. Plastic jugs are similarly useful but can be distorted by heat and hot liquids thereby often altering in shape and accuracy. The common measurements such as teaspoon or tablespoon are always for a level, not heaped, spoonful. A set of measuring spoons is an essential addition to kitchen equipment and will show accurately a $\frac{1}{4}$ teaspoon to a tablespoon. Very small quantities, such as salt or spices, are best indicated by 'pinch'.

Basic equipment

There are naturally a few pieces of equipment which are essential for baking, one of these being an oven. This does not mean you have to have the sort of expensive oven used by professional chefs: a reliable oven without fancy trimmings will do the job just as well. Anyone with a serious interest in learning to cook should forget about electric mixers and food processors to start off with, for it is only by working with your hands that you can get a real feel for the products you are using. Eventually experience will show which processes can be done by machine without affecting the quality of the final outcome.

A good set of basic equipment should include the following. For mixing pastries and doughs, a flat, plastic, or preferably marble, worktop. A marble sheet is particularly useful when working with sugar or chocolate. A large wooden rolling pin. The plain rolling pin (without handles) is best. Basins and bowls. A set of three round-bottomed bowls in assorted sizes is all you need for beating cake mixtures in, although the more rounded stainless steel or copper bowls, 25 to 30-cm/10 to 12-in. in diameter are better still. These allow lots of room for using a balloon whisk and have the added advantage of being able to go direct on the stove without having to stand in water. Several smaller basins are useful for mixing icing, melting chocolate etc.

Whisks in various sizes. Balloon whisks are useful as well as an electric whisk. You will also need three or four wooden or plastic spoons (or spatulas) in different sizes.

A wooden-framed sieve may sound old-fashioned but is ideal (though regrettably it can be difficult to find nowadays). A sieve like this makes easy work of sifting together flour, cornflour and other ingredients, whereas it can be a long process in a small plastic sieve.

Knives needed for baking include a serrated knife (25-cm/10-in long), a fruit-knife and particularly two or three palette knives in assorted sizes. These are the pastry-cook's universal tool. A flexible palette knife is by far the best thing to use to ice a large area. A chopping knife will also be necessary to chop dried fruit, etc. You should aim at good quality even with your small kitchen utensils: pastry brush; plastic or hard rubber spatula with wooden handle for scraping mixing bowls; plain and fluted pastry cutters and wheel. Also piping bags in various sizes and a selection of plain and star nozzles.

These are all the essential utensils. There are a host of small implements used in cake decoration but these are by no means necessary. With a little imagination you can produce excellent designs with the minimum of piping nozzles and cutters. Just think of the effects that can be achieved with a piping tube made solely of greaseproof paper. Nor do you really need a large number of cake tins although with the large choice and different varieties which are available it seems almost impossible to avoid amassing quite a collection.

Baking tins

Baking tins make an important contribution to the final result in baking, and you don't necessarily have to go for the most expensive. For sponges, yeast mixtures and most cakes you can now get very inexpensive tins in aluminium or tinplate, both of which are excellent conductors of heat, or in sheet-iron. Tins with a non-stick plastic coating are now widely available and these give excellent results in the oven. Traditionally the best materials for baking tins used to be copper and good-quality ceramic. These were fired at over 1,000 C/1,832 F and are excellent for deep cakes. They can sometimes be obtained today and one advantage is that both copper and ceramic containers are extremely attractive to display in the kitchen.

For sponge bases there are a variety of tins you can use. The most popular for home use is the loose-bottomed tin whose base can be removed for ease of turning out. Professional chefs use plain aluminium rings which are simpler and better since they produce a more even sponge. French chefs prefer ordinary tins with slanting edges, and with these it is essential to cover the base with greaseproof paper so that the sponge will come out easily once you have cut round the sides.

Sponge rings are extremely popular in the trade and have several advantages over the loose-bottomed tins which are usually found in the domestic kitchen (see step-by-step instructions, page 29). When the sponge is cooked all you have to do is to peel off the paper and cut round the ring with a knife.

Electric gadgets can make the job a lot easier. Regardless of whether he or she is kneading a dough using his or her hands or whipping a cake mixture with a whisk, the experienced chef seems to do the job in exactly the right way automatically. Here a Genoese sponge mixture is illustrated. However the time and energy saved by using electric food mixers or processors must be balanced against a few disadvantages.

They can be expensive to buy and as with any machine liable to break down. They also place the cook at one remove from the food being prepared, but this should not be a great disadvantage to those cooks who have first tried a recipe by hand and realise when the correct consistency has been reached in a mixer or processor.

The oven

It is worth considering carefully the type of oven that you require. Generally it is better to buy a larger oven if possible because otherwise there can be problems when entertaining or at such times as Christmas when the oven is in almost constant use. Nowadays one can buy either free-standing or built-in cookers; those with one or two ovens (the smaller of which often converts to a grill); and the choice will be between gas, electricity or a convection oven. The manufacturer's instructions should be read through and carefully followed to ensure good results. However the majority of ovens will vary slightly and there can be slight irregularities in the temperature and the only way to get to know your oven is to test-bake various kinds of pastry and cake mixtures.

Preheating the oven?

This is a question which comes up repeatedly and which has been revived once more by the convection or hot air ovens. One should work on the basic principle that the oven should be at the required temperature when the baking goes into the oven. You will need to check on the manufacturer's instructions how long your oven takes to preheat since it varies from model to model. Electric ovens take 10 to 20 minutes to reach temperatures around 200 C, 400 F, gas 6, gas ovens take only a few minutes, while the circulatory ovens are even quicker. It is essential to preheat the oven and all the recipes in this book work on this assumption. Equally problematical can be some manufacturer's instructions to take advantage of the after-heat of the oven – i.e. to turn off the oven before the food is completely done and to allow it to finish cooking in the slowly cooling oven. This is a highly questionable way of saving energy which can have an extremely adverse effect on your baking. Be sure to take food out of the oven and not merely to turn the oven off at the end of the recommended time. There are a few exceptions to this rule but if this is the case it will be made clear in the recipe in question.

Correct temperatures and baking times

In principal all baking recipes should be followed as closely as possible and this is certainly true of the measuring of ingredients and method of preparation. The weak link in any recipe, however, is always the recommended temperature and baking time. The problems with ovens, as discussed above, may affect the recommendations made in the recipe and experience alone can show when this is the case. The longer the baking time the more necesary it will be to check times and temperatures from experience. With any new recipe you try it is a good idea to make a note of the exact temperature and baking time, even though this may involve writing in the margin of a brand new cookery book. The next time you make the same recipe you will be glad for the guidance this provides. Small and very thin cakes and pastries can be cooked more or less 'by sight'; this means that when you think the cakes will be almost ready you keep an eye on them until they look done. If your oven has a window this is quite simple as you can see when the cakes are done without having to open the oven door. If there is no window you will have to keep opening the oven door to have a look at the cakes. Don't worry too much about this as cakes are not likely to fall during the final stages of baking.

1 **Place the eggs**, egg yolks, sugar and grated lemon rind in a large, clean mixing bowl.

Genoese Mixture

a basic sponge mixture

Sponge mixtures – of which Genoese sponge (known as Viennese in Germany) is one of the most common – can be mixed cold or whisked in a bowl over a saucepan of hot water (see the instructions on the right). The whole eggs can be whisked with the sugar or just the yolks whisked with the sugar and the whites whisked separately until stiff but not dry and then folded in (see opposite page). The higher the sugar content the denser and richer the sponge will be. Cutting down the sugar content makes for a lighter sponge but it will also be more fragile. Whisking the mixture over hot water gives a better volume quicker than in a cold bowl. The flour and cornflour also bind with the egg whites more easily and the final result is an even textured, stable sponge. The recipe below makes an excellent light sponge with success more or less guaranteed!

Ingredients:
5 eggs
2 egg yolks
150 g/5 oz caster sugar
½ teaspoon grated lemon rind
150 g/5 oz plain flour
25 g/1 oz cornflour
75 g/3 oz unsalted butter
25-cm/10-in deep cake tin or springform tin

Baking time: 30–35 minutes in a moderately hot oven (190 C, 375 F, gas 5).

2 **Stand the bowl** over a saucepan half full of hot water over a very low heat so that the water barely simmers; it should not be allowed to boil. Whisk the mixture with a balloon whisk or electric whisk until it is pale and thick enough to leave a trail for a few minutes when the whisk is lifted.

3 **Remove the bowl** from the saucepan and whisk until cooled, about 5 minutes. The mixture will be very pale, thick and creamy and will have visibly increased in volume.

4 **Sift the flour and cornflour together** and then sift on to a piece of greaseproof paper. Fold the paper in half and slowly sprinkle into the whisked mixture, folding them in lightly but thoroughly with a metal spoon.

5 **Melt the butter** in a small saucepan over a moderate heat to about 40 C/105 F. Skim off the froth then slowly trickle into the sponge mixture and fold it in gently but thoroughly.

28

6 **Grease the base of the cake tin**, line with greaseproof paper or non-stick baking paper then grease the paper. (Do not grease the sides of the tin as the mixture should adhere to the sides for a perfectly smooth edge.)

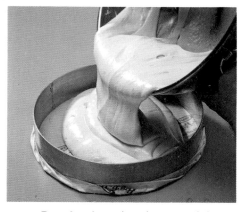

7 **Pour the mixture** into the prepared tin. While you are pouring keep an eye open for any lumps of flour in the mixture. These can either be gently stirred into the mixture or removed using a teaspoon.

8 **Lightly smooth the surface of the mixture**. It is a good idea to make a slight hollow in the middle so that the risen, cooked cake will have a flat surface. Bake in a moderately hot oven (190 C, 375 F, gas 5) for 30–35 minutes.

9 **When the mixture is cooked** the sponge will feel set and slightly springy in the middle. Leave the cake to cool in the tin for a few minutes. Run a palette knife around the inside edge of the tin to loosen the sponge. Lightly dust a baking sheet with flour then invert the cake tin on to it and leave to cool completely.

10 **Turning the sponge** upside down gives it an absolutely flat top when cool, even though it may have risen slightly in the middle during baking. Cooling upside down in the tin also prevents the cake drying out.

Dobos mixture is an example of a fat-free sponge that is mixed cold – i.e. not over hot water. Ingredients: 9 eggs separated, 225 g/8 oz icing sugar, 175 g/6 oz plain flour. Whisk the egg yolks with about a third of the icing sugar until thick enough to leave a trail when the whisk is lifted. Whisk the egg whites until they are stiff but not dry then gradually whisk in the remaining sugar until the mixture is stiff and very glossy. Fold a little into the yolk mixture. Gently fold in the remaining egg white mixture alternately with the sifted flour. Cut six to eight squares of non-stick baking paper (depending on how many layers you want for the cake) and draw a 25-cm/10-in diameter circle on each, then place on baking sheets. Divide the mixture equally between the circles and spread it evenly to cover the circles you have drawn. Bake the rounds of mixture as quickly as possible one after the other in a hot oven (220 C, 425 F, gas 7) for about 7–8 minutes. If the mixture is left to stand too long before baking it may lose some of its air and weep slightly. Watch the cooking time carefully because these thin cakes soon burn.

Chocolate Mixture

a sponge with walnuts and biscuit crumbs

The step-by-step instructions on the right are a good example of a sponge mixture which has fat and other flavourings added. Since most flavourings – for example nuts or chocolate – contain fat it is important to add them to the mixture at the correct stage. For a light sponge the whisked egg white is. folded as thoroughly as possible into the basic egg yolk mixture. If at the same time you can avoid breaking up the whites too much the mixture will have the maximum volume. The melted chocolate and butter are added to the egg yolk mixture at this stage because if either of these ingredients were added at the end, as in the Genoese sponge, the egg whites would begin to collapse. Remember to prepare the tin before starting the recipe so that it is ready for when the cake is mixed.

Ingredients:
8 eggs, separated
50 g/2 oz walnuts, ground
½ teaspoon vanilla essence
175 g/6 oz caster sugar
75 g/3 oz plain chocolate or cocoa powder
75 g/3 oz butter, melted
50 g/2 oz plain flour
100 g/4 oz fine biscuit crumbs (e.g. digestive)
25-cm/10-in deep cake tin, the base lined and greased

Baking time: about 35 minutes in a moderately hot oven (190 C, 375 F, gas 5).

Classic Chocolate Mixture

can either be mixed warm or cold following the steps shown on pages 28–9.

6 eggs
175 g/6 oz caster sugar
100 g/4 oz plain flour
50 g/2 oz cornflour
50 g/2 oz cocoa powder
50 g/2 oz butter, melted
25-cm/10-in deep cake tin or springform tin, lined and greased

Whisk the eggs and sugar in a bowl over a saucepan of hot water; remove from heat and whisk until cold. Sift together the flour, cornflour and cocoa powder and fold into the egg mixture. Then slowly fold in the melted butter. Pour the mixture into the prepared tin and smooth the top.
Baking time: about 35 minutes in a moderately hot oven (190C, 375F, gas 5).

1 **Place the egg yolks,** ground walnuts and vanilla essence into a mixing bowl with about half of the sugar.

2 **Whisk the egg yolk mixture** until thick and pale, and doubled in volume. Use either a balloon whisk or an electric whisk on a medium speed.

6 **Now add the remaining egg white mixture** and fold it in very gently. Finally, sprinkle a mixture of the sifted flour and biscuit crumbs over the top and fold in very carefully until evenly mixed.

7 **Transfer the mixture** to the prepared tin. The base of the tin should have been lined with a greased circle of greaseproof or baking paper cut to size. Do not grease the sides as this will prevent the sponge coming away from the sides and falling when baked.

Swiss Roll

75 g/3 oz caster sugar
6 egg yolks
pinch of salt
grated rind of 1 lemon
3 egg whites
65 g/2½ oz plain flour
15 g/½ oz cornflour
36 × 25-cm/14 × 10-in baking tray, lined and greased

In this recipe the egg whites are not folded into the yolks as is usual but the other way round. Bake the roll in a hot oven (230 C, 450 F, gas 8) for about 10 minutes, but keep an eye on it after about 6 minutes.

1 **Stir a tablespoon of the sugar** into the egg yolks with the salt and grated lemon rind. Whisk the egg whites then gradually whisk in the remaining sugar. Fold the egg yolk mixture into the whites. Sift together the flour and cornflour and fold gently into the mixture.

3 **Melt the chocolate** in a basin over a saucepan of hot, but not boiling, water. Stir the melted chocolate into the egg yolk mixture while still warm. If you prefer to use cocoa powder it should be sifted with the flour and added at the end.

4 **Work as quickly as possible** so that the mixture does not become too cool, in which case the chocolate will set. (If necessary warm it quickly over a pan of hot water.) Add the melted butter in a slow trickle and fold in evenly.

5 **Whisk the egg whites until stiff** but not dry then whisk the remaining sugar until stiff and very glossy. Spoon about one-third of the whites on to the top of the chocolate mixture and fold in gently, using a metal spoon. The egg white mixture should be well blended into the egg yolk mixture.

8 **Lightly smooth the top** of the mixture. This is easiest using a plastic scraper or spatula. As with the Genoese sponge (see page 29) the surface can either be completely flat or slightly hollowed in the middle.

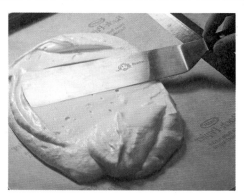

2 **Spread the sponge mixture** evenly over the prepared baking sheet, using a palette knife or pastry scraper. Bake in a hot oven (230 C, 450 F, gas 8) for about 10 minutes.

3 **Turn the baked sponge** out on to a damp tea-towel. Remove the paper, trim the edges as necessary, roll up the sponge and leave to cool. Unroll again before filling. Alternatively leave flat and cover with a second damp tea-towel.

4 **Fill the roll.** To use a fruit cream, as illustrated, the sponge must be completely cold. Do not spread the cream right to the edge along the long sides or it will spill out when the sponge is rolled. Use the tea-towel to help with the rolling.

Sponge Mixture

for a Marguerite cake, for example

There are three possible ways of mixing sponges:

A Warm melted fat is added as the last stage to the other well-mixed ingredients. This is the usual method for a Genoese sponge or other plain cakes.

B The fat is creamed with part of the sugar and the egg yolks are gradually beaten in. The remaining sugar is whisked into the whisked egg whites and gently folded in with the sifted flour and cornflour. This is the method used in the recipe for Marguerite cake on the right.

C The mixture is prepared in three separate stages. Egg yolks are beaten with sugar; sifted flour and cornflour creamed with the fat; egg whites whisked to soft peaks. The three mixtures are then combined in the order given.

Marguerite Cake

225 g/8 oz unsalted butter, softened
225 g/8 oz caster sugar
1 teaspoon vanilla essence
6 eggs, separated
150 g/5 oz plain flour
100 g/4 oz ground almonds
75 g/3 oz cornflour
20-cm/8-in plain or daisy-patterned
cake tin, greased and floured

First butter the tin or mould thoroughly and sprinkle lightly and evenly with finely sifted flour. Cream the butter with about a third of the sugar using a wooden spoon or an electric handheld mixer until the mixture is light and fluffy. Gradually beat in the vanilla essence and the egg yolks.

Whisk the egg whites until stiff but not dry then whisk in the remaining sugar. Stir about two-thirds of the egg whites into the butter mixture then fold in the remaining whites with the sifted flour, ground almonds and cornflour. Transfer to the prepared tin and lightly smooth the top. Bake in a moderately hot oven (190 C, 375 F, gas 5) for about 1¼ hours.

1 **Cream the butter** with about a third of the sugar until light and fluffy. Gradually beat in the vanilla essence and the egg yolks.

2 **Whisk the egg whites** until they are stiff but not dry then gradually add the remaining sugar in a slow trickle. Fold about two-thirds of the egg whites into the butter and egg yolk mixture using a metal spoon, taking care not to overmix.

3 **Fold in the remaining egg white mixture** with the sifted flour and cornflour. The first third of egg white must be completely mixed into the butter and egg yolk mixture before you fold in the remaining egg white with the flour and cornflour.

4 **Fill the prepared tin** with the mixture transferring the sponge mixture carefully to the tin.

5 **Level the top** with a rubber spatula or pastry scraper, leaving a slight hollow in the middle to compensate for the centre rising during baking. Smooth the mixture very gently to avoid loosing any of the air and bake as instructed.

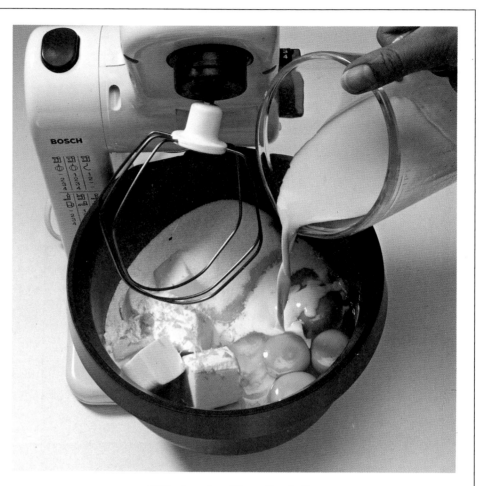

Victoria Sandwich

This is another basic mixture, but one which is much simpler to make than the Marguerite cake on the left. The creaming method and inclusion of baking powder makes this a very simple, and thus very popular, recipe.

With modern kitchen gadgetry (hand whisk or food processor) the basic mixture for a Madeira or marble cake can now be prepared in a matter of only minutes. The basic mixture can be varied by adding such ingredients as nuts or dried fruit, and the texture can be changed by substituting cornflour for part of the flour.

There are two possible methods of preparing the mixture. In the first the butter and sugar are beaten together until light and fluffy then the eggs are gradually folded in. The sifted flour, salt and flavouring if any is added at this stage. Finally fold in the milk to give a soft dropping consistency. The second method, in which all the ingredients are mixed in one go, is even simpler. The ingredients for the one-stage recipe are: 225 g/8 oz self-raising flour, 225 g/8 oz softened butter or margarine, 225 g/8 oz caster sugar, pinch of salt, 4 eggs, 75 ml/2½ fl oz milk, and 1 teaspoon baking powder which is not required if the creaming method is used but is needed in the one-stage method to make the cake rise properly. Sift the flour into a bowl and add all the other ingredients. Beat for 1 minute in the food mixer on the highest setting, then scrape round the edge of the bowl with a spatula and beat for a further 2 minutes, again at the highest setting. If flavourings such as nuts or dried fruit are to be included these should be quickly beaten in with the mixer on the slowest setting. Spoon into two 25-cm/10-in sandwich tins and level the top of the mixture. Bake in a moderate oven (180 C, 350 F, gas 4) for about 50 minutes.

Traditionally this cake is sandwiched together with jam and sprinkled with icing sugar. Alternatively the recipe can be varied and made into a chocolate cake by replacing 1 oz of the flour with the same amount of cocoa powder and sandwich it together with chocolate butter cream or Canache cream.

Meringue or Baiser Mixture

This is one of the most important basic mixtures for cakes and pastries. It can be varied by changing the sugar content or by flavouring with coffee, chocolate or, as in the case of Japonais, with almonds or other nuts. It can be used as a topping for fruit flans or can be piped and dried to make decorations.

A good basic recipe:
8 egg whites
225 g/8 oz caster sugar
225 g/8 oz icing sugar

The method of preparation is illustrated on the right. Flat meringue bases or small cakes should be baked for around 3 hours in a very cool oven (120 C, 250 F, gas ½) with the oven door slightly ajar.

These quantities make about fifteen small meringue nests or four rounds of 20-cm/8-in diameter. Pipe the meringue on to oiled greaseproof or non-stick baking paper using a 1-cm/½-in nozzle. Meringues without additional flavourings can be cooked and stored to be used as and when needed, but they must be stored in an airtight container to prevent them from becoming sticky and absorbing other flavours.

1 **First whisk** the egg whites without sugar. A balloon whisk is best for getting the largest volume, but an electric mixer fitted with a whisk makes the job much easier. Begin on a high speed and when the egg whites are stiff but not dry add a little caster sugar and turn down the speed to medium.

2 **Add the sugar** in a slow trickle. Turn the whisk down to the lowest setting while you add the sugar or you risk it being sprayed all round the kitchen. After each addition of sugar turn the whisk to high again and repeat the process until all the sugar has been incorporated.

3 **When all the sugar has been added** turn the mixer to medium and continue mixing until you can no longer see any sugar crystals. The mixture should be smooth, white, very glossy and firm enough to cut with a knife. When it is of the right consistency the whisk will leave cuts in it as you lift it out.

4 **Fold in the icing sugar.** Sift the icing sugar and fold into the egg whites gently but thoroughly with a metal spoon.

5 **Transfer to a piping bag** if the mixture is to be piped. Fold down the end of the bag and fill with the mixture using a rubber or plastic spatula. Fold back the edge, press the mixture down into the bag and twist the top of the bag. Use one hand to hold the bag and the other to guide it as you pipe.

Japonais

*Meringue mixture with almonds
or other nuts*

This mixture has a variety of uses in gâteaux and smaller cakes. Many different butter creams (mocha being used traditionally), as well as lighter flavoured creams or whipped cream all go well with this sweet, crispy base. Japonais is basically a meringue mixture with lightly toasted, finely ground almonds or hazelnuts added. Depending on how solid you want the Japonais mixture to be the amount of almonds can be up to two-thirds of the combined weight of egg white and sugar. Cornflour or flour (in very small quantities) are used as a stabiliser.

Japonais bases

*three bases of 20-cm/8-in diameter, to
make one cake*

5 egg whites
225 g/8 oz caster sugar
100 g/4 oz almonds or hazelnuts,
toasted and ground
25 g/1 oz cornflour
50 g/2 oz icing sugar
¼ teaspoon vanilla essence
1 quantity mocha butter cream (see page 55)

Place the egg whites in a large clean mixing bowl and whisk until stiff but not dry. Then gradually whisk in the sugar, until it is stiff and very glossy. Mix together the ground almonds (or hazelnuts), the sifted cornflour and icing sugar and fold into the egg whites together with the vanilla essence. Spread or pipe the mixture on to oiled greaseproof or non-stick baking paper in rounds and bake in a moderate oven (160 C, 325 F, gas 3) until golden brown, leaving the oven door slightly ajar to allow the steam to escape.

Cooked at this temperature, which is quite high for meringues, the bases will be crisp on the outside and sticky in the centre and the flavour of the nuts will be quite distinctive. The bases will take around 1½ hours, or even less, to bake and you will need to keep an eye on them as you get towards the end of the baking time. The more you reduce the heat (down to very cool, 120 C, 250 F, gas ½) the longer the cooking time, for the bases now 'dry out' rather than bake.

1 **The meringue mixture** must be of cutting consistency, prepared as on the previous page. The sugar (not the icing sugar) must be completely incorporated. The whites should form stiff peaks when whisked.

2 **Mix the finely ground almonds** with the sifted cornflour and icing sugar. Using a metal spoon, fold into the meringue mixture together with the vanilla essence. The mixture should be well mixed, but do not stir longer than is necessary.

3 **Draw circles** 20-cm/8-in. in diameter on to greaseproof or non-stick baking paper and lightly spread or pipe the mixture to fill the circle with a palette knife. Piping is rather time-consuming but does make for an even base.

4 **Cut round a stencil or plate.** While still warm the Japonais bases can be cut with a sharp, pointed knife. Alternatively leave the bases to cool, fill with butter cream, chill the cake and finally trim the edge smooth using a round stencil or plate as a guide.

5 **Place the first base**, uneven side uppermost, on a large cake stand or flat plate and spread with the mocha butter cream. Place the second base on top and spread similarly with butter cream. Top with the third base, flat side uppermost. Cover the top and sides with the remaining butter cream.

6 **The finished Japonais cake** with the traditional dot of pink fondant icing in the centre. The cake is sprinkled with finely grated, toasted almonds which should be pressed down gently with a palette knife. Small Japonais cakes of around 8-cm/3-in diameter are made in exactly the same way.

Choux Pastry

Choux pastry is made on the hob because the liquid ingredients – milk or water, butter and salt – are first boiled. Remove from the heat then add the flour to the pan all at once and beat in well. Stir vigorously until the mixture forms a fairly firm, ball of paste which leaves the sides of the pan clean. The eggs are beaten in one at a time off the heat and the mixture is thoroughly beaten until smooth, glossy and of piping consistency. The mixture is baked to make éclairs, puffs and profiteroles, but is also used for larger cakes, such as the Flaky Choux Gâteau on page 149.

100 g/4 oz butter
300 ml/½ pint milk
pinch of salt
150 g/5 oz plain flour
4 eggs, lightly beaten

Alternatively here is a mixture made with water which is particularly crisp:

100 g/4 oz butter
300 ml/½ pint water
pinch of salt
150 g/5 oz plain flour
4 eggs, lightly beaten

Cream puffs are the classic, cream-filled choux cakes. Choux pastry should be both light and moist. The less fat in the pastry the better it will rise. The more steam in the oven during baking the higher it will rise too. To create steam place a small, ovenproof bowl of water in the bottom of the oven when you put in the baking sheet and close the door quickly so none of the moisture can escape. Bake choux pastry in a hot oven (220 C, 425 F, gas 7) for between 15 and 20 minutes, then continue cooking at a lower temperature if necessary. Do not open the oven until the end of the baking time or the pastry will fall and become doughy and unusable.

1 **Melt the butter** in the milk or water with the salt over a low heat. Bring rapidly to the boil then remove from the heat and immediately beat in the sifted flour all at once. Stir the mixture until it comes away from the sides of the pan and forms a ball. Do not over beat the mixture or it will become oily.

2 **Transfer the mixture** from the saucepan to a mixing bowl and when it has cooled slightly beat in a little egg. Do not add any more egg until the first quantity is completely incorporated into the mixture and continue in this way with the remaining egg. Beat thoroughly until the mixture is smooth and glossy and of the right consistency for piping.

3 **To make cream puffs** spoon the mixture into a piping bag fitted with a star nozzle. On a lightly greased baking tray pipe large rosettes, remembering to leave plenty of space between them because choux pastry swells considerably during cooking. Keep the piping bag vertical and try to finish exactly in the centre of each rosette.

Shortcrust Pastry

Shortcrust is a traditional pastry made with two essential basic ingredients – fat and flour. In some cases – for sweet flan pastry for example – sugar and egg are added. Mixed by hand or electric mixer shortcrust is a very versatile pastry and can be used to make flans, pies, tarts and tartlets. Spices, whether sweet like cinnamon or cardamom or savoury like paprika and curry, can be added to the basic pastry mix to give variety and flavour.

All shortcrust pastry is by its very nature short and there is no better way of describing its consistency. There is the slightly salted, unsweetened or slightly sweetened classic rub-in shortcrust pastry, known in French as *pâte brisée*. This makes an ideal basis for many cakes and flans as it can be completely neutral in flavour or, as many prefer, very lightly salted. It is excellent with fruit flans and very sweet fillings like almonds or other nuts.

Obviously there is also a sweet version of shortcrust. This is known in French as *pâte sucrée* or *pâte sablée* (sand pastry).

Any shortcrust can be kept in the refrigerator. Wrap it in cling film or aluminium foil so as to be completely airtight and it will keep for eight to ten days. It also freezes well for up to three months, but beyond this period the butter in it turns rancid. Shortcrust pastry also freezes well after baking. Whatever you are freezing – flan or tartlet cases or small pies – should be under-baked so that once they have defrosted they can be put back in the oven for a short time to bring out their fresh buttery flavour.

The recipe in this section can be halved or doubled depending on quantities required. The following table will give an indication of the quantity of pastry you need.

Quantities of shortcrust for:

25-cm/10-in circle	225 g/8 oz
25-cm/10-in flan	350 g/12 oz
8-cm/3-in tartlet	about 40 g/1½ oz
10-cm/4-in tartlet	about 50 g/2 oz

Rubbed-in Pastry

The name comes from the way in which it is made, for in this method the fat and flour are first rubbed into crumbs using the finger tips, in the same way as you make a crumble topping. Two parts flour to one part fat with additional liquid gives a short, but firm pastry which is suitable for lining tins. Since it contains little sugar it is a good base for a fruit pie or tart.

150 g/5 oz butter, chilled
275 g/10 oz plain flour
1 tablespoon icing sugar
generous pinch of salt
1 egg yolk
2 tablespoons water

Using your fingertips rub the butter into the sifted flour until the mixture resembles fine breadcrumbs, then stir in the sugar and salt. Make a well in the centre and add the egg yolk then finally the water. The amount of water can be varied slightly to obtain the right consistency. Work quickly together into a dough. Roll the pastry into a ball, wrap in cling film or aluminium foil and leave to stand in the refrigerator for an hour. This quantity makes about two flan cases of 25-cm/10-in diameter or ten 10-cm/4-in tartlets. Bake in a moderately hot oven (200 C, 400 F, gas 6).

Shortcrust made with the mixer

This method is better for pastries which contain a lot of fat, for the fat is quickly mixed with the relatively small quantity of flour without overworking the pastry and making it too brittle, a problem rarely encountered with larger proportions of flour. Of course there is no reason why this pastry cannot be made by hand.

350 g/12 oz butter, softened
50 g/2 oz icing sugar
generous pinch of salt
2 eggs
1 tablespoon milk
675 g/1½ lb plain flour

Cream the butter with the icing sugar and salt in a mixing bowl. The butter should become smooth but not fluffy. Then beat in the eggs and milk. Finally add all the flour at once and, at the lowest speed, mix until just incorporated. This pastry should be quite soft, but easy to use and extremely short.

Sweet Shortcrust Pastry

This is the wonderful flan or tart pastry which the French call *pâte sucrée*. It is essential to use icing sugar as this dissolves much quicker in the pastry than caster sugar. Sugar also makes the gluten in the flour softer and the pastry shorter.

Ingredients:
675 g/1½ lb plain flour
50 g/2 oz cornflour
350 g/12 oz butter
225 g/8 oz icing sugar
pinch of salt
2 eggs

For extra flavour you can add either vanilla or grated lemon peel to the pastry.

3   **Mix in the flour.** This can be done using the hands, gradually working the flour into the centre and working it into the butter mixture. Alternatively use a wide knife or palette knife to bring the flour into the centre and then quickly work it in with your hands.

6   **First roll the pastry** into a ball then wrap it in cling firm or aluminium foil to prevent it from drying out. After an hour the pastry will be ready for rolling.

1   **Sift the flour and cornflour** on to a worktop and make a wide well in the centre. Place the butter, cut into cubes, the sifted icing sugar with the salt and eggs into the well. Add other flavourings such as vanilla or lemon peel at this stage also.

4   **Chop the butter mixture** with the flour using a large knife or palette knife, working from the outside inwards until all the flour has been incorporated. This should give a consistency of large breadcrumbs. You will have to work quickly to prevent the butter becoming too soft.

7   **Roll the pastry on a cold worktop.** A marble surface is ideal. First sprinkle the surface with a little flour to prevent the pastry sticking and work quickly to prevent the pastry becoming too soft.

2   **Remove the butter** from the refrigerator 10 minutes before use: it should be just firm. Lightly knead the butter then, still working within the flour well, work the icing sugar, flavouring and eggs into the butter to give a crumbly texture.

5   **Work the ingredients together** using your hands. The quicker this can be done, the lighter will be the pastry. If the pastry nevertheless becomes crumbly and will not bind together you can remedy this by working a little bit of egg white into the dough.

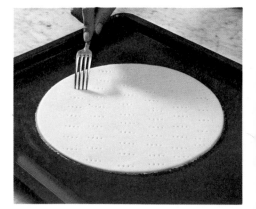

8   **It is best to cut the pastry** once it is on the baking sheet, for in transferring it from the worktop to the baking sheet it can easily go out of shape. Prick the pastry all over with a fork to prevent bubbles forming underneath as it cooks.

Flan Case

for Cinnamon cake, for instance

For many flans and tarts you will need a pastry shell to hold soft, or even runny, fillings. The shell is often first baked empty, to half cook the pastry, the filling will cook quickly, and to prevent any liquid filling from seeping into the pastry and making it soggy. To stop the empty shell from bubbling up in the middle it should be weighed down. This process is known as 'baking blind'–see the illustrations on the right. Dried pulses such as peas, lentils or beans are ideal, having the extra advantage that they can be used over and over again. For a 25-cm/10-in flan tin you will need about 1 kg/2¼ lb pulses.

Here is the recipe for Cinnamon cake in a pastry case which is first baked blind:

500 g/18 oz Sweet Shortcrust Pastry
(see page 38)
25-cm/10-in fluted flan tin or sponge tin
150 g/5 oz butter, softened
175 g/6 oz caster sugar
pinch of salt
pinch of ground cloves
1 teaspoon cinnamon
3 eggs, separated
200 g/7 oz unpeeled almonds, ground
100 g/4 oz ginger biscuit crumbs
cocoa powder or drinking chocolate for
sprinkling

The flan case should be baked blind for about 10 minutes in a moderately hot oven (190 C, 375 F, gas 5). Cream the butter with 50 g/2 oz sugar and spices until light and fluffy then gradually beat in the egg yolks. Whisk the egg whites until stiff but not dry then gradually whisk in the remaining sugar. Fold a little of the whisked egg whites and sugar into the egg yolk mixture. Then add the remaining egg white mixture and the mixed almond and biscuit crumbs and fold in gently until the mixture is of uniform consistency. Pour the mixture into the baked pastry case and bake. Leave the cake to cool and dust with cocoa powder or drinking chocolate.
Baking time: 40–45 minutes in a moderately hot oven (190 C, 375 F, gas 5).

Baking blind is the technical term for pastry cases baked empty, or pre-baked before the filling is added. Wrap the rolled-out pastry around the rolling pin and unroll over the tin. Press the pastry to the edges of the tin using a ball of left-over pastry or your forefinger. Cut off any excess pastry. Prick the base of the flan case using a fork. Cover the base with greaseproof paper then fill the case with dried peas or baking beans. The pastry should not brown as it will have to cook again with the filling. After baking it is very simple to lift out the greaseproof paper and peas or beans. Leave the pastry case to cool slightly, then fill with the cinnamon cake mixture and smooth the top.

You can see from this photograph that the shortcrust pastry has baked evenly. Despite the moist filling, pre-baking has kept the pastry light and short. With really runny fillings such as fruit custards the base has to be protected with a special baking wafer or layer of biscuit crumbs to prevent the liquid soaking into the pre-baked case.

Flavoured Shortcrust Pastry

as used for Linzertorte

Pastries made with ground almonds or other nuts are very short and melt in the mouth. However the natural fat content of nuts means that pastries of this kind, like other high-fat pastries, can very easily become crumbly. If the pastry is too crumbly to manage, making the lattice for the Linzertorte will be difficult.

Linzertorte

350 g/12 oz unpeeled almonds, ground
450 g/1 lb plain flour
350 g/12 oz butter
225 g/8 oz icing sugar
3 egg yolks
$\frac{1}{4}$ teaspoon ground cloves
pinch of cinnamon
grated rind of 1 lemon
$\frac{1}{2}$ teaspoon of vanilla essence
225 g/8 oz seedless raspberry jam
1 egg yolk to glaze
25 g/1 oz flaked almonds

Prepare, shape, fill and bake the pastry as shown on the right.
Baking time: pre-bake in a moderately hot oven (200 C, 400 F, gas 6) for around 10 minutes then reduce to a moderate oven (160 C, 325 F, gas 3) for about 45 minutes. If preferred the almonds can be replaced with hazelnuts. For the sake of completeness and since experts differentiate between Linzertorte and Linz pastry, here is also the recipe for the latter:

Light Linz Pastry

100 g/4 oz ground almonds
225 g/8 oz plain flour
175 g/6 oz butter
100 g/4 oz icing sugar, sifted
4 egg yolks
pinch of salt
grated rind of $\frac{1}{2}$ lemon
2 tablespoons milk
175 g/6 oz seedless raspberry jam
20-cm/8-in cake tin or sponge ring

Preparation is the same as for the Linzertorte. The top can be sprinkled with flaked almonds or, alternatively, dusted with icing sugar after baking.

1 **Pour the ground almonds** on to the worktop. Sift the flour over the almonds and make a wide well in the centre. Place the cut-up butter, icing sugar, 3 egg yolks and the flavourings in the well.

2 **First flake the butter then,** still using your fingers, work in the sugar, egg yolks and flavourings and work together into a smooth mixture.

6 **Using about a third** of the remaining pastry roll it out to form a long strip. Roll this into a cylindrical shape and place in a spiral on a floured cake-tin base or plate. This will make it easier to place around the edge of the tin. Press down using your thumb as shown.

7 **Spread the jam.** This is easiest with a plastic pastry scraper or spatula as these are quite flexible. Make sure no jam goes over the edge of the pastry.

3 **Work in the almonds and flour,** rubbing it in to make large crumbs. Lightly knead the mixture together into a dough, working quickly to make sure it binds well and does not become crumbly. Crumbly pastry makes preparation of the lattice topping extremely difficult.

4 **First wrap the pastry** in cling film or foil and leave it to stand for at least an hour in the refrigerator. Then take half the pastry, shape it into a ball and sprinkle the worktop with flour. Roll the pastry evenly to 1-cm/½-in thick. The remaining pastry will be needed later for the lattice.

5 **Cut out the pastry base** on the baking sheet. First cover the baking sheet with a piece of greaseproof or non-stick baking paper, as this will make it much easier to remove the cooked tart from the baking sheet. Use a 20-cm/8-in cake or flan ring to cut the pastry to size.

8 **Strips of pastry** about 1-cm/½-in. in diameter are rolled on a lightly floured worktop. You will need twelve of varying lengths. Place at regular intervals over the cake to make a lattice. Either cut the strips to length in advance or, using a sharp knife, on the tart itself.

9 **Beat the remaining egg yolk** with the milk and brush over the pastry. Sprinkle flaked almonds around the edge and bake.

Puff Pastry

Light, deliciously crispy and yet so tender that it melts in the mouth. A good puff pastry should have a rich buttery flavour and a baked crusty taste.

However it does require quite a lot of care and precision to make and it is not a job that can be rushed. There are various ways of making puff pastry, but the method illustrated here has the following advantages. The butter is used in thin layers rather than in a thick block and is therefore easier to roll into the pastry and more evenly distributed. If the edges are firmly sealed it is impossible for the butter to come out at the edges as you make the turns. When making puff pastry it is essential that the butter and pastry should both have the same firm texture. The flour and water pastry can be kneaded by hand or mixed using the dough hook in a food mixer. Using a mixer makes the job a little easier but makes little overall difference to the total time involved because the bulk of the time is taken up by rolling the dough, which can only be done by hand, and allowing the pastry to rest.

One tip on how to make the turns: to help you remember how many turns you have made mark the pastry with the corresponding number of fingers after each turn.

Our recipe:
450 g/1 lb plain flour
300 ml/½ pint water
2 teaspoons salt
450 g/1 lb butter, chilled
50 g/2 oz plain flour

2 **Knead the dough** until the surface is smooth and glossy. Wrap the dough and leave it to stand in the refrigerator for 15 minutes. Meanwhile dice the butter, sprinkle with the 50 g/2 oz flour and knead to soften it to the same consistency as the pastry. Be careful not to allow the butter to become soft.

3 **Roll out the flour and water dough** into a rectangle 36 × 52-cm/14 × 20-in. Roll the butter to 25 × 30-cm/10 × 12-in. Place the butter in the centre of the rolled dough and brush the edges of the dough with water or egg white.

5 **Roll out in two directions,** alternately from front to back and from left·to right. Try to keep the pressure even as you roll. With each change of direction the layers will become progressively thinner. Roll out to 36 × 52-cm/14 × 20-in and chill for 20 minutes.

6 **To make a single turn,** fold over one-third of the pastry and then fold over the remaining third. Try to fold exactly so that the edges are straight. Precision and care in making the turns are extremely important to ensure that the pastry rises evenly.

1 **Sift the flour** on to the worktop and make a wide well in the centre. Pour the cold water and salt into the well. Mix the flour and water together working outwards from the centre, while using a pastry scraper in the other hand to bring more flour into the centre.

4 **Fold both sides of the dough** over the butter so as to overlap slightly in the centre, and press down the edges. Press the narrow edges firmly together with your thumb to seal them securely. The butter is now securely wrapped in the dough.

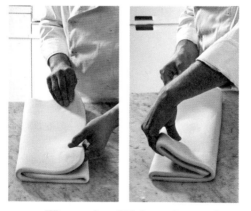

7 **When you have folded over** the second third of pastry, chill for 20 minutes. To make a double turn roll out the pastry once more, fold both sides into the centre and then fold over once more lengthways. Give the pastry two single and two double turns.

8 Here is an example of good, even turns after the second turn – i.e. after one single and one double turn. The layers of pastry and butter should be absolutely even – the idea is that when it is baked the butter will melt away to leave air between the layers of pastry.

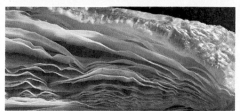

9 Pastry uncooked and cooked after the third turn. The layers in the uncooked pastry are now very thin but still distinguishable. After baking the pastry is nice and flaky and looks more like a puff pastry, but it still needs one more double turn which will make it better still.

10 Delicate flaky layers make up the finished pastry as in this flan case. After the fourth turn the separate layers are hardly visible in the uncooked pastry. When the turns have been given carefully the pastry should rise as easily as in the illustration.

Puff Pastry Flan Case

675 g/1½ lb puff pastry
1 egg yolk mixed with a little water
25-cm/10-in flan ring
20-cm/8-in flan ring
Suggested filling:
300 ml/½ pint double cream, whipped
225 g/8 oz fresh strawberries, puréed

Roll out the puff pastry evenly to about 7-mm/¼-in thick and so it is slightly larger than the 25-cm/10-in flan ring. Using the flan ring cut out a circle exactly as shown in the picture. It is important to use a really sharp knife for a clean cut and to ensure even rising.

Using the smaller ring, cut a circle from the middle of the large pastry circle then cut around the outside of the ring. Do not remove this inner circle of pastry yet. Press the pastry trimmings together and reroll these to about 3-mm/⅛-in thick. Lay the rolled out trimmings on a baking tray then carefully slide the pastry circles on top. Lift out the inner round of pastry and reserve this for another use. Sit the small flan ring in the pastry ring to ensure even rising. Trim off the edges of the pastry base. Using a fork prick the base of the flan case all over to prevent it from rising during cooking. Brush the top of the flan case with the egg yolk mixture making sure that you don't get any egg yolk on the ring. Chill the case for 20 to 30 minutes and then bake in a hot oven (220 C, 425 F, gas 7) for 15 to 20 minutes. Leave to cool. Fold the puréed strawberries into the whipped cream and use to fill the flan case.

Quick Puff Pastry

for Dutch Cherry Gâteau, for instance

This quick variation on classic puff pastry gets its flaky texture from the quick and incomplete way in which the butter is incorporated. While the pastry does not rise as much, or as evenly, as other puff pastries, it is very short and good for cake bases.

Here is the recipe:
1 kg/2 lb plain flour
800 g/1¾ lb butter
15 g/½ oz salt
450 ml/¾ pint water

Make up the pastry following the instructions below. When rolling out the pastry remember to roll it evenly in only two directions, from back to front and from left to right. With quick puff pastry, as with classic pastry, you cannot work too carefully. This applies to making the turns as much as to rolling out. Here is a reminder as to how to make the turns:

Roll out the pastry into a rectangle, fold over one-third of the width and then fold the remaining third on top. This is a single turn. Leave the pastry to stand for 5 minutes, or continue if you are short of time. Roll out the pastry again to a rectangle, fold both sides in to meet at the centre and fold the pastry again in half to make four layers. This is a double turn. Again with this quick pastry you will need to make four turns in all; two single turns alternating with two double turns.

Dutch Cherry Gâteau

3 Quick Puff Pastry bases
100 g/4 oz cherry jam, warmed and sieved or redcurrant jelly
75 g/3 oz fondant icing
1.15 litres/2 pints double cream
100 g/4 oz icing sugar
1 (450 g/1 lb) jar morello cherries
50 g/2 oz caster sugar
pinch of cinnamon
1 tablespoon cornflour
25-cm/10-in loose bottomed flan tin or springform tin

Prepare the morello cherry filling while the bases are baking to allow it time to cool. To make the filling bring the cherry juice to the boil with the sugar and cinnamon, stir in the blended cornflour, simmer for a few minutes and then add the cherries.

1 **Sift the flour** onto the worktop and make a well in the centre. Place the diced butter around the well and cover with a little of the flour. Sprinkle with the salt and then carefully pour the water into the well.

2 **With one hand** work as much of the flour as possible into the water without including any of the butter. Stir round and round with your hand until the water and flour have made a soft dough.

3 **Work the diced butter** into the flour and water dough, kneading it in well. As with classic puff pastry give the pastry two single and two double turns, but you can omit or reduce the resting time between each turn.

4 **Roll into a rectangle** and make the required turns, remembering to roll only from front to back and from left to right. When all the turns have been completed roll the pastry into three sheets about 3-mm/⅛-in thick and slightly larger than the cake tin.

5 **Place the sheets of pastry** in turn on a baking sheet covered with greaseproof paper. Place the cake tin upside down on the pastry and cut round the outside of the rim with a pointed knife. This should give bases 2.5-cm/1-in wider than the diameter of the tin. Leave to stand for 15 minutes.

6 **Prick the bases all over** with a fork to prevent bubbles forming underneath and bake for about 15 minutes in a hot oven (220 C, 425 F, gas 7). If necessary trim the bases to fit the cake tin while still warm, by placing the ring of the tin on the pastry and cutting round the inside with a sharp knife.

This is what the Dutch Cherry Gâteau looks like when cut. A delicious cream and cherry filling between crisp puff pastry. The separate layers of pastry and cream are clearly visible, and it is easy to see whether or not the pastry has been prepared carefully enough. The rings of cherry and cream in the bottom layer should appear at perfectly regular intervals.

7 **Ice the most even base.** Place the base upside down on the worktop and spread with warm sieved jam or warmed redcurrant jelly. Leave it to set slightly and then brush evenly with fondant icing to give a shiny pink surface.

8 **Leave the icing to dry** and as soon as it is firm cut into portions. Use a long knife and first cut the lid into quarters, then cut the quarters into smaller segments, cutting right across the whole width each time.

9 **Whip the cream with the icing sugar** until stiff. Place one pastry round in the cake tin and spread thinly with cream. Using a piping bag with a large plain nozzle pipe a circle of cream around the edge of the tin, and then two more rings at regular intervals.

10 **Arrange the morello cherries** and their sauce evenly between the circles of cream. Using a cake tin base slide the second round of pastry into the tin and press down gently onto the cream and cherries.

11 **Cover the second round of pastry** with a layer of cream up to the rim of the cake tin and smooth the top, preferably with a pastry scraper. To get rid of any air bubbles in the filling lift the tin and drop it gently on to the worktop.

12 **Remove the ring** and cover the edges of the cake with cream. Place the prepared lid on top of the cake and press gently into position. Garnish each portion with a whirl of cream and a drained morello cherry.

Yeast Dough

Although one complete chapter of this book is devoted entirely to baking with yeast, included here are two basic methods for making a yeast dough. This dough is very versatile and forms the basis of a variety of cakes and pastries, from the simple plaited loaf to the finest croissants. The typically sourish taste and the airiness of the dough are produced by the yeast cells which reproduce in warm, moist conditions. The yeast causes a process of fermentation, turning the starch in the flour into glucose, then into alcohol and carbon dioxide.

Yeast for baking comes in two forms. Compressed or fresh yeast is obtainable in block form from bakers or health food shops. It is sold by the ounce and will keep in the refrigerator for a couple of weeks. Dried yeast will keep for several months in a cool, dry place. It usually needs a slightly warmer liquid than fresh yeast in which to dissolve. As a general rule only half the quantity of dried yeast is needed to that of fresh.

Yeast dough can be made by two different methods. In the first method the yeast is dissolved in lukewarm milk and mixed immediately into the flour and other ingredients to form a dough. In the second method, the one illustrated below, the yeast is mixed with milk and a little of the flour to make a starter dough. Eventually this produces better and quicker fermentation, but one has to wait first for the preliminary dough to rise then for the fully mixed dough to rise. The remaining ingredients are mixed in but the starter dough has to be allowed time to rise first. When the starter dough has risen they are added in the form of melted butter mixed with sugar, eggs and salt.

Basic recipe for yeast dough using preliminary dough:

450 g/1 lb strong plain flour
25 g/1 oz fresh yeast or 15 g/½ oz dried yeast
300 ml/½ pint lukewarm milk
2 eggs
50 g/2 oz butter, melted
50 g/2 oz caster sugar
1 teaspoon salt

1 **Sift the flour** into a bowl and make a well in the centre. Crumble the fresh yeast into the well and add the milk. Stir gently to dissolve the yeast in the milk and to work in a little of the flour. If using dried yeast dissolve it in the milk, leave until frothy then place in the flour well and work in a little flour. Sprinkle this starter dough thinly with flour.

2 **Place the bowl** out of any possible draught and leave to stand for about 15 minutes at room temperature. Clearly defined cracks in the layer of flour over the mixture indicate that the starter mixture has been left long enough.

3 **Beat the eggs and melted butter together** and add to the dough. Sugar, salt and any other flavouring should also be added at this stage. Beat the ingredients together until all are thoroughly mixed and the dough has become slightly lighter.

4 **Then knead the yeast dough** on a lightly floured surface for about 10 minutes until smooth and elastic. If the dough is too soft you can add a little more flour at this stage.

5 **Shape the dough into a ball,** return it to the bowl, sprinkle with a little flour and cover with a cloth. Leave the dough to rise for 1–2 hours depending on how warm the room is, or until the dough has doubled in size.

6 **After proving the dough** should at least have doubled in volume. It has then risen sufficiently. You can give the dough a particularly light texture by kneading it again and leaving it to stand in a covered bowl for a further 15–30 minutes.

Croissant Dough

Yeast dough with extra butter

The basic croissant dough is a yeast mixture which is rolled and folded with butter in the same way as puff pastry.

Basic recipe:
900 g/2 lb strong plain flour
100 g/4 oz butter, softened
100 g/4 oz caster sugar
2 teaspoons salt
4 eggs
50 g/2 oz fresh yeast or 25 g/1 oz dried yeast
450 ml/¾ pint lukewarm milk
450 g/1 lb butter for rolling
100 g/4 oz plain flour for the butter

Sift the flour on to the worktop, make a large well in the centre and add the soft butter, sugar, salt and eggs. Crumble the fresh yeast into a basin and dilute with the lukewarm milk. If using dried yeast dissolve it in the lukewarm milk and leave for 10 minutes or until frothy then continue as above. Pour this mixture into the well in the flour. Using a wooden spoon, or better still just your hand, work the ingredients together, working out from the centre and gradually working in all the flour to give a soft dough. Knead the dough vigorously on the worktop, using extra flour if necessary, until the surface is smooth. Wrap the dough in oiled cling film and keep in the refrigerator for 2 to 3 hours. Meanwhile bring the butter to room temperature and work in the flour. Shape the butter into a square about 20 × 20-cm/8 × 8-in. Chill for 30 minutes in the refrigerator. Take the yeast dough out of the refrigerator and roll out evenly on the lightly floured worktop into a square about 40 × 40-cm/16 × 16-in. Place the slab (which should be of similar consistency to the dough) in the middle of the rolled-out dough, brush the edges of the dough with water and fold over so that the butter is completely wrapped in dough. As with classic puff pastry roll out the dough and pastry together to about 40 × 71-cm/16 × 28-in. Fold one-third of the dough over and cover with the third from the other side. This is a single turn. After each turn cover the dough and leave it to stand for 20 minutes in the refrigerator. Make a total of three turns and then shape the dough to make croissants or other shapes.

Fine Fillings

For as long as cakes have been in existence there have been a variety of fillings to enhance their flavour. Even in early medieval times there was a 'porridge', a 'fine monastic speciality' which consisted basically of barley, oats or millet boiled in milk, but which could be varied in many different ways: by being coloured with pollen or flower petals to make it look more appetising; mixed with dates, raisins, figs and nuts; made lighter with eggs; sweetened with honey; or made richer with cream. However it was not until the nineteenth century that delicate gâteaux with delicious fillings and decorations were invented. Cake makers and pastry cooks competed with one another to bring out new and different creations. While patissieres cooked for the coffee house, the best restaurants have always employed a pastry cook, and still do so today.

If pastries and cakes are the basics of baking then the fillings are the creative luxuries. There are many cakes and pastries which need no extra touches. Take nut cake, for example, poppy-seed cake or the traditional rich fruit cake which is iced only in honour of special occasions such as weddings or birthdays.

Simple fillings, like jams, fruit jellies and marmalades, require no special preparation and are therefore not included in this chapter. Other fillings suitable for small cakes made from puff pastry or yeast dough can contain fresh or preserved fruit, nuts or poppy seeds and these are all included in the appropriate recipes. In addition, creams and custards provide the basis for many filling variations which you can use as the basis for your own creations, and these will be dealt with in this chapter.

Light, airy creams are suitable for filling gâteaux, sponge rolls or cream slices. The simplest and lightest of these is cream itself. Double cream gives the best consistency for a cake filling. It is important to whip it correctly: stiff enough to hold its shape but not over whisked to look 'granular' in texture. Whipping cream can also be used as a filling for light cakes, however, it does not retain its whipped consistency for many hours but tends to weep very slightly and loose body if left for a long time. Vanilla cream is another light filling. Made with sugar, cornflour, egg yolk, vanilla pods and milk, this is none other than the familiar custard. Mixed hot with whisked egg white we get the delicate Chiboust cream. Custards made with fresh cream are other light fillings, and these include Bavarian cream which goes with almost any flavouring – fruit, nuts or chocolate – or the various wine creams which are excellent with citrus fruit.

Following these are the heavier butter creams, led by the less rich vanilla butter cream, a mixture of butter and custard. Next come the light butter creams with eggs, sugar and vanilla, and Italian butter cream which is made lighter with meringue. One of the richest of all fillings is French butter cream, *crème au beurre nature*, made from boiled sugar, vanilla, egg yolk and butter. One of the best fillings is Canache cream, an exquisite mixture of melted chocolate and fresh cream. Now it is up to you to make the most of the choices available. You have only to develop the art of combining the various ingredients to enhance each of them to the full and to create wonderful delicacies.

1 **Place half the sugar** into a basin with the cornflour and egg yolks. The eggs should be separated very carefully since any traces of egg white will form lumps when the cream is boiled. Add about a quarter of the milk.

Simple Vanilla Cream or Custard

or *crème pâtissière* as French chefs call it. This cream is popularly known as confectioner's custard and in this form it is one of the most popular creams. It is made by boiling milk with sugar and thickening it with starch. Egg yolks help to thicken and enrich the cream. The traditional flavouring is vanilla.

With or without vanilla this cream is one of the basic fillings and it has a multitude of culinary uses. Combined with whisked egg white while still hot it forms the basis of the deliciously light Chiboust Cream which is used in cream slices or Gâteau Saint-Honoré. It also forms the basis of the so-called 'German Butter Cream' or French

Almond Cream and a whole variety of other fillings. If it is to be used cold as a basic cream, it will stay smooth if it is stirred as it cools, but it does become looser in the process. Alternatively, the surface of the cream can be sprinkled with sugar or covered with a piece of greaseproof paper to prevent a skin forming. If necessary the thick, cold cream can be strained through a fine sieve and stirred until smooth. If it is covered, it can be kept in the refrigerator for up to two days.

100 g/4 oz caster sugar
50 g/2 oz cornflour, sifted
4 egg yolks
600 ml/1 pint milk
1 vanilla pod

2 **Beat with a small balloon whisk,** mixing slowly and carefully until all the ingredients are thoroughly blended. Meanwhile bring the rest of the milk and sugar to the boil in a large saucepan with the vanilla pod.

3 **Beat the cornflour mixture** once more with the whisk before pouring it in a slow, even trickle into the milk. Beat continuously as you add the cornflour mixture to the milk and then bring to the boil over a high heat.

4 **Boil the vanilla cream,** whisking it continuously. Continue to cook for 2–3 minutes to get rid of the starchy taste of the cornflour. Beating will prevent the cream sticking to, or even burning on, the base of the saucepan.

5 **Pour the vanilla cream** into a bowl to cool and sprinkle the top with sifted icing sugar. The layer of melting sugar prevents a skin forming and means that none of the cream is wasted when you come to use it.

6 **Cold, thick custard** will become smooth again if pressed through a fine sieve. This is easiest through a wooden-framed hair sieve used upside down. Press the cream through with a pastry scraper.

7 **Beat the cold cream smooth.** Return the vanilla cream to the bowl after straining and then whisk vigorously until it regains its smooth, creamy consistency. The cream is now ready to use.

Chiboust Cream

To make this the vanilla cream (made according to the recipe on the opposite page, but with only 25 g/1 oz caster sugar) must be ready at the same time as the meringue.

For the meringue:
6 egg whites
175 g/6 oz caster sugar
4 tablespoons water

Whisk the egg white until stiff but not dry then whisk in 1 tablespoon of sugar. Dissolve the remaining sugar in the water bring to the boil and boil steadily stirring occasionally until the syrup reaches a soft ball stage (116 C/240 F) then add it in a fine trickle to the whisked egg white. Fold in the boiling vanilla cream and use at once. The cake must also be ready to be filled immediately since this cream sets very quickly.

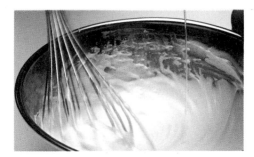

1 **Whisk the egg white** until it forms soft peaks then add the sugar. Beat for a few minutes more and then add the syrup in a slow trickle and gradually whisk it into the egg whites.

2 **Pour the boiling vanilla cream** into the meringue straight from the hob and fold it in with a metal spoon.

Whipped Cream

This is both one of the most popular and the easiest of the cake fillings to make. Alongside sugar and eggs, cream is one of the main ingredients of patisserie. As a pure natural product cream comes in different qualities and should be used accordingly.

These days cream is heat treated, like milk, to ensure its safety and to improve its keeping qualities. There are several different types of cream available: half cream, single cream, whipping cream, double cream, and clotted cream are all fresh creams whose consistency depends on the percentage of butterfat contained in them. Only whipping cream and double cream will whip successfully but care must be taken not to over whip or else the cream will start to turn granular and will eventually turn into butter if the whipping is continued. Always keep cream in the refrigerator and remember to look at the sell-by date on the top of the carton – an easy and efficient method of telling if the cream is fresh.

One of the basic rules when whipping cream is to thoroughly chill all your utensils (whisk and bowl), and when possible it is best to whip the cream in a cool room. You can sweeten the cream (with 25–40 g/1–1½ oz icing sugar to 600 ml/1 pint cream) before you begin whipping. If you prefer to use an electric whisk, don't use the highest setting, switch off the whisk before the cream is completely stiff and finish off with a hand whisk. Only by hand whisking can you judge the right consistency properly. If you are using the whisk of a food processor start at full speed and finish at a slower one.

Flavoured Whipped Cream

Whipped cream can be mixed with various flavourings such as chocolate, cocoa, nuts, or small quantities of spirits. Cream can be flavoured with the following (in each case quantities are for 600 ml/1 pint unsweetened cream):

25 g/1 oz icing sugar, 75 g/3 oz melted chocolate
50 g/2 oz icing sugar, 2 tablespoons dissolved instant coffee
100 g/4 oz finely crushed praline (see page 147)
50 g/2 oz icing sugar, 100 g/4 oz toasted hazelnuts, chopped
50 g/2 oz icing sugar, 2 tablespoons cherry liqueur

If larger quantities are to be mixed with the cream it will need a stabiliser if it is to retain its texture. Gelatine is excellent as it is neutral in taste, gives the cream a good consistency and helps prevent it separating. The result is a flavoured, stable cream which will keep for a whole day in the refrigerator.

A third way of using cream for cake fillings is to make a cream custard, a mixture of a basic custard and whipped cream. Basic flavourings for creams of this kind can be fruit purée or juice, wine, or a combination of fruit and wine. The flavour and acidity of citrus fruit goes best with white wine, but light red wines also go well with fruit, the only disadvantage with red wine is that it makes the cream rather an unattractive colour.

Orange Wine Cream

The basic orange sauce can be made in advance and stored in the refrigerator. When you want to use the sauce all that is required is to warm it through over a pan of hot water, then to allow it to cool again before combining it with the whipped cream. The quantities given are sufficient to fill and cover a 25-cm/10-in cake.

3 oranges
250 ml/8 fl oz white wine
225 g/8 oz icing sugar
25 g/1 oz cornflour
4 egg yolks
8 leaves gelatine or 25 g/1 oz powdered gelatine
600 ml/1 pint double cream

1 Grate the rinds of the oranges. Scrub the oranges thoroughly in hot water before grating. Be careful to grate only the thin outer rind because the white pith has a bitter taste.

2 Squeeze the orange juice. Reserve 2 tablespoons of wine and add the remainder to the squeezed orange juice. The total quantity of liquid needed is 450 ml/¾ pint. Gently simmer the juice mixture with the grated rind and sugar over a low heat for about 10 minutes.

3 Strain the wine and orange mixture to avoid having pieces of orange peel in the finished cream. Then bring the sauce to the boil in a fairly large saucepan. It is best to use a stainless steel or enamel saucepan to avoid any danger of the sauce oxidising.

4 Blend the cornflour with the reserved 2 tablespoons wine and the egg yolks. Whisk this mixture into the boiling sauce. Continue to cook for 2 minutes to make sure the cornflour is completely cooked.

5 Add the gelatine. Soak the leaf gelatine in cold water for 10 minutes, then squeeze it out and stir into the hot sauce or dissolve the powdered gelatine in 6 tablespoons hot water. Leave the sauce to cool, stirring from time to time to prevent a skin forming.

6 Whip the cream until stiff. Pour the sauce into a large bowl and when almost completely cold fold in the whipped cream, stirring it in gently with a hand whisk, or metal spoon. Do not whisk in the cream or the filling will become too loose.

Bavarian Cream

This is the classic dessert cream, a combination of custard and whipped cream. It makes a delicious filling for gâteaux and Swiss rolls and can be flavoured in almost any way imaginable.

4 egg yolks
100 g/4 oz caster sugar
600 ml/1 pint milk
1 vanilla pod
8 leaves gelatine or 25 g/1 oz powdered gelatine
600 ml/1 pint double cream, whipped

Prepare the cream as shown below. The quantities given will fill a 25-cm/10-in gâteau or a Swiss roll from the recipe on pages 30–1.

A combination of Bavarian cream and raspberries is the filling for this cake. The raspberries sink into the bottom layer of chocolate Bavarian cream and are then covered with vanilla Bavarian cream. The cake needs at least an hour in the refrigerator to cool and set fully.

1 **Cream the egg yolks and sugar.** Ideally a hand whisk is better than an electric whisk for this process because the sugar has to dissolve slowly. The mixture should be thick and creamy.

2 **Bring the milk to the boil** in a saucepan with the vanilla pod. Then beat the hot milk a little at a time into the egg and sugar mixture, whisking continuously. Then pour the mixture back into the saucepan.

3 **Cook the sauce** over a very gentle heat until it is thick enough to coat the back of a spoon, or to form rose-like ripples when swirled on the spoon with a clean finger. If the ripples remain the custard is thick enough. Do not allow the custard to boil or it will curdle.

4 **Soak the gelatine** in the cold water for 10 minutes, squeeze it out well, and stir into the warm sauce until completely dissolved or dissolve the powdered gelatine in 6 tablespoons of hot, not boiling, water and add to the sauce. Do not boil.

5 **Strain the sauce** to remove any lumps. Fill a large bowl with ice cubes and cold water and stand a smaller bowl (containing the custard) in it, but make sure that the smaller bowl is still large enough to allow you to whisk in the cream without too much difficulty.

6 **The final stage.** The sauce should not be too warm and runny, or it will make the whipped cream runny too. If, on the other hand, the sauce is too cold the cold cream will make it set solid. When the sauce runs off the spoon in a thick stream it is the ideal consistency.

53

Vanilla Butter Cream

German style

The high proportion of custard in this filling makes it the lightest of the butter creams and it has relatively little sugar too.

150 g/5 oz caster sugar
40 g/1½ oz cornflour, sifted
3 egg yolks
600 ml/1 pint milk
1 vanilla pod
350 g/12 oz unsalted butter, softened

Prepare the custard from the sugar, cornflour, egg yolks, milk and vanilla pod as shown on page 50 and sprinkle it with a little icing sugar before leaving it to cool. Strain through a fine sieve and beat until smooth. Then mix with the creamed butter.

Butter Cream

with eggs

This butter cream is much lighter than the 'classic French cream' and simpler to make, as you do not need to boil the sugar.

275 g/10 oz unsalted butter, softened
3 eggs
3 egg yolks
225 g/8 oz caster sugar
1 teaspoon vanilla essence

Cream the butter until light and fluffy. Beat the eggs, egg yolks, sugar and vanilla essence over a saucepan of simmering water and continue beating until cool, as shown in the Genoese sponge recipe (see page 29). Mix the two mixtures together when both are at the same temperature.

Italian Butter Cream

with meringue

225 g/8 oz unsalted butter, softened
5 egg whites
175 g/6 oz caster sugar
1 vanilla pod
6 tablespoons water

Cream the butter until light and fluffy. Whisk the egg whites until stiff but not dry then gradually whisk in 25 g/1 oz sugar. Meanwhile dissolve the remaining sugar with the vanilla pod in the water and boil steadily until it reaches a soft ball stage (116 C/240 F). Remove the vanilla pod then whisk the syrup slowly into the egg white. Continue whisking until the mixture is cool, and then fold into the butter.

1 **Make sure the butter** is at room temperature so that it is very soft, because only softened butter will become sufficiently fluffy and increase in volume when whipped. Use an electric whisk on the highest setting.

1 **Beat the egg mixture.** The technique is the same as for the Genoese sponge. The eggs, sugar and vanilla essence are beaten over a saucepan of hot water until thick enough to leave a trail when the whisk is lifted. Then remove the bowl from the water and continue beating until cold. The mixture should then be thick and creamy.

1 **Whisk the egg white** until stiff, adding 25 g/1 oz sugar as soon as it begins to form soft peaks. Whisk for a few minutes more and then add the sugar syrup in a thin trickle and whisk it slowly into the stiff egg white.

2 **Strain the custard** and make sure it is at the same temperature as the fat, then beat into the butter. If the custard is too cold the butter cream may separate. Use an electric whisk at medium speed.

2 **Cream the butter** until light and fluffy. Slowly add the egg mixture to the butter whisking continuously. Add a little at a time and make sure it is fully incorporated before adding any more.

2 **Add the creamed butter.** In contrast to the other creams we have described the butter here is incorporated into the meringue all at one go. Make sure that the meringue and butter are at the same temperature, for if the meringue is too warm the cream will not be firm enough.

Butter Cream –
the versatile filling

Butter cream is one of the most useful fillings and despite its name butter is not absolutely necessary in a cream of this kind: good quality margarines can also be used. Only the light-flavoured, soft margarines should be used instead of butter however as the more strongly flavoured, cheaper kinds are likely to taint the filling even if another flavouring is added.

Butter creams are a combination of two basic ingredients, butter and sugar, made lighter by the addition of eggs, egg white or custard. The quality of the main ingredient, the butter, determines the flavour of the butter cream, with the butter taste coming through quite distinctly in the delicately flavoured vanilla butter cream. Use only fresh, best quality unsalted butter.

The length of time the butter cream will keep is determined by the ingredients which are added to lighten the filling: German butter cream which is made with custard goes off fairly quickly; the cream made with whole eggs keeps slightly better, and Italian butter cream, which contains only egg white, keeps best of all.

Butter cream is the most versatile of all the fillings and icings and it can be flavoured with a multitude of different ingredients. The basic creams on these two pages are all vanilla flavoured, but omit the vanilla if you decide to make a cream of a different flavour.

These basic recipes are all suitable for a cake of an average to large size. Some contain more sugar than others and, depending on the chosen flavouring, you may need to add extra sugar. This would not be necessary with chocolate as this itself contains sugar, but with powdered cocoa you will probably need extra sugar. Coffee flavour will certainly need extra sugar as the coffee needs to be sweet to bring out the full flavour.

Liquid flavourings, such as liqueurs, may make the cream separate, and it is important that, whatever the flavouring, it should be at the same temperature as the butter cream.

French Butter Cream

Known in French as *crème au beurre nature*, this is the classic basic butter cream which can be varied to almost any flavour.

225 g/8 oz caster sugar
6 tablespoons water
1 vanilla pod
6 egg yolks
350 g/12 oz unsalted butter, softened

With the addition of the boiled sugar the egg yolks are first beaten warm, and then cold. You can use a bowl of water and ice cubes to cool the mixture more quickly. If you prefer an even lighter cream you can fold in 225 g/8 oz Italian meringue.

1 **Dissolve the sugar** in the water with the vanilla pod. Bring to the boil and boil steadily, stirring occasionally, until the syrup reaches the soft ball stage (116 C/240 F).

2 **Beat the egg yolks** and when they are nice and creamy pour the sugar syrup in a slow trickle down the side of the bowl, whisking continuously. This is very easy to do in a food mixer.

3 **Cream the butter** until light and fluffy and then gradually beat in the egg yolk mixture.

Almond Cream

Classic *crème d'amandes* is a filling cream which goes extremely well in puff pastry, yeast dough or even shortcrust pastry.

175 g/6 oz unsalted butter, softened
175 g/6 oz icing sugar
3 eggs
175 g/6 oz ground almonds
25 g/1 oz plain flour, sifted
4 tablespoons brown rum

Cream the butter and sugar until light and fluffy then add the eggs one after the other, making sure each is fully incorporated before adding the next. Mix the almonds into the sifted flour, then fold this into the creamed mixture. This basic mixture can be flavoured with rum at this point or (if you are not using it all at once) when you are ready to use it, when it is also mixed with the same quantity of custard (see page 50).

Simple Almond Cream

Made without custard, this cream is heavier and more strongly flavoured.

100 g/4 oz marzipan
50 g/2 oz unsalted butter, softened
50 g/2 oz caster sugar
1 egg
50 g/2 oz ground almonds
2 tablespoons cornflour, sifted

Cream the marzipan with the butter and sugar then gradually beat in the egg and continue beating until creamy. Fold in the ground almonds and cornflour.

1 **Cream the butter and sugar** until light and fluffy and then beat in one egg at a time. Each egg must be completely worked in before you add the next otherwise the mixture might curdle.

2 **Mix the ground almonds** with the sifted flour and fold into the butter mixture in two or three portions. Again each portion of flour and almonds must be well incorporated before you add any more.

3 **Add the rum.** This combines with the flavour of the almonds to give the cream an unforgettable taste. If you are not using all the cream, store the unused portion in the refrigerator without adding rum to it in case you eventually decide to give it some alternative flavouring.

4 **Mix equal quantities** of the basic almond mixture and custard to obtain the finished almond cream. Stir each thoroughly before combining them. If you are using almond mixture from the refrigerator you will have to warm it to make it smooth and creamy.

Canache Cream

as used in Truffle Cake

This classic chocolate cream is also known as Paris cream (in France *ganache*). The basic cream requires only two essential ingredients – chocolate and fresh cream – and the consistency can be altered by the way in which these two are combined. A light Canache cream is used as a filling for cakes and pastries.

The basic Canache cream allows for variation. Bitter chocolate can be replaced with milk chocolate. By adding butter the cream becomes nice and light. Almonds or other nuts go very well with the chocolate cream, as do a range of spirits. Rum, brandy or fruit liqueurs tend to be strongly flavoured and should be added only in limited quantities. With milder-flavoured liqueurs where you would have to add a lot of liquid and thus affect the consistency, you should reduce the amount of cream by the volume of liqueur. It is important with spirits not to add them until the cream is quite cool because heat evaporates alcohol and thus some of the flavour will be lost.

Truffle Cake

300 ml/½ pint double cream
350 g/12 oz plain chocolate, roughly chopped
75 g/3 oz unsalted butter, softened
5 tablespoons brown rum
1 chocolate sponge (see pages 30–1)
1 tablespoon Cointreau
100 g/4 oz plain chocolate, grated to decorate
icing sugar for dusting
16 chocolate truffles

Bring the cream to the boil and stir in the chopped chocolate until fully dissolved. Leave the cream to cool for about 30 minutes, whisking occasionally to prevent a skin forming. When the cream is cool but not set whisk thoroughly. Beat in the butter which should be of the same consistency. Finally stir in the rum and use the cream immediately.

1 **Pour the cream** into a saucepan large enough to allow you to stir in the chocolate without difficulty. Bring the cream to the boil taking care that it does not boil over. Remove the saucepan from the heat and immediately add the chopped chocolate.

2 **Whisk the chocolate** into the cream. The cream should still be hot but not boiling. The chopped chocolate soon melts as you stir it and the larger lumps will disappear after a few minutes to leave a smooth, glossy cream.

3 **Pour the hot cream** into a large mixing bowl in a cool place and stir occasionally with a whisk to prevent a skin forming. When the cream is almost cold whisk it until it is light and fluffy and has doubled in volume.

4 **Cream the butter** until light and fluffy then whisk it into the light, whipped cream and chocolate mixture. The butter must be of the same fluffy consistency as the cream if it is to mix in properly. Then gradually add 3 tablespoons of rum. Chill for 1–2 hours in the refrigerator.

5 **Fill the cake** with the chilled Canache cream. If it is still not firm enough put back in the refrigerator. Do not whip any further or the cream will fall.

6 **Chocolate truffle cake.** The sponge is cut into three layers. Spread the first layer with Canache cream and cover with the second layer of sponge. Sprinkle this sponge with half each of the remaining rum and Cointreau and another layer of cream. Cover with the third layer, again moisten it with the spirits and then cover the cake with cream. Sprinkle immediately with the grated chocolate before the cream sets. Do not allow time for the cake to chill, rather divide it immediately into 16 portions and garnish each with a whirl of cream and a chocolate truffle. Dust the top of the cake with a little icing sugar.

Icing and the Art of Decoration

Although fashions may change and cake decoration may vary from the elaborate to the simple, the art of cake decoration will always be with us as part of the repertoire of a good cook. As long as professional cooks continue to make such a wide variety of gâteaux and cakes, slices and tarts, their example will be followed and people will continue to take pleasure in decorating their home baking. The art of cake decoration does not stand still and the best pastry chefs are continually introducing new ideas.

Just as the modern ideas about afternoon tea developed from Victorian times, so did the cakes and pastries we eat at this meal develop from baking in the Middle Ages. The large cakes now known as gâteaux reached the apex of their development in the nineteenth century. As one might expect in that age of ease and luxurious living, these were elaborate cakes, richly decorated, in a host of shapes both large and small. But just as the Modernist movement had a purifying influence on the decorative excesses of nineteenth century art, the same trend towards purity of line became evident in the area of patisserie. Gâteaux were now decorated modestly, geometrically, stylishly. The piping bag with its swirls, whirls and rosettes was suddenly taboo. Henceforth there was to be nothing of the confectioner's skills of construction in cake decoration.

Since then contrasting styles have developed side by side. Many confectioners and chefs are proud of having developed their own individual style of decoration. And there is no doubt about the fact that many of them are real artists. Yet it is silly to argue about whether aesthetic style is better than pretty flourishes. Obviously no-one finds an over-decorated cake particularly attractive, yet clearly geometric lines will always have to compete with pretty frippery. We have attempted to work as timelessly as possible utilising plain and fluted piping nozzles; marzipan and chocolate; and fondant and velvety chocolate icing. We have combined chocolate with nuts and croquant. We have no objection to gold and silver balls – in the right place. Yet we have not decorated over-lavishly for we believe that too little is better than too much. We have attempted to explain the separate techniques without advocating any particular style. Quite the contrary. This is the area of confectionery which best lends itself to new creations and the cook should be left completely free to put his or her own ideas into practice.

Apricot Glaze

150 g/5 oz caster sugar
6 tablespoons water
1 tablespoon lemon juice
225 g/8 oz apricot jam

Dissolve the sugar in the water and lemon juice. Bring to the boil and boil steadily for 2–3 minutes. Add this mixture to the apricot jam and boil vigorously. Strain through a fine sieve to get a transparent glaze. Professional chefs usually make apricot glaze with liquid glucose which can be obtained from the chemist.

50 g/2 oz liquid glucose
3 tablespoons water
225 g/8 oz apricot jam, sieved

Fondant Icing

Place 675 g/1½ lb granulated sugar in a saucepan with 300 ml/½ pint water and heat gently until the sugar has dissolved. Add 1½ tablespoons of liquid glucose *or* ¼ teaspoon cream of tartar then bring to the boil slowly. While heating brush the sides of the saucepan with a brush dipped in cold water to prevent crystals forming. When the fondant has reached 115C/240F pour on to a slab of cold, wet marble or, if not available, into a large, cold, wet bowl. Work the fondant until white and firm. As the mixture begins to set knead well until smooth. It is now ready to be stored until needed or thinned down and re-heated for use. Thin as necessary with sugar syrup, egg white or milk. It must be stirred continuously while warming and should not be heated beyond 35C/95F or it will crystalise.

1 **Warm the fondant icing** in a bowl over a saucepan of hot water. The water temperature should not exceed 40C/104F. If you want a runnier fondant add a little sugar syrup and egg white and stir until smooth. The fondant itself should not be allowed to exceed 35C/95F on the sugar thermometer.

1 **Add the liquid glucose and water** to the sieved apricot jam. Boil vigorously for about 5 minutes until the mixture has reduced by about one-third.

2 **When the glaze is ready** it should be clear and transparent on the wooden spoon. Since the glaze can only be used hot sensitive cream gâteaux will need the protection of marzipan before glazing. Used as an icing in its own right apricot glaze never sets completely hard.

2 **When the fondant** runs off the spoon in a thick stream it is the right consistency to use for icing cakes. The cake should first be covered with apricot glaze to provide extra moisture and keep the fondant shiny. Fondant is not restricted to icing large cakes, however. It can be used for small puff pastries and croissants that need icing. In these cases the fondant should be transparent to allow the colour of the baking to show through. To get a transparent fondant you will have to dilute it further by adding extra syrup or alcohol.

Icing a Large Cake

Before you ice a cake with fondant it must first have an insulating layer of apricot glaze. This ensures that the fondant will keep its familiar glossy finish as it dries. A layer of marzipan under the glaze is also necessary if the cake has a custard or cream filling and, where used, should be kept as thin as possible. It is made by working 150 g/5 oz icing sugar into 200 g/7 oz almond paste. You should work as quickly as possible since overhandling makes the marzipan short and crumbly so that it is impossible to roll out. If you do find the marzipan difficult to roll mixing in a little egg white should remedy the situation.

3 **Brush with apricot glaze.** You need a very thin layer of apricot so dilute the glaze with a little water. Make sure that the glaze is warm enough to brush on to the cake but not too hot or it may melt the filling in the cake. Brush the glaze over the marzipan as thinly and lightly as possible.

4 **When the glaze is set,** pour the fondant icing over the cake. If the cake has a cream or custard filling which is sensitive to heat, it is a good idea to chill the cake between glazing and icing.

1 **Roll the marzipan** until very thin and slightly larger than necessary to cover the top and sides of the cake. Roll the marzipan around the rolling pin to prevent it stretching or tearing as you transfer it to the cake.

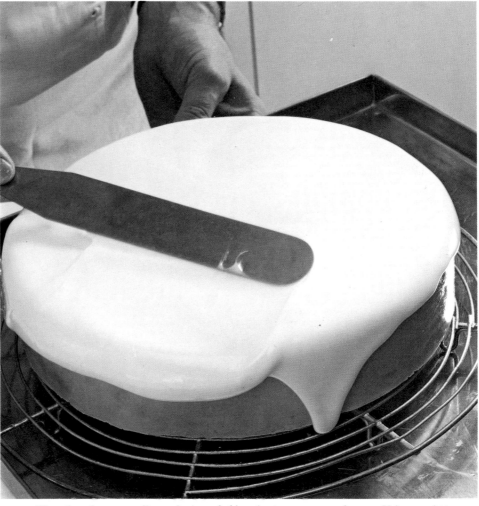

2 **Press smoothly over the edges.** A palette knife is the best thing to use for this. Try to avoid getting any folds, but should they develop, pinch the fold together between your fingers and cut off the excess with scissors. Smooth the join using the palette knife.

5 **Place the cake on a cooling rack** over a baking sheet or greaseproof paper. Using a palette knife, or long kitchen knife, spread the fondant very gently until even. Make sure that the icing is not too thick on the top of the cake and that it runs evenly down the sides, again use the knife to spread it evenly over the sides. Providing the cake itself is not too fragile you can spread the warm icing very effectively by lifting the cooling rack and gently tapping it on to the worktop.

Icing and Decorating

at the same time – as with this Punch cake – is the easiest way of making your cakes more appetising. Only the top is glazed and decorated. The end product is extremely attractive given that the operation involves only one step.

Punch Cake

1 Genoese sponge of 25-cm/10-in
4 tablespoons brown rum
3 tablespoons fresh orange juice
225 g/8 oz redcurrant jelly
½ quantity of Apricot Glaze (see page 60)
250 g/9 oz marzipan
150 g/5 oz fondant icing
brown food colouring
100 g/4 oz flaked almonds, toasted
16 glacé cherry halves

Cut the sponge into three layers. Mix 3 tablespoons of the rum with the orange juice. Moisten the middle and top layers with the orange juice and rum, then sandwich all three layers together with the redcurrant jelly. Cover the cake with a metal sheet and weight down with 2 kg/4 lb weight. Leave the cake to compress for 1 to 2 hours. This gives the cake a nice flat top.

Stir the apricot glaze until smooth and brush it over the cake. Then continue as shown in the photographs. The fondant icing should be diluted with rum in a bowl over hot water (see page 60) and, if necessary, thinned even more with syrup or water.

2 **Brush the remaining apricot glaze** thinly over the marzipan. This is essential, for it is this that gives the fondant its shine – as we have already said. Without the glaze the fondant would develop dry spots which look unsightly and would be difficult to decorate.

3 **Colour a little of the fondant icing on** a metal sheet with a little brown food colouring, mixing well with a palette knife until even throughout. Spoon this fondant into a greaseproof piping bag and cut off the point with sharp scissors.

1 **Roll the marzipan** out until quite thin. Lightly sprinkle a metal sheet with icing sugar and place the marzipan on it. Cut the marzipan to fit the cake by cutting round the inside of the sponge ring and then slide the marzipan on to the cake making sure there are no folds or wrinkles.

4 **While the rum fondant** is lukewarm (about 34 C/93 F on the sugar thermometer) pour it on to the top of the cake and spread evenly with a palette knife. You will have to work very quickly to prevent the fondant setting before properly spread. Make sure that none runs down the sides.

5 **While the rum fondant is still soft,** pipe a spiral of the brown fondant on to the cake. It is important that both lots of fondant should be of the same consistency, otherwise they will not combine properly to make the desired design.

6 **Using the edge of a palette knife** or the blunt side of a knife, lightly draw across the cake from the centre outwards. After each stroke wipe the blade clean with a damp cloth, for any brown fondant already on the knife would spoil the design.

7 **To prevent the icing cracking** leave the cake on the metal sheet while you cover the edge with toasted flaked almonds. Press these on to the cake with a palette knife as you slowly turn the cake around. Each portion should then be decorated with half a glacé cherry.

Mocha Cake

For the almond sponge:
6 eggs, separated
150 g/5 oz caster sugar
75 g/3 oz ground almonds
75 g/3 oz plain flour
50 g/2 oz biscuit crumbs

For the filling:
1½ tablespoons instant coffee dissolved in
2 tablespoons hot water
Vanilla Butter Cream (made with
100 g/4 oz butter, see page 54)

For the icing:
175 g/6 oz marzipan,
½ quantity of Apricot Glaze (see page 60)
150 g/5 oz fondant icing
1 teaspoon instant coffee diluted in
3 teaspoons hot water *and* 1 tablespoon
mocha liqueur to flavour the fondant
100 g/4 oz chocolate, grated, for the sides
16 edible chocolate coffee beans
25-cm/10-in cake tin, base lined with
greaseproof paper

Beat the egg yolks with about a third of the sugar until pale and thick. Whisk the whites until stiff then whisk in the remaining sugar. Fold the whites into the yolks and then fold in the ground almonds, sifted flour and biscuit crumbs. Bake in a moderately hot oven (190 C, 375 F, gas 5) for 35 to 40 minutes.

Stir the dissolved coffee into the butter cream. When the sponge is cool, cut into three layers. Sandwich together with half the butter cream and use the remaining to cover the cake thinly. Cover the top with marzipan, brush with apricot glaze and cover with the flavoured fondant icing (as shown on the right). Press the grated chocolate around the edge. To decorate the top pipe 16 whirls of butter cream and top each with a chocolate coffee bean.

Boiled Chocolate Icing

This is the sweet velvety icing used for the world-famous Sachertorte. It is a traditional Austrian icing.

Ingredients:
275 g/10 oz caster sugar
100 g/4 oz plain chocolate
50 g/2 oz cocoa powder
8 tablespoons water

3 **Pour into** a wide heatproof bowl and beat the icing with a wooden spoon, stirring the mixture away from the sides of the bowl. This eventually makes the icing thick and glossy.

1 **Place the sugar,** chocolate, broken into pieces, and sifted cocoa into a heavy based saucepan. Add the water and stir all the ingredients thoroughly with a wooden spoon. Bring the mixture to the boil, stirring.

4 **To make the icing thick and creamy** more quickly pour half on to a marble slab and work with a palette knife until creamy, and then stir it back into the remaining icing.

2 **Cook over a moderate heat** until a temperature of 108C/220F is reached or mixture forms a long dhread when tested between two teaspoons. Brush the edge of the saucepan frequently with water to prevent any crystals forming.

5 **Place the cake** on a cooling rack and stand it over a sheet of greaseproof paper or a large plate. Pour the thick, smooth chocolate icing on to the cake and spread it over with a palette knife, using as few strokes as possible.

Piping Icings

Royal Icing

225 g/8 oz icing sugar
1 egg white
1 teaspoon lemon juice

The quantity of icing sugar given should be treated as a general guide, for the smallest difference in the amount of egg white means quite a substantial difference to the quantity of icing sugar. To make decorations you will usually require less icing than that produced with one egg white. The consistency of the icing must be just right for piping – soft enough to give a continuous line but firm enough to hold its shape.

1 **Place the sifted icing sugar** and egg white in a bowl. It is a good idea to keep back a little of the icing sugar and to add it as necessary after you have mixed the icing and have a better idea of its consistency. Begin whisking slowly then gradually increase the speed. Lastly add the lemon juice.

2 **This is what royal icing should look like.** Thick and light, so that the marks of the whisk are clearly visible. When you have finished whisking the icing cover the bowl immediately with a damp cloth to prevent the surface drying out.

Chocolate Piping Icing

Melt 50 g/2 oz plain chocolate in a double-boiler over a low heat or a bowl over a saucepan of hot water. Stir the lukewarm chocolate to a smooth paste then gradually add the sugar syrup a teaspoon at a time, beating well after each addition. The consistency will depend on the amount of syrup you add (you will need about 7 teaspoons).

Piping Chocolate

This is used for decorations which are piped on to greaseproof paper or foil. When set they come easily away from the paper. They can be made with plain or milk chocolate. The warmed chocolate is mixed with icing sugar and then a few drops of water are added to give a piping consistency. Keep the chocolate at a constant temperature of 32 C/90 F over a saucepan of hot water to prevent it setting.

Make a piping bag with greaseproof paper: 1 Fold a square of paper diagonally in half. Hold the middle of the long side between your left thumb and index finger and twist the paper to the left with your right hand. **2** Keep twisting, holding the pointed end in your left hand. **3** Fold the extra paper in at the end to secure the bag. **4** Spoon in the icing taking care not to get any on the rim of the bag. **5** Before you fold the top make sure that the seam (the side edge of the paper) is at the back. First squeeze the air out of the bag and then fold in the ends. **6** Cut off the end with sharp scissors; remember that the size of the hole determines the thickness of the piped thread.

Ingredients:
225 g/8 oz plain or milk chocolate
50 g/2 oz icing sugar
few drops water

With a steady hand you can pipe delicate butterflies and flowers which you can decorate with silver balls and violets. Right: the correct consistency for piping chocolate.

Chocolate

Chocolate makes a delicious cake covering but has the disadvantage of being quite difficult to work with. It must be warmed before use, as this both improves the flavour and the appearance. Chocolate consists of cocoa with cocoa butter and sugar and there are different types of chocolate available. The best kind to use is dark, bitter chocolate intended for use in cooking but should not be confused with the lower quality 'cooking chocolate'. The 'real' cooking chocolate is less sweet and has more of a chocolate flavour than the dessert variety and is easier to melt as it can stand higher temperatures. Couverture is a special kind of cooking chocolate which is very expensive but gives a very smooth, glossy appearance and a strong chocolate flavour. Instructions on the packet will inform you how to use the couverture.

Dessert chocolate will give perfectly good results if melted carefully. Great care should be taken when melting chocolate as heat and moisture can spoil the texture quite easily. Cooking chocolate or chocolate-flavoured cake covering is something quite different. Its ease of use makes it quite popular but the inferior quality of this chocolate (lower cocoa content and vegetable fat base) is obvious in the inferior flavour.

5 **Spread the chocolate** on the marble slab. You will have to work quickly if the chocolate is to be evenly spread before it begins to set. Many decorations have to be made before the chocooate is completely hard, as with the chocolate rolls in the next photograph.

1 **Chop the chocolate,** so that it will melt more quickly and easily, by holding the block vertical and cutting down the side with a strong knife. Two hands may be needed on the knife if the chocolate is very hard. Melt half the chocolate in a bowl over a saucepan of hot water.

3 **Cooling on a marble slab** is a method that many prefer to cooling in the refrigerator. Pour half the melted chocolate on to the slab and work continuously with the palette knife until the chocolate is the consistency of thick cream. Return this thicker chocolate to the warm chocolate and reheat.

6 **Use a metal spatula** to make chocolate rolls. Work with the chocolate when half-set. Hold the spatula at a slight angle and push along the top of the chocolate for 2–3 cm/1–1½ in to form a thin roll of chocolate.

2 **Add the remaining chocolate.** This will help cool the melted chocolate. Remove the bowl from the hot water and stir until all the chocolate has completely dissolved. Should some chocolate refuse to melt, return the bowl to the warm water to rewarm the chocolate slightly.

4 **Place the cool, creamy chocolate** over a saucepan of hot water and warm slowly to 32 C/90 F, stirring continuously. Test with the palette knife. In 2–3 minutes the chocolate should become glossy and firm enough to cut into decorations.

7 **To make fans:** use a spatula to scrape a triangle from the soft chocolate; if you hold one corner firmly as you push the chocolate will concertina into a fan shape. Another method is to add a little oil to the chocolate to prevent it setting so hard.

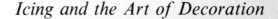

8 **To cut shapes** with a cutter spread the chocolate on to greaseproof paper. The chocolate should be thicker than that used to make rolls or fans.

9 **Cut shapes with cutters** before the chocolate has completely set. It is more difficult to cut chocolate once it has set, but it can be done by dipping the cutter into warm water. Wipe the cutter each time with a damp cloth before you cut out another shape.

The other illustrations on this page show attractive flower decorations made from chocolate. These can be made for the store cupboard but must be stored carefully, perferably in an air-tight container. They can be used in combination with other decorations such as nuts or glacé fruit. Here the chocolate has been combined with marzipan and praline (see Frankfurt Ring cake, page 146). The marzipan is rolled out before cutting. Praline is poured hot on to an oiled marble slab, rolled out and then cut with oiled cutters or a sharp knife. The chocolate you use with it should not be completely set.

10 **Very thin chocolate flakes** for decorating cakes are easy to make. Simply scrape your block of chocolate with a sharp knife. Keep the knife almost vertical otherwise you will cut large pieces rather than thin shavings.

11 **You can grate chocolate** with a cheese grater to get small, fine flakes. Since these flakes are extremely thin and fragile it is best to grate directly on to the cake. This also ensures that the chocolate flakes are more evenly distributed.

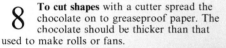

Cake Decorations

There are numerous decorations available for cakes and pastries and it is up to each individual to decide on their own preferences. Ingredients such as almonds – used whole, grated or flaked – toasted hazelnuts, walnut halves, candied violets, cherries and other fruit can be used. The food industry provides a motley collection of sugar-based decorations – gold and silver balls, hundreds and thousands in various sizes, sugar flowers, chocolate vermicelli, chocolate decorations in various shapes, mocha beans in sugar or chocolate, chocolate or sugar leaves. All these, together with crystalised sugar, are illustrated on this page, but the display is by no means complete. Everyone will have seen other colours and shapes in the shops – you can even buy sugar letters. These ready-made decorations are used by professional cooks as well as housewives, and there is no reason why they should not be. Not everyone is artistically inclined however and it may be useful for us to offer a few words of advice without trying to advocate any particular style of decoration. Go sparingly with the decorations; it is better to have too little than too much. It is up to everyone to decide for themselves how far they want to go with decoration. All that is offered here are some helpful suggestions. Anything that cannot be made at home, such as gold and silver balls or mocha beans to go on a coffee cake, should be brought ready-made. But with things that are easy to make – it is always better to do it yourself than to use inferior tasting, manufactured products. The final goal should be for the cake itself, the filling and the decoration to form an aesthetic whole.

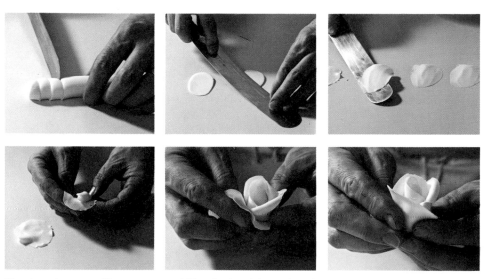

How to make a rose. You can use modelling fondant icing rather than marzipan for this. First cut the fondant into equal pieces and shape into balls. On a worktop flatten the balls, working outwards from the centre with a palette knife until nice and thin. Lift the petals from the worktop with the palette knife. Start with an elongated ball (the bud) and place one petal at a time around it, securing it at the base. Turn the tops of the petals outwards with your thumbs. Leave to dry and cut a flat edge across the base. This method can be used for both full-blown roses and buds.

Working with Marzipan

Almond paste, the basis of marzipan for cake coverings and decorations, can be mixed with up to an equal weight of icing sugar, but the following ratio brings out the almond flavour better:

450 g/1 lb icing sugar,
675 g/1½ lb almond paste

Sift the icing sugar on to a worktop. Break the almond paste into the icing sugar in small pieces and quickly incorporate into a smooth paste. If the marzipan is overworked it becomes crumbly and is then impossible to roll or shape. If this occurs add a little more icing sugar with egg white, but be prepared for a marzipan of lesser quality. The marzipan can be rolled on a surface sifted with icing sugar. An ordinary rolling pin can be used but there are also two special rolling pins developed specifically for marzipan which makes squares or furrows. To make marzipan golden brown use natural colourings like saffron or sugar colouring. Fruit extracts are not recommended for this can make the marzipan ferment when stored.

Piped Decorations

This is a simple and inexpensive method of decoration since it is normal practice to use the cream from the filling. If not using the filling itself for piping it is useful to bear in mind that the flavour of the alternative should go well with that of the cake and the filling. Apart from a piping bag and a selection of nozzles you need only a steady hand and a bit of practice. We would advise anyone who has not used a piping bag before to practise first. Use a piping icing made with 225 g/8 oz icing sugar and a little egg white, not too thick. Pipe on to greaseproof paper or a washable surface and have a go at all the patterns shown on the opposite page. It is only by trying it for yourself that you will get a feel for piping. Start with a plain nozzle and try a few lines, making them as straight as possible. This should give you confidence enough to try a star nozzle; again start with straight lines.

You should also have a go at rosettes, of all sizes. To make these: hold the piping bag vertical, and use a little pressure for a small whirl, more pressure for a larger one. Quickly pull the nozzle up away from the rosette to give a clean finish to the whirl. To pipe a wavy line with a star nozzle hold the piping bag at a slight angle and move it alternately from right to left as you squeeze out the icing. The illustrations show – from left to right in each case:

● Rosettes made with a fluted nozzle, for a nut-butter cream gâteau. For butter cream use a medium nozzle.

● Fluted decorations for meringue or whipped cream. You can use star nozzles of all sizes depending on the material used. For heavy butter creams use a smaller nozzle, and larger ones for light airy meringue or whipped cream.

● Whipped cream needs a large nozzle, either plain or starred.

● A lattice design in butter cream is made with small to medium nozzles, either plain or starred.

● Decorations with piping icing. Use small plain or star nozzles here, for piping icing is too sweet to be used in large quantities. The wedding cake is the exception that proves the rule! It is possible to make the most intricate designs with this soft icing – and chocolate icing is just as easy to use.

● This 'spaghetti icing' can be made with the smallest plain nozzle, but it is much quicker of course with this special nozzle which has five small holes.

● For decorations of this kind with butter cream small nozzles are used. The cream should be quite soft for piping to prevent air bubbles in the bag, for these would make breaks in the line as you pipe.

● You can buy special nozzles for intricate decoration like leaves, flowers, bands, whirls and other shapes. They are much smaller than the usual nozzles and are used with a paper piping bag (see page 75).

Filling a piping bag. Fold back the top of the bag. Hold the bag in one hand and use the other to fill it. Fold up the top of the bag, shake or press the icing down and twist or fold the top of the bag. With a paper piping bag cut off the end, insert a small nozzle and fill carefully with icing or cream, making sure that the rim of the bag stays clean and none of the cream escapes when you fold down the top.

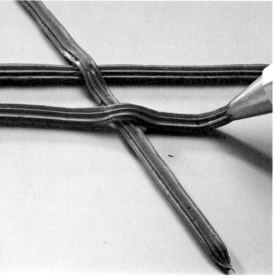

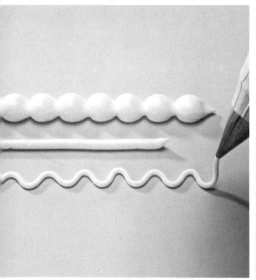

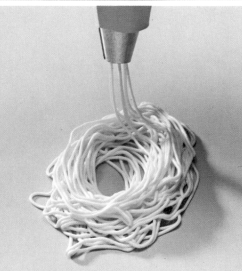

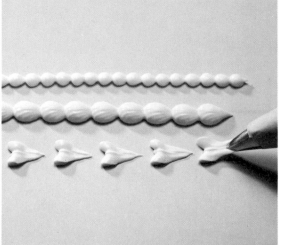

Cakes & Company

All over Europe housewives have taken a delight and pride in producing light sponges and mouthwatering cakes. These have traditionally been achieved either by creaming the butter and sugar then adding the eggs and flour, or by whisking the egg whites and sugar and folding them in to the flour and butter.

Whereas in the past this had to be done arduously by hand these days many cooks have recourse to electric food mixers or whisks which make the task a lot easier. Also the invention of baking powder (the perfect raising agent) has helped the home cook a great deal by rendering the old-fashioned hours of beating by hand unnecessary.

Many family recipes for sponge cakes and loaves were and still are surrounded in mystery, especially those mixtures which are more like a heavier traditional sponge than a quick, baking-powder sponge. Such recipes are handed down through the generations from grandmother to mother and from mother to daughter. The strict secrecy which envelops the ingredients is matched only by the strict adherence to the method of preparation. The aim is quite simply to make it impossible for the family recipe to be copied. The serving of a home-made marble cake, for example, can be the highlight of a coffee morning or afternoon tea for a hostess who hopes that her guests will like her baking and even congratulate her on it. The food industry has begun to make inroads in this area, however, and we should not underestimate the proportion of marble or Madeira cake eaten today which comes out of a packet. We should not forget either the excellent sponge cakes sold in small patisseries. This is a logical result of the fact that these cakes go particularly well with coffee and with tea. The traditional English 'tea-cake' was first baked in Bath by a lady by the name of Sally Lunn and put on public sale (and there is still a type of tea-cake known as a Sally Lunn). English afternoon tea was until quite recently something that one had in a cafe or restaurant rather than at home, so it is hardly surprising that this branch of cake making originated in cafes and pastry shops.

One of the most delicious types of sponge is the German 'Rehrücken' illustrated opposite. After baking the cake is stuck all over with almond spikes and covered with chocolate icing. The cake does in fact bear some resemblance to a saddle of venison (the meaning of the word *Rehrücken*) and it is not difficult to guess that this is a modern relic of the old fast days when no meat was eaten.

Sponges and raising agents

For cakes to rise successfully during cooking, air or gas in the form of carbon monoxide or steam must be introduced to the basic mixture, then trapped there to achieve a perfect result. Whisked sponge cakes rise well because of the bubbles which are incorporated into the mixture as the eggs and sugar are whisked to a foam. Whisking the egg whites on their own is more effective than whisking the whole egg, however the method of incorporating whisked whites into the creamed yolks and dry ingredients is more difficult than the traditional method. As the mixture cooks the egg yolk coagulates and holds in the trapped air.

The most well-known chemical raising agent is baking powder which consists of bicarbonate of soda and an acid-reacting chemical such as cream of tartar. This reacts with moisture and heat to produce carbon dioxide which is then trapped within the mixture to give a good rise. Creamed cake mixtures, like Victoria Sandwich, rely on baking powder or a similar raising agent, for success. Usually the raising agent is incorporated with the flour in the form of self-raising flour. For certain heavier cakes, for example fruited loaf cakes, extra baking powder is added to the self-raising flour.

There are a few cakes which rely upon a different chemical reaction to make the cake rise and do not use either eggs or baking powder. Vinegar cake is one of these where sodium is dissolved in milk and reacts with the vinegar to produce a gas which makes the cake rise.

Comparison of two sponges

The dramatic difference in the size of these two sponges shows what a difference using baking powder can make. The cakes are made from exactly the same recipe but the one on the right includes baking powder whereas the other does not. The sponges were made by the quick method, where all the ingredients are beaten together in a food mixer. The effect of baking powder is brought out very clearly here. The cake with no baking powder could have been improved however by using the classic method of preparation of beating the butter, sugar and eggs until light and fluffy and then folding in the flour. This would have produced a bigger sponge than that shown but still not as large as the one with baking powder.

1 **Draw round the cake tin onto paper.** There is no reason why the tin used for a sponge cannot be greased and evenly sprinkled with flour, but using greaseproof or baking paper ensures that the cake will come easily out of the tin and subsequently stay moist longer.

2 **Cut out the marked shapes,** cutting into each of the four corners at the end of the long sides and cut off half these ends. Fold the paper in along the lines marking the end of the tin and then along the side lines.

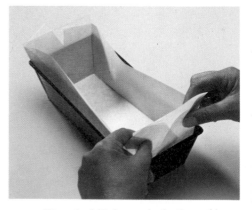

3 **Place the folded paper in the tin,** tucking the corners of the long sides behind the short end corners. If this makes a fold at the end take the paper out again and cut a bit off the side pieces until the paper lies flat in the tin.

4 **Whisk the eggs,** egg yolks, sugar and lemon rind over a pan of hot water until thick enough to leave a trail. Remove bowl from heat and beat until cold. Sift the flour, cornflour and salt together and fold into the mixture.

5 **Add the melted butter** in a slow trickle, folding it in until it is completely incorporated.

6 **Pour the mixture into the prepared tin.** The mixture must be completely free of lumps when it goes into the tin for this would give an uneven texture. Smooth the top gently with a spatula or pastry scraper taking care to keep the edges clean.

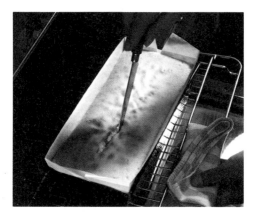

7 **After about 20 minutes** slide the cake very gently out of the oven and with a pointed knife, which you have first dipped in water, cut along the golden top of the cake. This allows the cake to rise more evenly.

First whisk the eggs, egg yolks, sugar, and lemon rind over a saucepan of hot water until thick enough to leave a trail when the whisk is lifted, but do not allow the temperature to rise beyond 40C/104F. Remove the bowl from the water and continue beating until cold. Sift together the flour, cornflour and salt and fold into the sponge mixture. Then slowly fold in the melted butter. Pour the mixture carefully into the tin and bake in a moderately hot oven (190C, 375F, gas 5) for about 40 minutes.

After 20 minutes, when the top of the cake is golden brown, cut along the top with a sharp knife dipped in water. This allows the cake to rise properly.

When cooked leave the cake to cool for about 15 minutes in the tin then transfer it to a wire rack keeping it the right way up. Dust the top with icing sugar and leave the paper on the cake until it is ready to serve as this will keep it nice and moist.

Classic Sand Cake

This is similar to a Madeira cake recipe and the result is particularly light and airy as well as fine and close in texture. This mixture is also a good basis for a jam or light cream sandwich, for which use a 25-cm/10-in round cake tin.

3 eggs
2 egg yolks
100 g/4 oz caster sugar
grated rind of 1 lemon
100 g/4 oz plain flour
50 g/2 oz cornflour
pinch of salt
75 g/3 oz butter, melted
icing sugar for dusting
1 loaf tin (25 × 10-cm/10 × 4-in)

Rum and Raisin Cake

100 g/4 oz raisins
50 g/2 oz candied lemon peel
3 tablespoons rum
100 g/4 oz butter, softened
175 g/6 oz caster sugar
grated rind of 1 lemon
6 eggs
225 g/8 oz plain flour
1 loaf tin (25 × 10-cm/10 × 4-in),
greased and floured
icing sugar for dusting

In a covered bowl steep the raisins and candied peel in the rum for an hour. Cream the butter with a third of the sugar and the grated lemon rind until light and fluffy. Separate the eggs and gradually beat the yolks into the creamed butter. Whisk the whites until stiff but not dry, then gradually whisk in the remaining sugar. Mix the soaked raisins and candied peel with the sifted flour. Beat about a third of the whisked egg whites into the butter mixture and then carefully fold in the remaining whites, adding the flour and fruit at the same time. Fold in very carefully to prevent the mixture falling. Transfer the mixture to the tin and smooth the top gently with a spatula. Bake in a moderate oven (180 C, 350 F, gas 4) for about 1–1¼ hours. Leave the cake to cool in the tin for about 10 minutes before transferring to a wire rack to cool completely. When cool dust with icing sugar. This cake is excellent with a thin covering of apricot glaze and melted chocolate, and will keep longer with this addition.

Light Fruit Cake

100 g/4 oz raisins
50 g/2 oz currants
100 g/4 oz chopped mixed peel
25 g/1 oz stem ginger, finely chopped
2 tablespoons rum
225 g/8 oz butter, softened
225 g/8 oz caster sugar
4 eggs, separated
grated rind of 1 lemon
275 g/10 oz plain flour
1 teaspoon baking powder
pinch each of ground ginger, nutmeg,
cloves and salt
1 loaf tin (25 × 10-cm/10 × 4-in),
lined and greased
icing sugar for dusting

In a covered bowl steep the raisins, currants, peel and stem ginger in the rum until the alcohol is absorbed. Cream the butter with a third of the sugar, the egg yolks, and grated lemon rind until light and fluffy. Whisk the egg whites until stiff but not dry, then gradually whisk in the remaining sugar. Sift together the flour and baking powder, spices and salt and mix with the fruit. First beat about a third of the whisked egg whites into the butter mixture, then gently fold in the remaining egg white mixture with the fruit and flour mixture. Spoon the mixture into the prepared tin and gently smooth the top. Bake in a moderate oven (180 C, 350 F, gas 4) for about 1½ hours. When completely cool dust the cake with icing sugar.

Walnut Spice Cake

100 g/4 oz butter, softened
175 g/6 oz caster sugar
4 eggs, separated
1 tablespoon brandy
1 tablespoon Cointreau
grated rind of 1 orange
100 g//4 oz plain flour
50 g/2 oz cornflour
50 g//2 oz cocoa powder
½ teaspoon ground cinnamon
pinch each of cloves, allspice, ground
ginger and salt
100 g/4 oz walnuts, ground
1 Balmoral tin (fluted, round-bottomed
loaf tin) (30-cm/12-in long), greased and
floured
275 g/10 oz plain chocolate, melted
chopped pistachio nuts to decorate

Cream the butter with a third of the sugar and the egg yolks until light and fluffy. Beat in the alcohol and add the orange rind. Sift together the flour, cornflour, cocoa powder and spices. Stir in the walnuts. Whisk the egg whites until stiff but not dry then gradually whisk in the remaining sugar. Beat about a quarter of the whisked egg whites into the butter and egg yolk mixture and then gently fold in the rest with the flour mixture. Pour the mixture into the prepared tin and bake in a moderate oven (180 C, 350 F, gas 4) for about 40 minutes. Leave the cake to cool in the tin for a few minutes before turning out on to a wire rack. When completely cool cover with the melted chocolate and sprinkle with the chopped pistachio nuts.

Rehrücken

(illustrated on page 72)

75 g/3 oz butter, softened
100 g/4 oz caster sugar
3 eggs, separated
1 teaspoon vanilla essence
75 g/3 oz plain chocolate, melted
75 g/3 oz blanched almonds, toasted
and ground
75 g/3 oz rich tea biscuit crumbs
1 Balmoral tin (30-cm/12-in long),
greased and floured
1 quantity of Apricot Glaze (see page 60)
75 g/3 oz blanched almonds, quartered
lengthways
1 kg/2 lb melted plain chocolate for icing

Cream the butter with a third of the sugar, the egg yolks and vanilla essence until light and fluffy. Then add the chocolate melted in a small bowl over a saucepan of hot water. Whisk the egg whites until stiff but not dry then whisk in the remaining sugar. Mix the ground almonds and biscuit crumbs. First beat in about one-third of the whisked egg whites until completely mixed into the egg yolk and chocolate mixture. Then fold in the remaining whites with the almond and crumb mixture, trying to avoid knocking all the air out of the mixture. Spoon the mixture into the greased and floured tin and smooth the top. Bake in a moderate oven (180 C, 350 F, gas 4) for about 50 minutes. Leave to cool in the tin for 15 minutes before turning out. Brush thinly with the hot apricot glaze and leave until completely cool. Stud the cake all over with the blanched almonds which have been quartered lengthways to form long spikes, place on a cooling rack and cover with the melted chocolate. To get an unbroken covering which also covers all the almond spikes you will need to work with about 1 kg/2 lb chocolate but you should find you have used only about 225 g/8 oz of the chocolate. Give the cooling rack a good shake to get rid of any chocolate drips. If you place paper beneath the cooling rack beforehand you can recover the chocolate that drips off the cake once it has set and keep it to use again, either as a cake covering as here or melted down again and used to make chocolate decorations as shown on pages 66–7.

Rehrücken is a popular German cake and its meaning is 'saddle of venison' to which the whole cake – as illustrated on page 72 – does in fact bear a strong resemblance.

Almond and Chocolate Cake

4 eggs, separated
175 g/6 oz caster sugar
½ teaspoon vanilla essence
1 tablespoon Benedictine
75 g/3 oz butter, melted
100 g/4 oz plain flour
pinch each of cinnamon, allspice and salt
75 g/3 oz plain chocolate, grated
175 g/6 oz ground almonds
1 Balmoral tin (30-cm/12-in long),
greased and floured
1 quantity of Apricot Glaze (see page 60)
275 g/10 oz plain chocolate, melted
1 tablespoon finely chopped pistachio
nuts to decorate

Whisk the egg yolks with 100 g/4 oz of the sugar, the vanilla essence and Benedictine until pale and thick. Whisk the egg whites until stiff but not dry then gradually whisk in the remaining sugar. Beat about half of the whisked whites into the egg yolk mixture. Then fold in the lukewarm butter in a slow trickle. Sift together the flour and spices then mix with the grated chocolate and ground almonds and fold this mixture carefully into the cake mixture with the remaining whites. Spoon into the prepared tin and bake in a moderately hot oven (190 C, 375 F, gas 5) for 50 to 60 minutes. Leave to cool for 10 minutes before turning the cake out of the tin. When cool brush with apricot glaze and cover with melted chocolate, then sprinkle with the chopped pistachio nuts.

Basque Cake

This round cake originated in the Basque region which is an area of the Pyrenees between France and Spain. The sponge often has a vanilla filling, but in the Basque area jam is also used as a filling, with black cherry jam being especially popular.

275 g/10 oz butter, softened
275 g/10 oz caster sugar
450 g/1 lb plain flour
pinch of salt
2 teaspoons baking powder
1 teaspoon vanilla essence
3 eggs
two 18-cm/7-in sponge tins,
greased and floured
½ quantity of Simple Vanilla Cream (see page 50)
1 tablespoon brown rum
icing sugar for dusting

Grease and flour the two 18-cm/7-in sponge tins or a 25-cm/10-in deep cake tin. Cream the butter with the sugar until light and fluffy; the butter should be very soft and the sugar completely dissolved. Sift the flour with the salt and baking powder. Beat in the vanilla essence then the eggs one at a time, adding 1 teaspoon of the flour with each egg. Then fold in the remaining flour with a spoon. Transfer the mixture to a piping bag with a plain 1-cm/½-in nozzle, and working inwards from the edge of the tins fill each with a spiral of mixture. Pipe an extra ring around the rim of the tins to prevent the filling coming into direct contact with the tin during baking.

Strain the vanilla cream and stir in the rum then spread the filling over the cake mixture inside the outer-ring using a small palette knife. Cover the filling by piping a second spiral of cake mixture into the tin and bake in a moderately hot oven (190 C, 375 F, gas 5) for about 50–60 minutes. When cool dust with icing sugar.

French Fig Cake

(not illustrated)

The finished *gâteau aux figues* is similar to a Scottish black bun, although the ingredients, dates, figs and walnuts, are typically Mediterranean.

100 g/4 oz dried figs
100 g/4 oz dates
100 g/4 oz walnut pieces
2 tablespoons Armagnac
½ quantity of sweet shortcrust pastry
(see page 38)
1 loaf tin (30 × 10-cm/12 × 4-in)
100 g/4 oz butter, softened
175 g/6 oz caster sugar
½ teaspoon vanilla essence
6 egg yolks
4 egg whites
50 g/2 oz plain flour
pinch each of salt and ground cloves
½ teaspoon cinnamon
75 g/3 oz ground almonds
icing sugar for dusting

Steep the dried figs overnight in lukewarm water. Wipe the figs dry with kitchen paper and then coarsely chop them with the dates. Chop the walnuts and place in a basin with the dates and figs, pour in the Armagnac and leave to steep for 1 to 2 hours.

Roll out the shortcrust pastry to a thin sheet and use to line the tin. Cream the butter with a third of the sugar until light and fluffy (the French describe this consistency very accurately as *en pommade*). Beat in first the vanilla essence and then more gradually the egg yolk until the mixture is light and fluffy. Whisk the egg white until stiff but not dry then gradually whisk in the remaining sugar. Beat about a third of the egg whites into the mixture, then gently fold in the remaining whites. Fold in the flour, sifted with the salt, cloves, cinnamon and ground almonds, and fruit. Spoon the mixture into the pastry-lined tin and gently smooth the top. Bake in a moderate oven (180 C, 350 F, gas 4) for 1¼ hours. When cool dust the cake with icing sugar, or brush with apricot glaze and cover with melted chocolate. you can also use fresh figs for this cake; the fresh fruit will not require the overnight steeping.

Traditional British Cakes

Cakes were originally a combination of bread dough and dried fruit, often mixed with spices. A lot of traditional cakes and buns are still based on this history of making use of left-over dough. In Britain many housewives set aside one particular day of the week as a 'baking day', rather like Monday is often regarded as the traditional 'washing day'. Bread and cakes were made to last the week and that is why rich fruit cakes have always been popular in Britain, as they keep so well and are sometimes actually better if eaten a few days after cooking. The fruit cake is a particular British institution and relies upon the quantity of fruit to flour and eggs to keep it moist. A heavy mixture of fruit to the other ingredients will preserve the cake for many months, not to say years – as in the case of the wedding or Christmas cake for instance.

One of the best-known old recipes for a British cake is that of the Pound Cake, named after the pound in weight of each ingredient that was incorporated: butter, sugar, eggs and flour. This quantity does, however, produce an extremely large cake and today the recipe can be adapted to a quarter pound of each ingredient. There are many variations on this basic recipe, using different flavourings, or the addition of a varying quantity of fruit.

Another basic recipe which can be adapted is that of the Madeira cake. This has always been a very popular cake in Britain. The name is said to have originated from the eighteenth and nineteenth-century custom of drinking a glass of the sweet Madeira wine as an accompaniment to the cake. One of the most appealing variations to the Madeira cake is the addition of glacé cherries to turn it into a delicious Cherry cake. Alternatively the addition of carraway seeds will turn it into a traditional seed cake.

One of the most favoured occasions to make use of the wide range of cakes that can be made is the traditional 'afternoon tea'. This custom has been preserved by the British love of tradition almost unchanged since its conception to the present day. Afternoon tea would normally be taken around four o'clock and is an opportunity for home-baked cakes and pastries to be temptingly displayed. Each person will have their own favourite be it a fruit cake like the Dundee, or a sponge mixture like the Victoria Sandwich filled with jam or butter cream. Perhaps the choice will be for a mouth-watering meringue instead. These cakes are usually baked at home but there are also a large number of old-fashioned teashops around the country where the cakes are baked fresh on the premises each day and the ritual of afternoon tea is observed.

Tea drinking became a passion within Britain from the eighteenth century onwards. At first only China tea was available and it was very expensive to buy – thus the invention of small tea caddies with locks to prevent anyone taking the precious commodity without permission. Such was the popularity of tea that in the nineteenth century tea plantations were established in India and Ceylon to supply the growing requirements for more and cheaper tea. Tea drinking became a national pastime and has continued to flourish today.

The Rolls Royce – symbol of British quality – is a fitting frame in which to admire the traditional glass of sherry and its accompanying cakes: the simnel or Easter cake, the fruit Dundee and the Madeira cake.

Simnel Cake

This is undoubtedly one of the oldest known English cakes. Tradition ascribes its origin to Ancient Greece, at least as far as the decoration goes – twelve marzipan balls to honour the gods of the Pantheon. It still remains a cake for special occasions, especially for Easter Sunday or Mothering Sunday.

225 g/8 oz butter, softened
225 g/8 oz caster sugar
6 eggs
350 g/12 oz plain flour
1 teaspoon baking powder
pinch each of salt, allspice, ginger and cloves
1 teaspoon cinnamon
50 g/2 oz ground almonds
grated rind of 1 orange and ½ lemon
350 g/12 oz currants
100 g/4 oz raisins
1 tablespoon orange liqueur (Cointreau or Grand Marnier) or brandy
575 g/1¼ lb marzipan
20-cm/8-in deep cake tin, lined and greased
1 quantity of Apricot Glaze (see page 60)
75 g/3 oz fondant icing
royal icing to decorate

Cream the butter and sugar until light and fluffy. Break the eggs into a separate bowl and whisk for a few seconds. Beat the eggs a little at a time into the butter and sugar and continue beating until the mixture is pale and airy and has increased visibly in volume.

Sift together the flour, baking powder, salt and spices, add the almonds and rind and stir into the cake mixture with the fruit and alcohol. Fold in very carefully so that the mixture looses as little air as possible. Pour half the mixture into the tin and gently smooth the top. Divide the marzipan into three. Roll one third to the same diameter as the cake tin. Place on top of the cake mixture and spread the remaining mixture over, making a slight hollow in the centre to allow for the rise in the middle when baking. Bake in a moderate oven (180 C, 350 F, gas 4) for about 2 hours. Remove the paper from the cake and brush thinly with hot apricot glaze. Roll the second third of marzipan to the same diameter as the cake. Glaze the top once more. Cut the remaining marzipan into 3-cm/1-in rounds and place around the edge of the cake. Brown slightly under the grill. Warm the fondant icing and spread over the top of the cake and add the lettering in royal icing.

Dundee Cake

Whether it is true that there are more types of cake in Scotland than types of whisky is a matter of debate, but it is certainly true that Dundee Cake is probably the most popular tea-time cake both in Scotland and throughout the rest of Britain.

225 g/8 oz butter, softened
225 g/8 oz brown sugar
6 eggs
1 tablespoon marmalade
350 g/12 oz plain flour
2 teaspoons baking powder
½ teaspoon salt
100 g/4 oz ground almonds
575 g/1¼ lb raisins
100 g/4 oz chopped mixed peel
2 tablespoons brown rum
about 225 g/8 oz blanched almonds, halved for the topping
20-cm/8-in cake tin, lined and greased
Baking time: 2 hours in a moderate oven (160 C, 325 F, gas 3)

1 **Cream the butter** with the brown sugar until light and fluffy. This is best done in a food mixer for it can take up to 15 minutes for the sugar to dissolve fully and the mixture to become fluffy.

2 **Break the eggs** into a jug or bowl and beat them lightly with a whisk. Then gradually beat them into the creamed mixture, adding a little at a time and beating each portion in well before adding the next.

3 **The mixture** should have increased considerably in volume. It is the long beating process which gives the Dundee Cake its fine texture. Now add the marmalade and beat until it is completely incorporated into the mixture.

4 **Sift the flour,** baking powder and salt into the bowl, stir in the ground almonds but do not fold in yet. Add the fruit and peel which you have first soaked in the rum and fold in the flour and fruit with a spoon.

5 **Fill the prepared tin** with the mixture, smooth the top gently and cover with the traditional blanched almond halves.

Most fruit cakes will keep excellently and many take several days for their full flavour to develop. Dundee cake is one of these. Once cooked leave the paper on the base and sides and store the cake in an airtight container in a cool place. The almonds will have an attractive shine if you brush them with a thin apricot glaze while still hot.

Baumkuchen

The Baumkuchen stands at the summit of German baking and has come to be regarded as the symbol of quality baking. It appears in the coat-of-arms of the Society of German Pastry Cooks, and it is a cake that is always mentioned in connection with typical German baking.

The cake is not entirely German in origin, however, because it can be traced back to ancient Greece. Just as other cakes have mythological associations, this cake is thought to have been a fertility symbol. The discovery that the cake had been baked on a rotating spit provided a clue to its original texture, which evidently was heavy, probably similar to a bread dough. Over the centuries this kind of cake appeared in various forms in many cultures. The precursors of the modern Baumkuchen had names such as spit cake, makeshift bread, spit loaf, or Prügelkuchen. We know that in early wars, soldiers baked cakes like these on a spit. Even the colonists in America baked similar spit cakes over camp fires fueled with buffalo dung. The process of improving the dough from a plain bread dough to the rich mixture of today was undoubtedly a slow one. It can be assumed that, as with most culinary advances, the cooks and confectioners working in the European courts must have played a major role in developing the recipe. With the organisation of trade guilds and the growing availability of sugar, regional centres to make Baumkuchen were established in central Germany – in Dresden, Cottbus, Salzwedel, etc. – and because sugar was available, it was possible to make changes in the recipe that ultimately brought the Baumkuchen close to the form in which we know it today. It also made it possible to advance from making the cake on a spit to using a wooden roller, still found in the Tirol and known as a 'Prügel'.

No one seems very sure of the origin of the name Baumkuchen (tree cake). The way the cake is made tends to create a bark-like effect. When the cake is cut horizontally, it closely resembles the age rings on a tree. It has been suggested that the name comes from the 'Prügel' or wooden roller on which the cake is cooked, but this argument is unconvincing.

This unusual cake certainly merits its lofty position in the culinary world and, despite all the modern kitchen equipment available, it remains a hand-made masterpiece. Both the preparation of the mixture and the cooking process requires a great deal of experience and skill if the end result is to be successful. But nowadays, when one hears talk of 'one-step methods' and 'emulsifiers', even this, the masterpiece of the baker's art, seems to be in danger.

Although space does not allow room to provide the method used in the preparation of this cake in detail, there is enough space to give the recipe for a typical Baumkuchen, the Salzwedel Baumkuchen. Beat 25 egg yolks with 225 g/8 oz caster sugar until frothy. Cream 450 g/1 lb butter with the pith of a vanilla pod until fluffy and then add 6 tablespoons rum. Sift together 225 g/8 oz plain flour and 225 g/8 oz cornflour and stir into the butter mixture, stopping as soon as the flour is incorporated. Whisk 20 egg whites with 225 g/8 oz caster sugar until very stiff. Stir the egg yolks into the butter mixture then gently fold in the whites. After baking the first few layers it may be necessary to thin the mixture down with a little single cream. This recipe will make a Baumkuchen about 60 cm/24 in tall.

The wooden roller, or Prügel, is first wrapped in greaseproof paper then secured in place with thread. The first layer is cooked over the open fire with the spit being turned carefully for even browning.

Here is a home-made Prügelkuchen from Brannenberg in the Tirol. The method of making it, though similar to that for a Baumkuchen, employs a wood fire, which gives the end result a distinctive flavour.

Katharina Marksteiner carries on the traditional methods of making a Prügelkuchen. She uses only beech wood for her fire, as it burns slowly with a constant heat. The fire does, of course, need careful tending during the two hours it takes to cook the cake.

The Tirolean Prügelkuchen

This cake was one of the forerunners of the modern Baumkuchen and the identical method of preparation is used for them both. The Prügel – which is a slightly tapering wooden roller – is first wrapped with greaseproof paper and this is secured in place with a cotton thread. This roller is then placed over a hand-worked spit which is held up by two old-fashioned iron supports. Although similar ingredients are used to those of the Baumkuchen the mixture does differ. The quantities of butter, sugar and flour used are based upon, and are the same as, the weight of the eggs. The eggs are whisked with the sugar and butter then finally the flour is folded in. This gives quite a thick mixture which must be kept near the fire during baking so that the warmth keeps it runny. The end result is a long-lasting cake that is baked until it is relatively dry. If properly stored it will keep for over six months. In this it is different from the Baumkuchen which needs to be iced if it is to stay fresh for long.

The Prügelkuchen was traditionally made by the peasants for special occasions such as christenings and weddings. On these occasions the cake was decorated with flowers. The Prügelkuchen is never iced as the gleaming brown surface with its irregularities is attractive enough to stand on its own. The irregularities are the result of using a hand crank since it is possible to vary the speed of the roller to achieve the required effect.

Fruit Flans and Tarts

Sponge cakes tend to be dominated by tradition and convention in the basic recipes and in the fillings whereas fruit flans tend to leave more to the individual's imagination. When considering the range of possible ways that fresh fruit can be used in flans and tarts there would seem to be no recognised classic recipes and no hard-and-fast rules. There are innumerable recipes and every pastry cook will have experimented and come up with his or her own favourite.

Fruit flans, especially simple baking-sheet flans, form part of the standard repertoire of home baking. Originally these forms of patisserie were made in the summer and autumn making use of the abundant fruit that these seasons provide. Each area of Europe has invented its own specialities, which differ not so much in the type of pastry used but more through the choice of fruit. It is up to the individual cook to decide whether they would rather bake plums on a shortcrust pastry or on a thin yeast dough, as is customary for example in southern Germany. One of the most popular of the fruit flans throughout Europe is the apple flan or pie and since apples have always been available all the year round because they store well numerous apple recipes have been invented. There are shortcrust pies with lids, yeast dough flans and more unusual recipes such as the French *Tarte Tatin* in which the thin layer of pastry serves only as a container for delicious, caramelised stewed apples.

There is no fruit which seems unsuitable for a fruit flan filling. Cooks have invented a number of ways of using the various qualities of each individual fruit. One of the best known is to fill a pre-baked flan case made of shortcrust or flaky pastry. Frequently a sponge is used as a base with a layer of jam and custard cream between the fruit and the sponge. Both methods make it unnecessary to cook soft fruit such as raspberries or strawberries.

More robust fruits, such as plums, apples, pears, cherries and currants, can be cooked with the flan. These two methods both provide a wide range of combinations and adaptations. The 'covered' pie has a pastry lid, while in a 'sunken' flan the pastry rises to cover the fruit during baking. In Alsace it is customary to take a flan out of the oven half way through the cooking time and to cover it with a 'Royale' made with cream, eggs and flavouring. This sets over the fruit during the remaining baking time and is wonderfully creamy. France has its own light tarts with very thin puff-pastry bases and fruit covered in sparkling jelly. Typical of British and American baking are the flat pies made either with or without lids. For special occasions fruit flans can be covered with meringue and browned under the grill.

The latest development, however, is the use of exotic fruit in our baking. In recent years previously unknown fruit have become well-established in the shops and are now taken for granted just as bananas or oranges are. The most popular is the delicious kiwi fruit with its unpromising exterior, but extremely decorative interior when cut open, and mangoes, persimmon and lychees all compare well with our native fruits for flavour.

Pear Flan

⅓ quantity of shortcrust pastry
(see page 37)
675 g/1½ lb pears
juice of 1 lemon
1.15 litres/2 pints water
150 g/5 oz caster sugar
½ quantity of Simple Vanilla Cream
(see page 50)
50 g/2 oz marzipan
150 ml/¼ pint single cream
25-cm/10-in flan tin

Use the shortcrust pastry to line the flan tin. Peel, halve and core the pears, dipping them in the lemon juice to prevent discolouration. Bring the water to the boil with the lemon juice drained from the pears and 100 g/4 oz sugar. Blanch the pears for about 2 minutes.

Cover the base of the flan with the vanilla custard then drain the pears and arrange in the flan. Work an egg into the marzipan until creamy, then add the second egg with the cream and remaining sugar and beat well. Pour the mixture over the pears and bake in a moderately hot oven (190 C, 375 F, gas 5) for 40 to 45 minutes.

Virginia Apple Pie

For the pastry:
450 g/1 lb plain flour
¼ teaspoon salt
75 g/3 oz block margarine
100 g/4 oz butter, finely diced and chilled
6–8 tablespoons iced water
25-cm/10-in pie tin or plate

For the filling:
1.5 kg/3 lb cooking apples
75 g/3 oz soft light brown sugar
2 tablespoons lemon juice
pinch each of nutmeg, allspice and ginger
2 teaspoons cinnamon
40 g/1½ oz butter, diced
1 egg yolk to glaze

Sift the flour and salt in a mixing bowl. Rub in the fat until the mixture resembles fine breadcrumbs. Sprinkle on the iced water and lightly mix the ingredients to make a short dough. Leave the pastry to stand in the refrigerator for at least an hour then divide in half and use one portion to line the pie tin or plate. Peel, core and thinly slice the apples, toss them with the sugar, lemon juice and spices and transfer them to the pie dish. Dot with the butter. Roll out the remaining pastry to make a lid. Dampen the

Using your fingers press the shortcrust pastry case so that it hangs slightly over the rim of the tin and flute the edges. Prick the base with a fork, spread with vanilla custard and top with the pears. Finally the cream and egg mixture is poured over the pears.

Virginia Apple Pie is a country-style fruit pie, associated with real home baking and for this same reason a popular feature in the repertoire of many professional chefs. A pie dish is lined with pastry and filled with the prepared apple mixture. It is important for the pastry to cover the rim of the plate so that the lid can be properly sealed to enclose the filling. The fluted edge, made with two fingers and the handle of a wooden spoon is the traditional decoration for this pie.

edge of the pastry base, lift the lid on top and press the edges well to seal in the filling. Beat the egg yolk with a little water and brush over the pie. Bake in a moderately hot oven (200 C, 400 F, gas 6) for about 45 minutes.

Tarte Tatin

Madame Tatin's legendary apple flan is by far and away the best known of the many French regional variations. It is not really a genuine flan for the thin pastry is only there to hold the delicious, tender, caramelised apples together. Like most apple pies this one tastes best when served fresh, just out of the oven. Success depends to a large extent on the type of apples used: they should become soft during baking but retain their

shape. Cooking apples are unsuitable as they break up during cooking. The type of pastry used is a matter of personal preference; puff pastry would be just as good as the sweet flan pastry recommended in this recipe.

It is important that the cooking container is a good conductor of heat to caramelise the fruit successfully and deep enough to hold the apple halves neatly in place.

For the pastry:
175 g/6 oz plain flour
75 g/3 oz butter
2 teaspoons icing sugar
½ teaspoon salt
1 egg yolk
2 tablespoons water

For the filling:
1.5 kg/3½ lb dessert apples

100 g/4 oz butter, softened
175 g/6 oz caster sugar
25-cm/10-in pie tin (preferably with slanting sides)

Make the pastry as for Rubbed-in pastry on page 37 and then leave to stand in the refrigerator for an hour. Meanwhile peel, quarter and core the apples and prepare the tin. Prepare the tart as shown below.

There is also a slightly simpler method that makes it easier to check when the apples are cooked. Place the tin full of apples on the hob and place over a high heat for about 15–20 minutes until the sugar caramelises. Then bake for a few minutes in a preheated oven to soften the apples slightly. Remove the tin from the oven, cover with the pastry lid and cook until the pastry is done.

1 **Butter and sugar the tin.** The butter should be nice and soft, as you are going to use quite a lot of it and you want to be able to spread it evenly. Pour the sugar into the tin and shake the tin until the sugar evenly coats the base.

2 **The cored apple quarters** should be arranged on end in the tin. They should be placed close together so that they support one another. Continue filling the tin until it is tightly packed and there are no gaps.

3 **Roll the pastry** into a round about 30-cm/12-in. in diameter. The pastry should be slightly larger than the top of the tin. Wrap the pastry round a floured rolling pin and unroll again over the tin, making sure that it is as straight as possible.

4 **Seal the tin completely.** Carefully lift the very edge of the pastry and dampen it underneath, then press it securely to the sides of the tin so as to seal in the apples. Prick the top several times with a fork to allow the steam to escape during cooking.

5 **Bake the tart** in a hot oven (220C, 425F, gas 7) for about 45 minutes. Allow to stand for 5 minutes but no longer then invert the tin on to a large serving plate, quickly run the point of a knife between the pastry and the tin and lift off the container.

6 **The upside-down tart** should be covered with a thin layer of caramel. The apples should keep their shape but be soaked in butter and sugar and soft enough to melt in the mouth. Golden Delicious, Cox's or Reinettes are the best types of apple to use.

Swiss Apple Flan

Like many baked fruit flans from Germany and Alsace, the Swiss flans or *Wähen* form part of the tradition of country baking. They were seasonal dishes served only when the particular fruits were in season. While the season was short for plums, apricots or berries, apples with their relatively long shelf-life (especially cooking apples) were the exception and were used more or less continuously throughout the year. In several regions the shortcrust base was often replaced with yeast dough and, regardless of the choice of pastry, these flans were usually made in very generous quantities which would not fit in our modern ovens. In the recipe given here it is easy to reduce the quantities if you want to.

For the pastry:
275 g/10 oz plain flour
½ teaspoon salt
100 g/4 oz butter
50 g/2 oz lard
25 g/1 oz caster sugar
1 egg
2 tablespoons iced water
30-cm/12-in flan tin

For the filling:
1 kg/2 lb apples (Bramleys or Cox's)
75 g/3 oz caster sugar
juice and grated rind of 1 lemon
100 g/4 oz ground almonds
75 g/3 oz biscuit crumbs
2 eggs
300 ml/½ pint single cream
2 tablespoons brandy or rum

Sift the flour and salt into a bowl. Rub in the butter and lard until the mixture resembles breadcrumbs. Stir in the sugar. Add the egg and iced water and lightly mix the ingredients together. Shape into a ball, handling the pastry as little as possible, and leave to stand in the refrigerator for 1 to 2 hours. Roll out the pastry and use to line the flan tin. Press the pastry well to the sides and cut off any excess. Prick the base of the flan with a fork.

Peel and core the apples and cut into wedges about 1-cm/½-in thick. In a basin sprinkle the apples with half the sugar, the lemon juice and grated rind (you can add a little cinnamon too if you like). Mix together the ground almonds and biscuit crumbs and sprinkle over the base of the lined tin. Cover with the apples, trying to get as smooth a surface as possible. Bake in a moderately hot oven (200 C, 400 F, gas 5) for about 20 minutes. Meanwhile beat the eggs with the cream, brandy and the remaining sugar and pour the mixture over the partly cooked apples. Bake for a further 30 to 35 minutes until golden brown. To give the flan a nice shiny surface brush with a thin layer of apricot glaze.

Apple and Bilberry Flan

For the dough:
225 g/8 oz strong plain flour
15 g/½ oz fresh yeast or 1½ teaspoons
dried yeast
6 tablespoons lukewarm milk
25 g/1 oz lard
25 g/1 oz caster sugar
pinch of salt
grated rind of ½ lemon
pinch of allspice
1 egg
baking sheet (36 × 28-cm/14 × 11-in),
greased
1.25 kg/2½ lb cooking apples

For the cream:
300 ml/½ pint soured cream
50 g/2 oz caster sugar
3 tablespoons cornflour
2 egg yolks
grated rind of ½ lemon

350 g/12 oz stewed bilberries
icing sugar for dusting

Sift the flour into a bowl and make a well. Crumble the fresh yeast into the well and stir into an initial mixture with the lukewarm milk. Alternatively dissolve the dried yeast in the milk and leave for 10 minutes or until frothy then pour into the flour well. Sprinkle this mixture with a little of the flour, cover the bowl, and leave to stand for 10 to 15 minutes in a warm place. Meanwhile heat the lard (until just warm) and beat with the sugar, flavourings and egg. When the yeast mixture develops bubbles on the surface, add the lard mixture, mix into the yeast mixture and the flour to give a smooth, fairly soft yeast dough. Knead lightly on a floured surface for 10 minutes. Put in a large bowl, cover with oiled cling film and leave to rise for 1–1½ hours or until doubled in size. Knead for a further 2–3 minutes then roll it out to

the size of the baking sheet. Spread the dough over the greased baking sheet and prick with a fork then cover again with oiled cling film and allow to rise for a further 45 minutes. Peel, core and slice the apples.

To make the cream heat the soured cream, sugar, cornflour, egg yolks and lemon rind in a saucepan to just below boiling point, whisking continuously with a balloon whisk. Cool until lukewarm. Spread the cream evenly over the pastry and top with overlapping rings of apple. Fill the holes in the rings with the stewed bilberries and bake the flan in a moderately hot oven (200 C, 400 F, gas 6) for about 30 minutes. Five minutes before the end of the baking time remove the flan from the oven, sprinkle with the icing sugar and caramelise the sugar under the grill. Apricot and plum flans can be made with this same recipe, the only difference being that the cream is mixed with 100 g/4 oz ground almonds and the bilberries are omitted.

Cherry Streusel Flan

For the dough:
225 g/8 oz strong plain flour
15 g/½ oz fresh yeast or 1½ teaspoons
dried yeast
6 tablespoons lukewarm milk
40 g/1½ oz butter
25 g/1 oz caster sugar
1 egg
grated rind of ½ lemon
pinch of salt
baking sheet (36 × 28-cm/14 × 11-in)

For the filling:
25 g/1 oz cornflour
300 ml/½ pint milk
3 egg yolks
1 vanilla pod
50 g/2 oz marzipan
1 kg/2 lb sweet cherries, stoned

For the streusel:
350 g/8 oz plain flour
175 g/6 oz butter
175 g/6 oz caster sugar

Sift the flour into a mixing bowl, make a well in the centre and dissolve the crumbled fresh yeast in the lukewarm milk. Cover this mixture with some of the flour in the bowl, cover the bowl and leave to stand for about 15 minutes. If using dried yeast stir it into milk, leave in a warm place for 10 minutes. Melt the butter and stir in the sugar, egg, lemon rind and salt. Pour into the mixing bowl and work all the ingredients together. Knead until smooth and elastic, then replace the dough in the bowl, cover and leave to stand in a warm place for 1 to 1½ hours or until doubled in size.

Blend the cornflour with 2 tablespoons of the milk and the egg yolks. Bring the remaining milk to the boil with the vanilla pod. Remove the vanilla pod and pour on to the cornflour mixture, stirring well throughout. Return to the saucepan and bring to boil stirring continuously. Cut the marzipan into pieces and whisk into the mixture. Remove the saucepan from the heat and sprinkle the cream with a little icing sugar to prevent a skin forming as it cools. Roll out the dough to a rectangle 36 × 28-cm/14 × 11-in, then use to line the greased baking sheet. Prick all over with a fork. Cover and allow to rise for 45 minutes. Spread with cream and top with the cherries.

To make the streusel rub butter into flour until the mixture resembles fine bread-crumbs, stir in sugar, spread over the flan. Bake in a moderately hot oven (200 C, 400 F, gas 6) for 35 to 40 minutes. Leave flan to cool for 5 to 10 minutes. Remove from the baking sheet and cut into slices.

Apricot Streusel Flan

with curd filling

For the dough:
225 g/8 oz strong plain flour
15 g/½ oz fresh yeast or 1½ teaspoons
dried yeast
6 tablespoons lukewarm milk
25 g/1 oz butter
25 g/1 oz caster sugar
1 egg
pinch of salt
30-cm/12-in flan tin

For the filling:
1 kg/2 lb fresh, ripe apricots
575 g/1¼ lb curd cheese
3 eggs
150 g/5 oz caster sugar
grated rind of 1 lemon
4 tablespoons cornflour
40 g/1½ oz butter
150 g/5 oz walnuts, chopped
75 g/3 oz icing sugar
1 egg white
50 g/2 oz glacé cherries, chopped

For the streusel:
175 g/6 oz plain flour
100 g/4 oz butter
100 g/4 oz caster sugar
½ teaspoon cinnamon
icing sugar for dusting

Make the dough up following the previous recipe.

Drop the apricots a few at a time into boiling water (for 1 to 2 minutes at the most) and then remove the skins. Halve the apricots along the indentation and remove the stones. Line the sides and base of the flan tin with the dough and prick all over with a fork. Beat the curd cheese with the eggs, sugar, lemon rind and cornflour. Spread the mixture over the flan case. Place the apricots cut side uppermost over the curd mixture. Melt the butter in a saucepan, add the chopped walnuts and icing sugar and stir over a medium heat until the mixture caramelises. Pour the mixture on to an oiled surface or into an oiled tin. Allow to cool, then crush the caramelised nuts until they form a fine powder. Do this by placing the mixture in a polythene bag and crushing it with a rolling pin. Mix it thoroughly with the egg white and chopped glacé cherries. Spoon a little of this soft mixture into the centre of each apricot half.

Make the streusel as in the previous recipe and sprinkle over the flan. Leave the flan to stand for a further 10 to 15 minutes, then bake in a moderately hot oven (200 C, 400 F, gas 6) for 35 to 40 minutes. When cold dust with icing sugar.

Plum Streusel Flan

(not illustrated)

There are a lot of different combinations possible for plum flans: the base can be either shortcrust pastry or yeast dough; between the pastry and the fruit you can sprinkle almonds or spread vanilla or curd cheese custard; the top can be of streusel, almonds or other nuts. The following recipe is a basic recipe for a plain plum flan with streusel.

For the dough:
225 g/8 oz strong plain flour
15 g/½ oz fresh yeast or 1½ teaspoons
dried yeast
6 tablespoons lukewarm milk
40 g/1½ oz butter
25 g/1 oz caster sugar
grated rind of ½ lemon
generous pinch of salt
1 egg
baking sheet (36 × 28-cm/14 × 11-in)

For the filling:
1½ kg/3 lb ripe plums

For the streusel:
225 g/8 oz plain flour
175 g/6 oz butter
175 g/6 oz caster sugar

Make a yeast dough with the ingredients listed as instructed in the previous Cherry Streusel Flan recipe. Cover the baking sheet with the evenly rolled dough and prick with a fork. Cut the plums into quarters without cutting right through to the base so that the quarters are still joined together, and remove the stones. Cover the dough with a thick layer of overlapping plums. Make a streusel with the flour, butter and sugar and sprinkle over the plums. In case the pastry has not had time to rise fully while you have been filling the flan, leave it to stand for a further 10 to 15 minutes. Bake in a moderately hot oven (200 C, 400 F, gas 6) for 25 to 35 minutes. Towards the end of the baking time lift the dough from the tin with a knife to check that the bottom is not getting too brown.

Instead of using plums in this recipe other types of stoned fruit can be used when obtainable such as the greengage, damson or bullace (which is a wild European variety of plum related to the sloe but larger than it).

Baking-Sheet Flans with Fruit Toppings

The flans referred to here are large flans with fruit toppings baked on a rectangular baking sheet and served cut into slices or squares. These flat flans are one of the oldest ways of using fruit in baking. In the Near East and Mediterranean countries figs, sweet grapes, cherries and apricots were used for the topping. In the colder climate of central and northern Europe less exotic fruits such as apples, pears, plums and wild berries were used. Less exotic they might be, but these were no less tasty, and chefs and housewives were able to develop excellent recipes using these fruits.

The possible combinations and variations are endless. Yeast dough or various shortcrust pastries can be used: even a firm cake mixture can be used as a base, or as an intermediate layer. Choose fruit which are suitable for baking on the base which you are using. Apples, plums, apricots, cherries and rhubarb, which require a longish cooking time, are best on yeast pastry. Bilberries and gooseberries are also fruits that don't suffer when baked for a long time. Blackcurrants need a shorter baking time and it is a good idea to pre-cook the pastry partially before adding the fruit. Raspberries, strawberries or blackberries should be covered in meringue and browned very quickly so that they retain their shape and flavour.

Further variations are offered by the intermediate layer – the layer between the fruit and the pastry. This can be biscuit crumbs, nuts, or alternatively cream fillings with a milk, curd cheese or yogurt base flavoured to complement the fruit. The recipes on the right should be considered as guidelines and you can easily devise your own variations.

The finished products: redcurrant meringue flan, brown cherry flan and apricot flan. All these flans are best eaten fresh from the oven, they should not be kept for a long time. Preferably they should be eaten the same day. Do not cut the flan until it is served.

Bilberry Flan

Cover a baking sheet 36 × 28-cm/14 × 11-in with quantity of yeast dough (see page 46) and prick a over with a fork to prevent the pastry bubbling u during baking. Pick over 1 kg/2 lb bilberrie discarding any which are not perfect. Cover th dough with the bilberries and sprinkle with sugar t taste. Make a streusel from 350 g/12 oz plain flour 225 g/8 oz butter, 225 g/8 oz caster sugar and teaspoon cinnamon. Spread this over the bilberries Leave to rise for a further 15 minutes, then bake o the middle shelf of a hot oven (220 C, 425 F, gas 7) fo 30 minutes.

Morello Cherry Flan

Wash and stone 2 kg/4½ lb morello cherries, sprinkl with 150 g/5 oz caster sugar and leave to steep for hours. Cover a 36 × 28-cm/14 × 11-in baking shee with 1 quantity of yeast dough (see page 46) an prick with a fork. Mix 75 g/3 oz ground toaste hazelnuts with 50 g/2 oz biscuit crumbs and sprea evenly over the pastry. Drain the cherries well an reserve the juice. Arrange the fruit in a thick layer o the flan. Leave to stand for 15 minutes and the bake in a hot oven (230C, 425F, gas 7) for 30 minute Blend 1 tablespoon arrowroot with 150 ml/¼ pir water. Stir in the cherry juice, ½ tablespoo cinnamon and 1 tablespoon lemon juice. Bring t the boil and continue to cook for 2–3 minutes t form a thick glaze. Pour over the flan while warm

Rhubarb Flan

Line a 36 × 28-cm/14 × 11-in baking sheet with 750 g/1½ lb shortcrust pastry (see page 37), prick with a fork and bake in a moderately hot oven (200C, 400F, gas 6) for 10 minutes. Mix together 150 g/5 oz ground toasted almonds and 75 g/3 oz biscuit crumbs and spread over the pastry. Wash and peel 1¾ kg/4 lb rhubarb and cut into 5 cm/2 in lengths. Arrange the rhubarb on the flan and sprinkle with a mixture of 150 g/5 oz caster sugar and ½ teaspoon cinnamon. Bake on the middle shelf of a moderately hot oven (200C, 400F, gas 6) for about 40 minutes. Leave the flan to cool slightly. Whisk 4 egg whites until stiff but not dry, then gradually whisk in 225 g/8 oz caster sugar. Using a piping bag fitted with a 1-cm/½-in star nozzle, pipe a lattice of meringue on to the flan. Bake on the top shelf of the oven for 10 minutes.

Brown Cherry Flan

Cover a 36 × 28-cm/14 × 11-in baking sheet with 675 g/1½ lb shortcrust pastry (see page 37) and prick with a fork. Cream 225 g/8 oz butter with 100 g/4 oz caster sugar until pale and fluffy, then gradually add 6 egg yolks, a pinch of salt, the grated peel of 1 lemon, 1 teaspoon cinnamon, 225 g/8 oz ground almonds and 175 g/6 oz plain flour. Whisk 6 egg whites until stiff but not dry then whisk in 100 g/4 oz caster sugar and fold into the mixture. Finally stir in 225 g/8 oz grated plain chocolate. Spread half the mixture on the pastry, cover with 800 g/1¾ lb washed, stoned cherries, cover with the remaining mixture and smooth the top. Bake in a moderately hot oven (200C, 400F, gas 6) for 50 to 60 minutes. When cool dust with icing sugar.

Redcurrant Meringue

Cover a 43 × 33-cm/17 × 13-in baking sheet with 675 g/1½ lb shortcrust pastry (see page 37), prick the base with a fork and then bake blind in a hot oven (220C, 425F, gas 7) for 10 minutes. Leave to cool. Whisk 8 egg whites until stiff but not dry then gradually whisk in 275 g/10 oz caster sugar. String the redcurrants (scrape the fruit off the stalks with a fork), then fold them into the meringue. Spread this over the pastry and bake in a very hot oven (240C, 475F, gas 9) for 10 minutes. Keep the oven door slightly ajar during cooking (jam the handle of a wooden spoon in the opening) to allow steam to escape. Cool and cut into 7.5-cm/3-in squares.

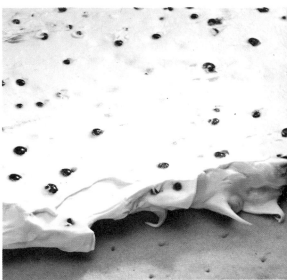

Apricot Flan

Cover a 36 × 28-cm/14 × 11-in baking sheet with 1 quantity of yeast dough (see page 46). Blend 1½ tablespoons custard powder with a little milk, 2 tablespoons sugar and 2 egg yolks. Bring 600 ml/1 pint milk to the boil. Pour the milk onto the custard mixture then return to the saucepan and boil vigorously for a few minutes. Allow to cool slightly before stirring in 225 g/8 oz marzipan. Spread the cream over the pastry. Blanch 1 kg/2 lb apricots and remove the skins. Halve and stone the apricots and arrange on the flan. Leave the flan to stand for a further 10 minutes then bake in a moderately hot oven (200C, 400F, gas 6) for about 30 minutes. Warm 225 g/8 oz apricot jam and brush over the cooked flan before sprinkling with 100 g/4 oz toasted flaked almonds.

Gooseberry Flan

Cover a 43 × 33-cm/17 × 13-in baking sheet with 675 g/1½ lb shortcrust pastry (see page 37), prick with a fork and bake in a hot oven (220C, 425F, gas 7) for 15–20 minutes until golden. Spread 225 g/8 oz redcurrant jam on the pastry base and top with a basic Swiss roll sponge (see pages 30–1). Wash 1 kg/2 lb gooseberries and cook with 100 g/4 oz caster sugar in boiling water for 2–3 minutes. Whisk 8 egg whites until stiff but not dry then gradually whisk in 225 g/8 oz caster sugar. Fold 175 g/6 oz ground almonds into the whisked whites and spread half this mixture on the sponge. Cover with the drained gooseberries and place the remaining meringue on top. Bake in a hot oven (220C, 425F, gas 7) for 12–15 minutes.

Plum Flan

Cover 36 × 28-cm/14 × 11-in baking sheet with 1 quantity of yeast dough (see page 46) and prick with a fork. Wash and stone 1½ kg/3 lb plums and cut lengthways into quarters. Cover the dough with a thick layer of plums. Rub in 150 g/5 oz plain flour with 75 g/3 oz butter and 150 g/5 oz caster sugar to make a streusel and spread thinly over the flan. Sprinkle with 100 g/4 oz flaked almonds. Leave the flan to stand for 15 minutes then bake in a moderately hot oven (200C, 400F, gas 6) for 20 to 30 minutes. When cool dust with icing sugar and cut into 7.5 × 10-cm/3 × 4-in slices.

Lemon Flan

The French *Tarte au citron* is usually made with a rich egg cream (with lots of butter). The following recipe is much lighter and airier but no less tasty, especially with the browned meringue topping.

For the pastry:
225 g/8 oz plain flour
100 g/4 oz butter
50 g/2 oz icing sugar
pinch of salt
1 egg yolk
2 tablespoons water
flan tin, 25-cm/10-in diameter and
2.5-cm/1-in deep, or similar sponge tin

For the lemon cream:
25 g/1 oz caster sugar
25 g/1 oz cornflour
3 egg yolks
300 ml/½ pint milk
grated rind and juice of 1 lemon

For the meringue:
225 g/8 oz caster sugar
6–8 tablespoons water
4 egg whites
icing sugar for dusting

Make the shortcrust pastry as described on page 37. Wrap in cling film or foil and place in the refrigerator for about an hour. Roll out and line the tin then bake blind for about 15 minutes in a moderately hot oven (190 C, 375 F, gas 5). Then remove the baking beans and greaseproof paper and bake at the same temperature for a further 5–10 minutes until golden brown. Make a custard with the sugar, cornflour, egg yolks and milk (as for Simple Vanilla Cream, see page 50) and then stir the lemon juice and finely grated rind into the hot cream.

Meanwhile dissolve the sugar in the water then bring to the boil and boil steadily, stirring occasionally, until the syrup reaches a soft ball stage (116 C/240 F). Whisk the egg whites until stiff but not dry and then whisk in the syrup in a slow trickle. Fold half the meringue into the lemon cream with a metal spoon and pour immediately into the baked pastry case, smoothing the top gently. Spoon the remaining meringue into a piping bag with 1-cm/½-in star nozzle and decorate the flan as shown in the picture below. Sift with icing sugar and lightly brown under the grill.

Apple Cake with Calvados Cream

500 g/1 lb quick puff pastry (see page 44)
1 kg/2 lb Cox's apples
50 g/2 oz currants
1 tablespoon Calvados (apple brandy)
50 g/2 oz caster sugar

For the cream:
3 egg yolks
75 g/3 oz caster sugar
300 ml/½ pint milk
1 vanilla pod
15 g/½ oz powdered gelatine
300 ml/½ pint double cream
3 tablespoons Calvados

For the glaze:
300 ml/½ pint dry white wine
50 g/2 oz caster sugar
4½ teaspoons cornflour
2 tablespoons water
50 g/2 oz flaked almonds, toasted

Roll the puff pastry and cut into two 28-cm/11-in rounds. Place the rounds on a moist baking sheet, prick all over with a fork and leave the pastry to stand for 15 minutes. Bake in a hot oven (220 C, 425 F, gas 7) for 12 to 15 minutes. If the rounds go out of shape during baking, reshape by cutting round a 25-cm/10-in ring.

Peel, core and quarter the apples and cut into 1-cm/½-in slices. Cook them in boiling water for about 3 minutes. Place the apples and currants in a bowl, pour on the Calvados and sprinkle with the sugar. Cover the bowl and leave to steep for at least an hour.

Beat the egg yolks with the sugar until thick and creamy. Bring the milk to the boil with the vanilla pod, remove the pod and stir the hot milk into the egg yolk mixture. Cook the custard in a heavy-based saucepan over a very low heat, stirring continuously, until thickened enough to coat the back of a wooden spoon. The custard must not overcook or boil or it will curdle. Dissolve the gelatine in 2 tablespoons of hot water in a basin over a saucepan of hot water then stir it into the custard. Leave to cool. Whip the cream until thick enough to hold its shape then stir it into the custard and Calvados before it begins to set.

Spread about three-quarters of the cream on one of the pastry bases, cover with the second round of pastry and then spread the top and sides of the cake with the remaining cream. Drain the apples and arrange on top of the cake, sprinkling with the currants.

Bring the wine and sugar to the boil. Blend the cornflour with the water and pour into the wine. Boil, stirring continuously, until the liquid is clear and then brush immediately over the apples. Press the almonds around the edge as shown below.

Blackcurrants with Vanilla Cream

Make a vanilla cream using 300 ml/½ pint milk, 1 vanilla pod, 50 g/2 oz caster sugar, 25 g/1 oz cornflour and 2 egg yolks (see page 50). Leave the cream to cool slightly, then stir until smooth and use to fill six 10-cm/4-in pastry cases. Dissolve 100 g/4 oz caster sugar in 2 tablespoons water over a gentle heat then, add 3 tablespoons crème de cassis and 2 tablespoons lemon juice. Bring to the boil and add 450 g/1 lb blackcurrants. Cook the fruit for 2 to 3 minutes then spoon into the tartlets. Garnish with pistachio nuts cut into spikes.
Makes six tartlets.

Plums on Almond Cream

Make a vanilla custard using 300 ml/½ pint milk, 1 vanilla pod, 50 g/2 oz caster sugar, 25 g/1 oz cornflour and 2 egg yolks (see page 50). Stir until cold and then stir in 1 tablespoon Amaretto and 100 g/4 oz ground almonds. Spoon the almond cream into six 10-cm/4-in pastry cases. Stone and quarter 675 g/1½ lb ripe plums. Bring 600 ml/1 pint water to the boil with the juice of 1 lemon and 100 g/4 oz caster sugar, quickly blanch the plums in this syrup and transfer to the pastry cases. Blend 4 teaspoons cornflour with 8 tablespoons white wine. Stir in 8 tablespoons of the syrup and bring to the boil stirring continuously. Cook until the liquid is clear then use to glaze the plums.
Makes six tartlets.

Caramelised Raspberries

Make a vanilla custard using 150 ml/¼ pint milk, 1½ tablespoons caster sugar, 1½ level tablespoons cornflour and 1 egg yolk (see page 50), pour into a basin and sprinkle with a little icing sugar. Strain the cold custard and stir in 2 tablespoons raspberry liqueur and 50 g/2 oz crumbled almond macaroons. Whisk 1 egg white until stiff then gradually whisk in 50 g/2 oz caster sugar. Fold into the vanilla cream. Spoon the cream into six 10-cm/4-in pastry cases and cover thickly with raspberries. Sift with icing sugar and brown quickly under the grill until the sugar begins to caramelise. Makes six tartlets.

Kiwis with Lime Cream

Bring 6 tablespoons dry white wine with the rind and juice of 2 limes and 50 g/2 oz caster sugar to the boil. Remove from the heat. Stir 1½ teaspoons powdered gelatine into the hot but not boiling liquid until completely dissolved. Whip 150 ml/¼ pint double cream and fold into the cooled liquid together with 150 ml/¼ pint natural yogurt. Leave on one side until half set. Meanwhile brush the insides of four 10-cm/4-in meringue cases thinly with melted chocolate and then fill with the cream, leave to set, then top with sliced kiwis (from about eight kiwis) and thin slices of peeled lime. Top with cranberry jelly.
Makes four tartlets.

Loganberries

Blend 2 teaspoons cornflour with 40 g/1½ oz caster sugar, 1 egg yolk and the juice of 1 orange. Bring 600 ml/1 pint soured cream to just below boiling point. Pour a little on to the cornflour mixture, stirring well. Return to the saucepan and cook for a few minutes until the mixture thickens. Spoon the mixture into six pastry cases and smooth the top. Bring 300 ml/½ pint white wine to the boil with 50 g/2 oz caster sugar and boil until reduced by half. Add the rind of half an orange and 275 g/10 oz loganberries. Bring to the boil, then cool and spread over the soured cream mixture.
Makes six tartlets.

Apples on Wine Cream

Peel and core 5–6 Cox's Orange Pippin apples and cut into equal slices. Bring 300 ml/½ pint white wine to the boil with 75 g/3 oz caster sugar. Add 40 g/1½ oz raisins. Blanch the apples in the wine for 1 minute. Drain the apples and raisins. Blend 1 teaspoon cornflour with 2 egg yolks, the grated rind and juice of 1 lime and 1 tablespoon Calvados. Stir in a little of the hot apple juice. Return to the saucepan and bring to the boil stirring continuously. Sprinkle 15 g/½ oz powdered gelatine over the mixture and stir until it has dissolved. Leave to cool and then fold in 300 ml/½ pint whipped double cream. Fill six 10-cm/4-in shortcrust pastry cases with the mixture. Top with the apples arranged to form a flower and sprinkle with raisins. Brush with a little apricot glaze.
Makes six tartlets.

Gooseberry Meringue

[Cr]ush six meringue nests with a mixture of [40]g/1½ oz ground almonds, 1 tablespoon Amaretto [an]d 3 tablespoons sugar syrup. Sprinkle with [toa]sted flaked almonds. Bring 8 tablespoons white [wi]ne to the boil with 50 g/2 oz caster sugar and 1 [ta]blespoon lemon juice. Add 675 g/1½ lb washed, [rip]e gooseberries and boil for a few minutes until [th]ey become transparent. Drain the gooseberries [an]d spoon into the meringue nests. Bring the fruit [sy]rup back to the boil, thicken with 2 teaspoons [co]rnflour blended with a little cold water and glaze [th]e gooseberries.

[M]akes six tartlets.

Blackberries with Meringue

Bring 8 tablespoons red wine to the boil with 50 g/2 oz caster sugar and 1 tablespoon lemon juice and boil to reduce it slightly. Add 450 g/1 lb fresh blackberries and 1 tablespoon rum and leave to steep for an hour in a covered bowl. Whisk 3 egg whites until stiff, then gradually whisk in 100 g/4 oz caster sugar. Spoon a third of the meringue into piping bag with a star nozzle. Fold 50 g/2 oz ground almonds into the remaining meringue and use to fill six 10-cm/4-in shortcrust pastry cases. Cover with the blackberries and their juice, garnish each tartlet with a whirl of meringue and brown under the grill. Makes six tartlets.

Morello Cherries in Burgundy

Bring 300 ml/½ pint Burgundy wine to the boil with 100 g/4 oz caster sugar and continue boiling for about 5 minutes. Remove the stalks and stones from 450 g/1 lb morello cherries, add to the wine and bring back to the boil. Remove the pan from the heat and drain the cherries. Bring the syrup back to the boil, thicken with 3 teaspoons cornflour blended with a little water and flavour with 1 tablespoon Kirsch. Return the cherries to the sauce and then spoon the mixture into six 10-cm/4-in shortcrust pastry cases. Decorate with toasted flaked almonds. Makes six tartlets.

Alpine Strawberries with Cream

[Ma]ke six 10-cm/4-in shortcrust tartlet cases (using [sw]eet shortcrust pastry recipe on page 38). Brush [thi]nly with 100 g/4 oz melted chocolate and leave to [set.] Stir 1 tablespoon brandy into 75 g/3 oz biscuit [cru]mbs and leave to soak for 30 minutes. Crush [10]0 g/4 oz Alpine strawberries with a fork, then mix [the]m into the biscuit crumbs. Whisk 300 ml/½ pint [do]uble cream with 25 g/1 oz caster sugar until stiff, [the]n fold in the crumb mixture. Spoon into the six [tart]let cases. Top with a further 100 g/4 oz [str]awberries and dust with icing sugar. [Ma]kes six tartlets.

Figs in Sauterne

Heat 150 ml/¼ pint Sauterne wine with 40 g/1½ oz caster sugar. Remove the saucepan from the heat just before the liquid boils and sprinkle over 1½ teaspoons powdered gelatine. Stir until the gelatine dissolves. Leave the mixture to cool and just before it begins to set fold in 300 ml/½ pint whipped double cream. Spoon into six 10-cm/4-in shortcrust tartlet cases and smooth the top. Peel and slice 10–12 ripe figs and arrange on the tartlets. Decorate the centre of each with a few peeled seedless grapes. Brush with an apricot glaze and sprinkle the edges with flaked almonds.
Makes six tartlets.

Cranberry Tartlets

Prepare a half quantity of Simple Vanilla Cream (see page 50) and set aside to cool. Work 2 tablespoons Kirsch into 100 g/4 oz marzipan until creamy, then stir this into the Vanilla Cream. If the mixture is too thick to spread easily, thin it with a little single cream. Fill six shortcrust pastry tartlets with this mixture. Boil 3 tablespoons white wine with 75 g/3 oz caster sugar until the syrup reduces slightly. Add 450 g/1 lb fresh cranberries and simmer the fruit until it turns translucent and begins to break up slightly. Spoon into the tartlets.
Makes six tartlets.

Cheesecakes

The Romans loved cheese and had at least thirteen different types. Although they were not responsible for creating cheesecake, they did develop it into a fine delicacy. To combine cheese with sweet ingredients in a cake was directly in line with the rather exotic tastes of the period. The combination of savoury and sweet things of which the Romans were so fond was best exemplified in the *savillum*, the ancient version of the cheesecake which developed over the centuries into the versions we know today. The recipe was extremely simple: 'Work together half a pound of flour, two and a half pounds of curds, a quarter of a pound of honey and one egg. Cook the mixture in a buttered clay pot with a close-fitting lid. When the cake is cooked pour honey over it and sprinkle it with poppy seeds.'

Cheesecakes are still eaten in modern-day Italy, with Ricotta often used as the main ingredient for the cheese filling. Ricotta is a type of curd cheese prepared from sheep's milk. Wonderful cheesecakes are still made in Italy, of which the crustless *crostata di ricotta* is just one example. It is not generally appreciated that the famous *cassata Siciliana* really belongs in this chapter as it should not properly be filled with ice cream but with curd cheese! The confusion arises from the fact that the *cassata* is chilled to make it firm. There is an excellent phrase to describe this delicacy decorated with the finest candied fruit or any other of the excellent cheesecakes: 'Tout est beauté, tout est charme en elle' – it contains everything of beauty and charm.

Cheesecakes were popular in seventeenth and eighteenth-century Britain and have always been popular in the United States where they were called curd cakes and originally brought over from Europe by Russian and Polish immigrants.

Yogurt originated in Eastern Europe and is still very popular there. It is claimed to be the secret of the longevity of the people in the Balkans and is claimed to have other health-giving properties. The first man in western Europe to realise its beneficial effects on stomach disorders is reputed to be Francis I of France.

Yogurt has been produced commercially in the second half of this century. Natural yogurt is popular both for sweet and savoury dishes especially because of its low-fat content. Fruit, nuts or honey can be added to natural yogurt as it goes well with any flavouring. Yogurt can be used in place of cream for many dishes but care should be taken to keep natural 'live' yogurt in the refrigerator otherwise the live bacteria in it will become active again in the warmth and the yogurt will separate.

Cheese Tart

This dish can have many variations and it is likely that you will come across different recipes for it. Either cream or curd cheese can be used to make the following tart depending on your individual preference. Curd cheese has a lower fat content than cream cheese as it is made from skimmed milk as opposed to whole milk or a mixture of whole milk and cream. In the past only natural curds could be obtained, and these had to be drained before use. Modern methods of cheesemaking have made this process obsolete however and prepared curd cheese can be bought over the counter ready for use.

For the pastry:
225 g/8 oz plain flour
100 g/4 oz butter, softened
50 g/2 oz icing sugar
pinch of salt
2 tablespoons water
1 egg yolk
tart tin of 25-cm/10-in diameter and
2.5-cm/1-in deep, or similar cake tin

For the curd cheese mixture:
450 g/1 lb curd or cream cheese
150 g/5 oz caster sugar
4 eggs
grated rind of 1 lemon
100 g/4 oz butter
50 g/2 oz plain flour
pinch of salt
75 g/3 oz raisins
1 tablespoon Kirsch or white rum
icing sugar for dusting

Make the pastry as shown on page 38. Leave the pastry to stand for an hour in the refrigerator, then roll into a round of about 30-cm/12-in. in diameter. Line the tin with the pastry, pressing it carefully to the sides and cutting off any excess. If possible use a loose-bottomed tin. Prick the base several times with a fork. Line the flan case with greaseproof paper weighted with dried beans (as shown on page 41) and bake 'blind'.

Prepare the curd mixture as shown in the photographs on the opposite page. One important factor if the cake is to be a success is to bake it in a moderate oven (160 C, 325 F, gas 3) for 45 minutes. If baked at a higher temperature it will rise too much and probably split open, before falling again. At the lower temperature it rises very little although the egg white still coagulates, and the cake remains lighter and moister. When the tart is cooked leave it to cool, dust with icing sugar and mark with a lattice using a heated wire mesh. This caramelised sugar goes well with the flavour of the cake.

Not everyone likes raisins in a cheese tart and they can be omitted without spoiling the recipe; but you could also try replacing them with something different – fresh fruit, for example, which must be ripe and firm. Morello cherries, sweet cherries or apricots are all excellent. If using raisins soak them for at least an hour beforehand in the Kirsch or white rum.

1 **Here the curds** are strained through a fine sieve. This is not necessary for modern curd or cream cheese but doing this will help the cheese whisk up more easily as it softens it.

2 **Place the curd cheese** and 75 g/3 oz of the sugar in a bowl. Separate the eggs. Add the yolks to the curd cheese and pour the whites into another clean bowl. Cover the bowl (to keep the whites clean) and leave to one side while you prepare the curds mixture.

3 **Whisk the curd cheese** with the sugar and egg yolks until light and fluffy, using a fairly strong whisk as the mixture will be quite stiff at first. As this will take some time it is a good idea to do this with a food mixer or electric whisk using a medium speed.

4 **Give the lemon** a good scrub under running water before use. Grate the rind very thinly and when you have finished grating tap the grater on the side of the bowl to make sure you get all the rind into the mixture.

5 **Melt and clarify the butter** by carefully removing the surface scum with a spoon without taking any of the butter with it. Using the whisk, beat the butter into the curd mixture, sift the flour and salt into the bowl and fold in.

6 **Add the steeped raisins.** For a cheesecake use only plump, seedless raisins and soak these in Kirsch or rum for at least an hour. Stir lightly into the curd mixture, but do not over-stir at this point or the mixture may take on a greyish colour.

7 **Whisk the egg white** until stiff but not dry then whisk in the remaining sugar. Stir in about a quarter of the whisked egg whites with a metal spoon and then fold in the remaining whites extremely carefully trying to avoid the mixture falling.

8 **Pour the mixture** gently into the pre-baked pastry case using a spatula to remove all the mixture from the bowl.

9 **Using a palette knife** spread the mixture to the edges of the tart and smooth the top. Bake immediately in a moderate oven (160 C, 325 F, gas 3) for 45 minutes.

Rich Cream Cheesecake

For the pastry:
175 g/6 oz butter
75 g/3 oz icing sugar
2 egg yolks
225 g/8 oz plain flour

For the filling:
4 egg yolks
225 g/8 oz caster sugar
grated rind of 1 lemon
pinch of salt
300 ml/½ pint milk
8 leaves gelatine or 25 g/1 oz
powdered gelatine
450 g/1 lb curd or cream cheese
600 ml/1 pint double cream, whipped
icing sugar for dusting

3 **Soften the leaf gelatine** for 10 minutes in cold water, then squeeze out the excess water. Dissolve the leaf or powdered gelatine in a little hot water, standing the basin over a saucepan of hot water. As soon as the egg yolk mixture is removed from the heat, stir in the dissolved gelatine. Strain through a fine sieve.

5 **Whisk using a strong whisk,** for the mixture is quite stiff at first. As soon as you have incorporated the first portion of the egg yolk mixture add a little more warm mixture. When you have added all the mixture whisk until you have a smooth creamy texture.

Make the pastry as shown on page 38. Chill then roll out to make two 25-cm/10-in rounds and bake in a moderately hot oven (200 C, 400 F, gas 6) for 10 minutes or until golden brown. Cut one round into portions while still hot.

1 **Place the egg yolks,** sugar, lemon rind and salt in a saucepan and add the milk. Mix the ingredients, first whisking vigorously and then stirring continuously with a wooden spoon while the mixture warms slowly over a moderate heat.

4 **Leave the basic cream** to cool slightly, then pour it over the curd cheese in a large bowl. The cream will stir in more easily if you add it in two or three stages. It should be added while still warm for it is soon cooled by the cold curd cheese.

Rich Cream Cheesecakes with Fruit Filling

With the inclusion of fruit, the quantities of curd or cream cheese can be reduced as follows.

2 **Cook the mixture gently,** stirring continuously, until it will coat the back of the spoon. The custard must not be overcooked or boiled or it will curdle. The spoon should be thickly coated with the mixture when lifted from the pan.

6 **Fold in the cream,** taking care not to let the whipped cream fall. The job takes longer with a metal spoon, rather than with a whisk, but you will get better results.

7 **Place a cake ring** around one of the pastry bases. This can be an aluminium ring from which the cake can later be loosened with a knife. Fill with the cheesecake mixture.

8 **Cover with a pastry lid.** This lid must be cut into the required number of portions immediately after baking (while it is still hot and soft). If you try to cut it once it is cold it will break. Using the base of a loose-bottomed tin to help you, slide the lid from the baking sheet on to the cake. Dust with icing sugar.

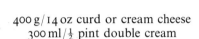

2 pastry bases (see recipe on opposite page)
4 egg yolks
175 g/6 oz caster sugar
grated rind of ½ lemon
pinch of salt
300 ml/½ pint milk
8 leaves gelatine or 1 oz powdered gelatine

400 g/14 oz curd or cream cheese
300 ml/½ pint double cream

The curd cream is prepared exactly as in the basic recipe. The fruit must be ready for use before you start making the cream, because it sets quite quickly. Place a flan ring round one of the pastry bases and spread with a thin layer of curd cream to protect the pastry from the moist fruit. Arrange the fruit on the cream. Do not take the fruit right to the edge but leave room for a good border of curd cream. Cover the fruit with the remaining cream and smooth the top. To get rid of any air bubbles lift the cake on its base and gently tap it on the worktop.

The cake should be firm enough to cut after 2 hours in the refrigerator. Remove the ring, top with the pastry lid which you have already cut into portions and dust the top with icing sugar.

Cherry Filling

450 g/1 lb stewed morello cherries
8 tablespoons morello cherry juice
1 tablespoon sugar
½ teaspoon cinnamon
1 teaspoon cornflour

Drain the cherries thoroughly in a sieve. Bring the cherry juice to the boil with the sugar and cinnamon. Blend the cornflour with a little water, then stir it into the juice. Simmer gently until the mixture has thickened then add the cherries and stir gently to avoid breaking them. Continue simmering for a few minutes, then remove the pan from the heat and leave the cherries to cool. Drain the cherries before filling the cheese cake.

Apricot Filling

675 g/1½ lb fresh apricots
300 ml/½ pint dry white wine
175 g/6 oz caster sugar
3 tablespoons apricot liqueur

Quickly blanch the apricots in boiling water and remove the skins. Halve and stone the apricots. Boil the wine and sugar for 2 to 3 minutes. Add the apricots, bring back to the boil and then remove the pan from the heat. Add the apricot liqueur. Leave the fruit to cool in the juice and drain thoroughly before use.

Tamarillo Yogurt Flan

For the pastry:
175 g/6 oz butter
75 g/3 oz icing sugar
grated rind of ½ lemon
pinch of salt
1 egg yolk
225 g/8 oz plain flour
25-cm/10-in flan tin

For the yogurt cream:
275 g/10 oz tamarillos or plums, stoned
150 g/5 oz caster sugar
3 egg yolks
juice of 2 limes
6 leaves gelatine or 20 g/¾ oz
powdered gelatine
225 g/8 oz thick-set natural yogurt
300 ml/½ pint double cream, whipped

To decorate:
300 ml/½ pint double cream, whipped
25 g/1 oz caster sugar
50 g/2 oz chocolate, grated

Make the pastry as shown on page 37. Line the flan tin and bake blind for 15 minutes then remove the baking beans and bake for a further 5 to 10 minutes until golden brown. Purée the fruit in a blender and strain through a sieve. Mix the purée with the sugar, egg yolks and lime juice, place in a saucepan and heat until slightly thickened. Do not boil. Soften the leaf gelatine in cold water for 10 minutes, then squeeze out the excess water and stir into the mixture until melted, or sprinkle the powdered gelatine over and stir until dissolved. Strain the mixture through a sieve. Finally stir in the yogurt and keep stirring until the cream is cool. Just before the mixture begins to set fold in the whipped cream. Pour the mixture into the baked flan case and smooth the top. Chill in the refrigerator for about 2 hours or until set. Divide into 12 portions. Sweeten the whipped cream with the sugar, pipe on to the flan and sprinkle with the chocolate.

Orange Yogurt Ring

For the pastry:
100 g/4 oz butter, softened
65 g/2½ oz icing sugar
1 teaspoon vanilla essence
1 egg yolk
150 g/5 oz plain flour
65 g/2½ oz ground almonds
75 g/3 oz marmalade, sieved

For the cream:
8 tablespoons orange juice
juice of ½ lemon
grated rind of 2 oranges
100 g/4 oz caster sugar
4 egg yolks
8 leaves gelatine or 25 g/1 oz
powdered gelatine
225 g/8 oz thick-set natural yogurt
600 ml/1 pint double cream
25 g/1 oz caster sugar
50 g/2 oz flaked almonds, toasted
23-cm/9-in ring mould

Beat the butter, icing sugar, vanilla essence and egg yolk until creamy. Mix together the sifted flour and ground almonds and fold into the butter mixture to make a pastry. Chill for 2 hours then roll it out and cut out two rings the same size as the mould. Place on a baking sheet and prick with a fork. Bake in a moderately hot oven (200 C, 400 F, gas 6) for 10 minutes. Sandwich them together with the marmalade.

Beat the orange and lemon juice with the rind, sugar and egg yolks. Heat gently until slightly thickened. Soak the leaf gelatine for 10 minutes, squeeze out and dissolve in the mixture or sprinkle in the powdered gelatine. Strain the mixture and stir in the yogurt. Whip the cream with the sugar until stiff. When the yogurt cream begins to set add the cream. Pour into the mould and top with the pastry ring. Chill for 2 hours until set. Turn out then brush the edge of the pastry with marmalade and sprinkle with almonds.

Raspberry Yogurt Cake

For the sponge:
4 eggs
100 g/4 oz caster sugar
100 g/4 oz plain flour
25 g/1 oz cornflour
50 g/2 oz butter, melted
25-cm/10-in cake tin or ring

For the filling:
300 ml/½ pint milk
175 g/6 oz caster sugar
4 egg yolks
8 leaves gelatine or 25 g/1 oz powdered
gelatine
450 g/1 lb thick-set natural yogurt
225 g/8 oz fresh raspberries
1 tablespoon raspberry liqueur
300 ml/½ pint double cream
25 g/1 oz caster sugar
juice of 1 lemon

To decorate:
600 ml/1 pint double cream, whipped
1 tablespoon sugar
50 g/2 oz flaked almonds, toasted

Make a Genoese sponge as shown on pages 28–9, slice the sponge across into two layers and place a flan or cake ring round one layer. Heat the milk with the sugar and egg yolks until thick enough to coat the back of a spoon. Stir in the soaked and drained leaf gelatine or sprinkle in the powdered gelatine and stir until dissolved. Fold in the yogurt. Strain equally into two basins.

Purée the raspberries (reserving 16 for decoration) and stir into one portion of the cream with the raspberry liqueur. Whip the cream with the sugar until stiff and, before the yogurt cream begins to set, stir half the whipped cream into the raspberry yogurt cream and spread over the sponge base. Set in the refrigerator. Meanwhile stir the lemon juice into the remaining portion of yogurt cream and fold in the remaining whipped cream. Spread this over the firm raspberry cream, smooth the top and cover with the second layer of sponge base. Chill again, then cover the whole cake with the whipped cream. Divide into 16 and sprinkle with the almonds. Decorate with cream and raspberries.

Fruit Yogurt Flan

with Alpine strawberries and peaches

For the pastry:
175 g/6 oz butter, softened
75 g/3 oz icing sugar
grated rind of ½ lemon
pinch of salt
1 egg yolk
225 g/8 oz plain flour
25-cm/10-in deep-sided flan tin

For the chocolate yogurt cream:
8 tablespoons milk
50 g/2 oz caster sugar
2 egg yolks
40 g/1½ oz cocoa powder
4 leaves gelatine or 15 g/
½ oz powdered gelatine
1 tablespoon rum

150 g/5 oz thick-set natural yogurt
600 ml/1 pint double cream
1 tablespoon sugar
5 stewed peach halves, canned or peach halves lightly poached in syrup
225 g/8 oz Alpine strawberries or small strawberries quartered
50 g/2 oz caster sugar
50 g/2 oz grated chocolate to decorate

Cream the butter with the sifted icing sugar, lemon rind, salt and egg yolk until smooth and fold in the sifted flour as quickly as possible to prevent the pastry becoming too short and crumbly. Chill in the refrigerator for about 2 hours.

Line the deep-sided flan tin with pastry as shown on page 39 and bake blind. After 15 minutes remove the paper and baking beans and bake for a further 5 to 10 minutes until golden brown.

Heat the milk in a saucepan with the sugar, egg yolks and cocoa powder and simmer, stirring continuously, until thick enough to coat the back of a wooden spoon.

Dissolve the soaked and drained leaf gelatine in the mixture or stir in the dissolved powdered gelatine. Stir in the rum and yogurt. Whip half the cream with the tablespoon of sugar until stiff and stir into the cool mixture. Pour the mixture into the pastry case and leave in the refrigerator to set. Drain the peaches and cut into slices. Cover the cream in the flan case with successive rings of peach. Keep the best strawberries to one side to use for decoration and purée the remainder. Whip the remaining cream with the sugar until stiff. Keep a third of the cream back for decoration and stir the rest into the strawberry purée. If the mixture is too runny stir in 2 leaves of dissolved leaf gelatine, or 1 teaspoon powdered gelatine which has been dissolved in 2 tablespoons of hot water. Leave the strawberry cream purée until thick enough to spread then pour it in a mound over the peaches in the flan case and cover the top with grated chocolate. Divide the top into 12 or 14 portions and decorate with whirls of cream using a piping bag with a star nozzle. Top each whirl of cream with 3 Alpine strawberries as illustrated below.

Baking with Yeast

Bread is a staple product all over the world and the making of bread dates back to the Stone Age. There are various types of bread that are made without the use of yeast – such as Irish soda bread or Indian chapati – but since the discovery of yeast in the sixteenth century we have become used to leavened breads made with wheat flour.

As well as being baked in a loaf tin, yeast dough is very adaptable and lends itself well for shaping. At harvest time, for example, it is traditional to have a loaf baked in the shape of a wheatsheaf. Plaited loaves have always looked appealing and are ever popular.

The Gugelhupf, one of the best known German cakes, was once a middle-class status and wealth symbol. It was, and in many places still is, an essential feature of the middle-class family breakfast or the Sunday afternoon tea shop. The Gugelhupf is as much a feature of Sunday in Germany as an outing or visit to relatives. This can probably be explained by the time involved in making the cake so that the job was left for the weekend and the fact that all yeast cakes are best eaten fresh, preferably warm from the oven.

The strange etymology of the wonderful name 'Gugelhupf' is extremely interesting, and the spelling alone poses insoluble problems. Whether the word should begin with a 'K' or a 'G', whether the first syllable should be 'Gugel' or 'Gogel', whether it should be 'Hupf' or 'Hopf' are all matters of debate. Apparently the word 'Gugel' refers to the shape of the cake which, according to Zenker's *Kochkunst* (*The Art of Cookery*) should be tall in shape. The word 'Kugel' has similar connotations; in the Alps a high cone-shaped mountain is referred to as a 'Kogel', and in many areas peasant women still wear the spherical headdresses known as 'Gugel' which first became popular in the twelfth century. The syllable 'Hupf' or 'Hopf' on the other hand refers to the amazing way in which yeast dough rises and which brings to mind the term 'Hupfen' (to jump, leap).

These cakes were popular as long ago as Roman times. The excavations at Herculaneum produced tall, straight-sided bakeware and museums in Speyer and Berne include finds of bakeware with amazing similarities to the later Gugelhupf. Experts claim that the shape originally represented the 'rotating sun'. Admittedly the medieval version lacked the characteristic 'chimney' placed in the centre of the cake to ensure more even heat distribution. At that time the Gugelhupf was baked in a mortar, as a Viennese manuscript reveals. From the eighteenth century onwards richly decorated copper moulds began to appear and the range of recipes that could be cooked in them was widened. The 'ordinary' Gugelhupf was joined by sponge, almond or Malaga versions, the Waltersdorf Gugelhupf and even the Kaiser-Gugelhupf (the Emperor Franz Joseph was reputedly fond of what he referred to as this 'old German dish').

Whether for emperor or peasant these cakes, topped with almonds or glistening sugar, covered in chocolate or icing, with their light golden cake and juicy raisins, undoubtedly create a festive atmosphere of well-being.

Plaited Loaves

It is an ancient custom to make bread or cakes in the shape of a plait and an elastic, pliable yeast dough is very suitable for this purpose. The following recipe produces a firm dough which makes two plaited loaves.

1 kg/2 lb strong plain flour
25 g/1 oz fresh yeast or 15 g/½ oz dried yeast
450 ml/¾ pint lukewarm milk
100 g/4 oz butter, melted
150 g/5 oz caster sugar
1 teaspoon salt
egg yolk to glaze

The ingredients are made up as in the basic recipe (see page 46). Leave the dough plenty of time to rise both before and after plaiting, glaze and bake in a moderately hot oven (200 C, 400 F, gas 6).

This is a recipe for a richer yeast-dough plait. It is softer, more difficult to plait and loses its shape slightly during baking:

450 g/1 lb strong plain flour
25 g/1 oz fresh yeast or 15 g/½ oz dried yeast
150 ml/¼ pint lukewarm milk
100 g/4 oz butter, melted
75 g/3 oz caster sugar
½ teaspoon salt
grated rind of 1 lemon
1 egg
50 g/2 oz blanched almonds, chopped
25 g/1 oz chopped mixed peel
75 g/3 oz raisins
1 egg yolk to glaze
chopped almonds or sugar crystals for decoration

Mix the dough ingredients as in the basic recipe (see page 46). Work in the almonds, peel and raisins after the dough has been left to rise for the first time. Knead again and leave for 45 minutes, then glaze and decorate. Bake in a hot oven (220C, 425F, gas 7) for 25 to 35 minutes.

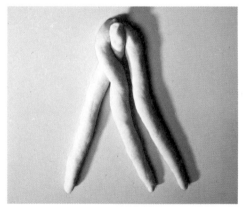

1 **Three-stranded plait.** This is the simplest plait to make. Whether the plait is to be of even breadth along all its length or to taper at the ends depends on how you roll the strands from which it is made.

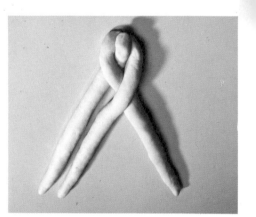

2 **Begin plaiting** by arranging the strands on the worktop and press them together at one end. Place the left strand over the centre one, so that the left strand is now in the centre and the centre one is now on the left. Now place the right strand over the centre one.

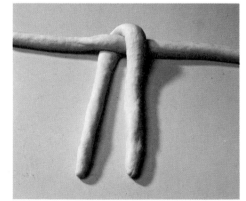

1 **Making a four-stranded** flat plait from two lengths of dough. Roll the strand to taper slightly at the ends. Place one strand across the worktop. Place the second strand, which should be the same length as the first, around the first strand so that the centres of each are together and separate the two ends.

2 **Begin plaiting** with the middle strands in the following way: hold the second strand from the left in your right hand and the second from the right in your left hand. Cross one over the other and drop back on to the worktop.

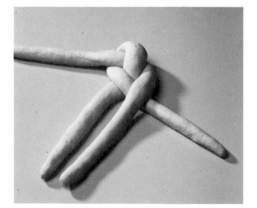

3 **Hold the right half** of the first horizontal strand in your right hand and place it over the second strand from the right so that it is parallel with the second strand from the left. As you plait make sure to weave the strands as closely as possible and not to leave any spaces between.

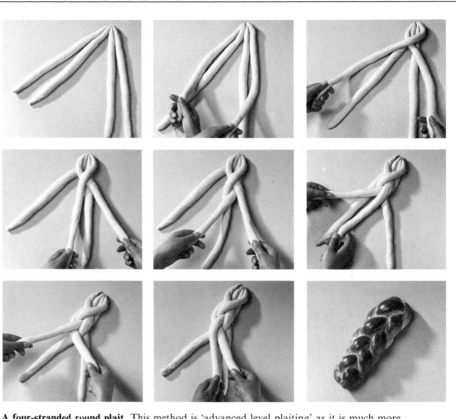

A four-stranded round plait. This method is 'advanced level plaiting' as it is much more complicated than the flat plaits shown in the two series of photographs below. It makes the job much easier if you spread out the strands, two on each side, after each step. This makes it much easier to see which strands you need each time. The photographs above illustrate the complete process which is merely repeated until you reach the ends of the strands.

3 **Fold the left strand** over the centre one once more. Continue placing the outer strands alternately over the centre one until you reach the end of the strands. Squeeze the ends firmly together to prevent them coming apart during baking.

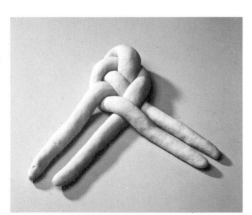

4 **Lift the second strand** from the left in your left hand. Using your right hand bring the second half of the first horizontal strand under the strand you are holding in the left hand and over the second strand from the right. Repeat this step with the right strand and continue until finished.

Poppy Seed Stollen

For the dough:
350 g/12 oz strong plain flour
15 g/½ oz fresh yeast or 1½ teaspoons
dried yeast
8 tablespoons lukewarm milk
50 g/2 oz butter, melted
40 g/1½ oz caster sugar
1 egg
½ teaspoon salt
grated rind of 1 lemon
25 g/1 oz ground almonds

For the filling:
150 g/5 oz poppy seeds, ground
450 ml/¾ pint milk
40 g/1½ oz cornflour
1 egg yolk
50 g/2 oz caster sugar
25 g/1 oz butter, melted

To decorate:
50 g/2 oz Apricot Glaze (see page 60)
50 g/2 oz fondant icing
1 tablespoon rum
25 g/1 oz flaked almonds, toasted

Sift the flour into a mixing bowl, make a well in the centre, crumble the fresh yeast into the well and stir with the lukewarm milk and a little of the flour to make a starter dough. If using dried yeast dissolve the yeast in the lukewarm milk and leave for 10 minutes or until frothy then mix with a little of the flour. Sprinkle this mixture with some of the flour in the bowl, cover the bowl and leave it in a warm place for 15 minutes.

Meanwhile beat the melted butter with the sugar, egg, salt, grated lemon rind and ground almonds. While this mixture is still lukewarm add it to the starter yeast mixture. Beat the two mixtures together also working in all the flour in the bowl and knead until you have a firm, malleable dough. Cover and leave to stand for a further 1–1½ hours or until doubled in size.

Bring the poppy seeds to the boil in 300 ml/½ pint of the milk and simmer for 10 minutes. Blend the cornflour in the remaining milk, then add the egg yolk, sugar and melted butter. Stir this mixture into the poppy seeds and milk and bring to the boil. Leave to cool. Knead the risen dough and then roll it into a rectangle about 30 × 40-cm/12 × 16-in. Spread the dough with the poppy mixture and roll both of the long sides in towards the centre. Place the loaf on the lightly greased baking sheet, cover and leave to rise for a further 45 minutes or until it has doubled in volume. Bake in a moderately hot oven (190 C, 375 F, gas 5) for 30–40 minutes.

Brush the loaf while still warm with hot apricot glaze, leave to dry for a few minutes, then cover with the fondant icing flavoured with the rum and thinned if necessary. Sprinkle the centre of the loaf with the flaked almonds.

Almond Plait

For the dough:
350 g/12 oz strong plain flour
15 g/½ oz fresh yeast or 1½ teaspoons
dried yeast
8 tablespoons lukewarm milk
50 g/2 oz butter, melted
40 g/1½ oz caster sugar
½ teaspoon salt
1 egg

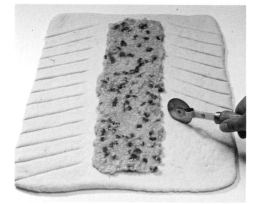

1 **Fill and cut the plait.** Roll the dough into a rectangle of 30 × 40 cm/12 × 16 in and spread the filling over an 7.5-cm/3-in strip down the centre. Using a pastry wheel or knife make diagonal cuts down each side of the pastry at about 2-cm/1-in intervals.

2 **Fold the pastry strips over.** Beginning at the top fold alternate left and right strips over one another into the centre. Then squeeze the ends firmly together to prevent the filling escaping. Place the plait on a lightly greased baking sheet.

For the filling:
50 g/2 oz each of marzipan, apricot jam,
raisins and chopped almonds

For the decoration:
1 egg yolk to glaze
50 g/2 oz Apricot Glaze (see page 60)
50 g/2 oz fondant icing
25 g/1 oz flaked almonds, toasted

Make a yeast dough as shown in the basic recipe on page 46. Cover and leave to rise for 1–2 hours. Mix the apricot jam with the marzipan and work until smooth, then fold in the raisins and chopped almonds. This filling should be of spreading consistency. Make up the plait as shown below and then leave it to rise on a lightly greased baking sheet for 45 minutes or until it has doubled in volume. Brush with the egg yolk and bake in a moderately hot oven (190 C, 375 F, gas 5) for about 30 minutes until golden brown. Brush with the apricot glaze while still hot. Leave to cool slightly before icing with fondant and sprinkling with flaked almonds.

Nut Plait

For the dough:
450 g/1 lb strong plain flour
25 g/1 oz fresh yeast or 15 g/1½ oz
dried yeast
8 tablespoons lukewarm milk
50 g/2 oz butter, melted
50 g/2 oz caster sugar
1 teaspoon salt
grated rind of ½ lemon
2 eggs

For the filling:
100 g/4 oz ground almonds
2 egg whites
50 g/2 oz caster sugar
½ teaspoon cinnamon
150 g/5 oz hazelnuts, toasted and ground

For the decoration:
1 egg yolk to glaze
100 g/4 oz Apricot Glaze (see page 60)
100 g/4 oz fondant icing
1 tablespoon each of lemon juice and Arrak

Make the ingredients into a yeast dough as for the Poppy Seed Stollen or as in the basic recipe on page 46. Beat the ground almonds with the egg whites, sugar and cinnamon until smooth and stir in the ground hazelnuts. When the dough has risen spread it with the filling and plait it as shown in the photographs below. Place on a lightly greased baking sheet, cover and leave until it has almost doubled in volume. Bake in a moderately hot oven (190 C, 375 F, gas 5) for about 40 minutes. Brush with apricot glaze while still hot and ice with fondant, thinned down with lemon juice and Arrak.

1 **Roll the risen dough** into a rectangle of 35 × 40-cm/14 × 16-in. Spread the filling evenly over the dough leaving a narrow space around the edges. Brush the edges with egg yolk to help the roll stay in place and then roll the long side up.

2 **Place the roll** on the worktop and using a sharp knife cut the roll in half lengthways. Try to cut exactly down the centre otherwise your plait will be uneven.

3 **Make the plait.** Place the two halves side by side on the worktop. Starting at the centre twist the two strands together. Turn the plait round and twist the remaining ends, again beginning at the centre. Press the ends firmly together.

Gugelhupf

This recipe gives a medium-heavy, not too fatty mixture. It could be thought of as a basic yeast-mixture Gugelhupf recipe which allows for variation, by adding extra raisins, candied lemon peel or almonds for example.

100 g/4 oz raisins
1 tablespoon rum
450 g/1 lb strong plain flour
25 g/1 oz fresh yeast or 15 g/½ oz dried yeast
8 tablespoons lukewarm milk
175 g/6 oz butter, softened
100 g/4 oz caster sugar
1 teaspoon salt
pinch of nutmeg
grated rind of 1 lemon
3 eggs
16 blanched almonds
20-cm/8-in Gugelhupf tin, greased and floured
icing sugar for dusting

Place the raisins in a basin, sprinkle the rum over and leave to soak. Sift the flour into a bowl and make a well in the centre. Blend the fresh yeast with the milk in the well in the flour. Cover and leave for 15 minutes. If using dried yeast dissolve in the lukewarm milk, leave for 10 minutes or until frothy then pour into the well. Beat the butter with

the sugar, salt, nutmeg, lemon rind and eggs, then work this into the yeast dough and leave to rise again for 1–1½ hours. Finally fold in the raisins soaked in rum. Let the mixture rise again, then transfer it to the tin lined with the almonds. When it has almost doubled in volume bake in a moderately hot oven (200 C, 400 F, gas 6) for 45 minutes. If the top gets brown too quickly cover it with folded greaseproof paper. With tall cakes like this it is essential to test with a skewer that the cake is cooked. Dust with icing sugar when cool.

2 **Beat the butter mixture** until creamy with a wooden spoon or electric whisk. Beat until the mixture has doubled in volume, which will take about 10 minutes. If the mixture curdles add a few tablespoons of flour.

1 **Remember to take the butter** out of the refrigerator so that it can soften. Then cut it into pieces and place in a mixing bowl. Add the sugar, salt, nutmeg and grated lemon rind then the eggs.

3 **Stir the butter mixture** into the yeast and flour dough using a wooden spatula and beat until the mixture is light and airy and comes away from the sides of the bowl. Cover with a cloth or oiled cling film and leave to rise for 1–1½ hours.

4 **Thinly coat the Gugelhupf tin** with soft butter. To make sure the tin is evenly coated place the tin in the refrigerator to harden the butter and then grease once more. Place the almonds in the bottom of the tin and then sprinkle it with flour.

5 **One hour in advance** soak the raisins in the rum in a covered basin, then drain them in a sieve and fold into the risen yeast mixture with a wooden spoon.

6 **Transfer the mixture** to the prepared tin and smooth the top. Cover the tin with oiled cling film and leave it to rise in a warm place until the mixture has doubled in volume.

Chocolate Gugelhupf

This chocolate-covered cake can best be described as a 'luxury Gugelhupf'.

450 g/1 lb strong plain flour
25 g/1 oz fresh yeast or 15 g/½ oz dried yeast
8 tablespoons lukewarm milk
175 g/6 oz butter, softened
100 g/4 oz caster sugar
3 eggs
1 teaspoon vanilla essence
½ teaspoon salt
pinch of allspice
pinch of ground ginger
3 tablespoons single cream
25 g/1 oz currants
50 g/2 oz raisins
75 g/3 oz chopped mixed peel
1 tablespoon rum
75 g/3 oz blanched almonds, chopped
50 g/2 oz plain chocolate, chopped
20-cm/8-in Gugelhupf tin, greased and floured

For the decoration:
1 quantity of Apricot Glaze
(see page 60)
plain chocolate, melted
50 g/2 oz flaked almonds, toasted

Work the ingredients together into a yeast dough as in the previous recipe, cover and leave to rise for 20 minutes.

Meanwhile place the currants, raisins and peel in a basin, pour on the rum, cover and leave to soak. Drain then mix with the almonds and chocolate and fold into the yeast mixture. Pour into the tin and smooth the top. Cover and leave to rise for 45 minutes then bake in a moderately hot oven (200c, 400 f, gas 6) for 45 minutes. Test with a skewer to see if the cake is cooked.

While still warm spread thinly with the glaze and leave until cool. Cover with the melted chocolate. Decorate the edge with flaked almonds before the chocolate has set.

Baking for the Morning

'It is the variety and ornamental complexity of our baking that reveals the long history of our culinary culture.' This is a quotation from Otto Stradal's book *Wiener Stadt, Wiener Leut* (*The City and People of Vienna*). Vienna does indeed seem to merit its reputation as the foremost city in the world for patisserie and for breakfast baking in particular. In Gdansk there are small rolls known as 'Vienna rolls', in Prague there are 'Vienna butter croissants', in Silesia there are 'Vienna horns', in Saxony 'Vienna knots' and in Copenhagen pastries in croissant dough are known as 'Vienna bread' (though the Viennese themselves call these same pastries 'Danish pastries').

The crescent-shaped Kipferl, one of the best known of the croissant-dough pastries, reputedly has close links with the history of Vienna. A master baker called Peter Wendler is said to have baked them after the Turkish siege of the city in mockery of the Islamic crescent moon which the defeated Turks had set up in front of the cathedral of St Stephan. There can however be no truth in the story for Peter Wendler had already been dead for three years in 1683 (the year of the siege), and the Kipferl is in fact much older than this. The Viennese Annals of 1670 mention 'knupfl' cakes, in the Baroque period Abraham a Santa Clara describes 'long, short, curved and straight Kupfel', while as early as 1227 a Viennese baker presented Duke Leopold the Glorious with a 'basket of Chipfen' at Christmas. Even earlier the Kipferl featured amongst Germanic Easter cakes and is thought to have represented the fertility symbol of the goat's horn.

It seems likely that the Kipferl spread from Germany not only to Vienna but also westwards towards France – where the crescent-shaped pastries were developed into the croissant. What better way could there be to start the day than to drink your breakfast coffee with fresh croissants, warm from the oven and smelling of butter! The same could also be said of brioches, a fine French roll of delicate yeast-dough. These extremely light creations come in a variety of forms, as small individual rolls or as loaves known as Nanterre and Brioche mousseline – all famous for the characteristic flavour of fresh butter.

Another traditional breakfast roll in Germany is the pretzel. Medieval monks called these pastries 'Brachitum' and the diminutive form 'Brachitellum' from the Latin *brachium* (arm) from the shape which resembles two linked arms. In the baking of small pastries in dough, the baker has always been able to give free rein to his imagination when it came to twisting and plaiting them into a multitude of different shapes. It would be impossible to try to list the wide variety of shapes and the richness of invention which pastry cooks have brought to breakfast baking. The Viennese for example make a very precise distinction between Kipfel and Kipferl. The latter is often subdivided into separate types such as butter Kipferl, brioche Kipferl or the flaky 'Splitterkipferl'. The first group on the other hand includes such items as hearth Kipfel, Radetzky Kipfel, ham Kipfel and baking sheet Kipfel, which is said to have been the favourite of Mozart's wife Konstanze. To sum up in the words of Otto Stradal, 'The speciality of the Viennese baker's basket could form the subject of a thesis.'

Brioches

These buttery, yeast-dough rolls from France can be made in a range of shapes and sizes. The best known, however, are the small individual brioches which are baked in small fluted tins. Eaten fresh they are one of the lightest of the yeast dough products.

Brioche dough can be made a day in advance and also freezes quite well, hence the quite large quantities given here, which can of course be halved if required.

900 g/2 lb strong plain flour
40 g/1½ oz fresh yeast or 20 g/¾ oz dried yeast
150 ml/¼ pint lukewarm water
9 eggs
2 teaspoons salt
100 g/4 oz caster sugar
225 g/8 oz butter, softened
1 egg yolk to glaze

Make the dough as shown on the right then leave it to rise for 2–2½ hours in a covered bowl in the refrigerator. At this temperature it will not of course rise very much but it will be sufficient to give an excellent result. Then knead the dough once more lightly and reshape into a ball. If the dough is required for breakfast you can leave it to stand overnight in a bowl covered with oiled cling film in the refrigerator. Otherwise leave to rise for a further 45 minutes in the lightly greased tins. When the brioches are fully risen brush evenly with beaten egg yolk and bake in a hot oven (230 C, 450 F, gas 8) for 10–15 minutes.

1 **Sift the flour on to the worktop** and make a well in the centre. Crumble the fresh yeast into the well and stir with the lukewarm water. Alternatively dissolve the dried yeast in the water and leave for 10 minutes or until frothy then place in the flour well. Cover this initial yeast mixture with flour.

2 **Break the eggs into the well,** then add the salt and sugar. Working outwards from the centre, use your hands to mix all the ingredients together, bringing the flour in from the edge with a spatula, until you have a soft dough.

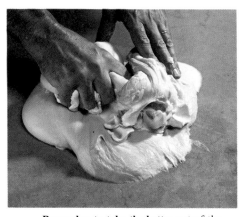

4 **Remember to take the butter** out of the refrigerator 1 to 2 hours in advance to bring it to room temperature. Cream the butter and then work into the dough. First pinch it into the dough with your finger tips, then knead the dough with the ball of your hand.

5 **The dough should be smooth and elastic.** This is achieved by beating the dough repeatedly on the worktop. Cover the dough in a bowl with oiled cling film and leave to rise in the refrigerator for 2–2½ hours.

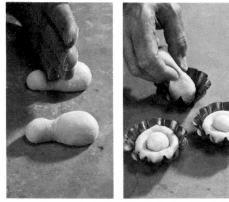

7 **First method of making brioches.** The ball of dough is rolled with the side of the hand. Place your hand one-third of the way along to divide the ball for the bottom and top of the brioche but without breaking right through it. Place the dough in the brioche tin pressing down on the larger of the two portions.

8 **Second method.** Roll the ball of dough in the same way under the side of your hand but this time separate the two pieces completely. Place the larger piece in the tin and press a hole in the centre with a fingertip and insert the smaller piece, narrow end first.

9 **Press the tops down well** to prevent them separating either while the dough is rising or during baking. Use one hand to turn the tin while you press down the dough between the top and the outer edge with the index finger of the other hand. The small ball of dough should now sit deeper in the base.

3 **Knead the dough thoroughly.** Use both hands, repeatedly lifting the dough and dropping it back on to the worktop to incorporate plenty of air. From time to time loosen any dough that is sticking to the worktop with a pastry scraper.

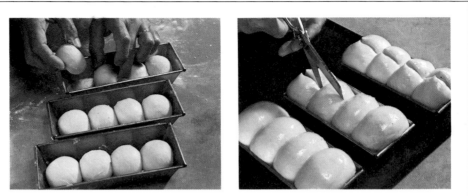

Brioches Nanterre. For this type of brioche the dough is baked in a loaf tin. You will need a third of the dough for a 25 × 10-cm/10 × 4-in loaf tin. Divide the dough into four equal parts and shape into balls as shown in photograph 6. Place the balls in the tin, leave to rise for about 45 minutes at room temperature before brushing with beaten egg yolk. Cut the tops of the brioches with scissors dipped in cold water, so that they open out as they bake. Baking time: about 30–40 minutes in a hot oven (220 C, 425 F, gas 7).

6 **Knead the dough again** for 2–3 minutes, then shape the dough into rounds. Weigh equal portions of dough and shape into balls in the palm of your hand. Since the dough contains a lot of fat it is essential to flour both your hands and the worktop.

10 **Leave the brioches to rise** at room temperature until they have at least doubled in volume, about 45 minutes. Do not put in a warmer place as because of the high butter content this would spoil the consistency. Glaze with beaten egg yolk and bake in a hot oven (230 C, 450 F, gas 8) for 10–15 minutes.

A selection of brioches all made from the recipe on the opposite page. Small individual brioches, larger brioches of the same shape, but with four cuts made in the outer edge. The Brioche Nanterre made of four sections and the tall Brioche mousseline which is baked in a 10-cm/4-in conical tin. The main characteristic of the dough – its lightness and lovely buttery flavour – come from the high egg and butter content.

Rich Breakfast Rolls

1 kg/2 lb strong plain flour
50 g/2 oz fresh yeast or 25 g/1 oz
dried yeast
300 ml/½ pint lukewarm milk
50 g/2 oz caster sugar
1 teaspoon salt
pinch of nutmeg
1 egg
50 g/2 oz butter, melted
1 egg yolk and 2 tablespoons single
cream to glaze
sugar crystals for decoration

Sift the flour into a bowl and make a well in the centre. In the well dissolve the fresh yeast in the lukewarm milk. Alternatively dissolve the dried yeast in a bowl with the lukewarm milk for 10 minutes or until frothy, then place in the flour well. Cover this mixture with a thick layer of flour, cover the bowl with a tea-towel or cling film and leave until the flour layer shows distinct cracks. Stir the sugar, salt, nutmeg and egg into the melted butter. Stir this mixture into the yeast mixture then work in the flour. Beat until you have a smooth, firm dough, and then knead well for about 10 minutes. Leave the dough to rise once more for 2–2½ hours then divide it into 50 g/2 oz pieces. Shape these into balls and cover with a moist cloth or oiled cling film. This will prevent them drying out and make the dough easier to shape. Use the balls of dough to make the shapes as shown on the photographs on the right. Transfer them to a baking sheet, cover with a cloth and leave to rise again for about 45 minutes. Beat the egg yolk into the cream and brush over the rolls. Sprinkle the sugar crystals over the rolls then bake in a hot oven (220 C, 425 F, gas 7) for 10–15 minutes.

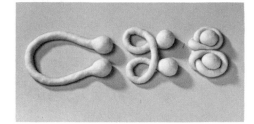

Streusel Cake

For the dough:
350 g/12 oz strong plain flour
25 g/1 oz fresh yeast or 15 g/½ oz
dried yeast
150 ml/¼ pint lukewarm milk
100 g/4 oz butter, melted
50 g/2 oz caster sugar
½ teaspoon salt
grated rind of 1 lemon
pinch of allspice
2 eggs
1 baking sheet (35 × 28-cm/14 × 11-in)

For the filling:
25 g/1 oz cornflour
250 ml/8 fl oz milk
100 g/4 oz caster sugar
225 g/8 oz curd cheese
juice and grated rind of ½ lemon
1 tablespoon rum

For the streusel:
350 g/12 oz plain flour
225 g/8 oz butter
225 g/8 oz caster sugar
½ vanilla pod

Make a yeast dough as in the basic recipe (see page 46). Cover and leave to rise for 20 minutes. Roll the dough to fit the baking sheet, cover the baking sheet with the dough and prick all over with a fork.

Dissolve the cornflour in a little milk and bring the rest of the milk to the boil with the sugar. Pour into the cornflour mixture. Cool slightly then stir in the curd cheese, lemon juice, grated rind and rum and spread over the dough.

Rub together the sifted flour, butter, sugar and pith from the vanilla pod to make a streusel and spread over the cake. Bake in a moderately hot oven (200 C, 400 F, gas 6) for 20 to 25 minutes.

Honey and Almond Slices

For the dough:
450 g/1 lb strong plain flour
25 g/1 oz fresh yeast or 15 g/½ oz
dried yeast·
8 tablespoons lukewarm milk
100 g/4 oz butter, melted
100 g/4 oz caster sugar
½ teaspoon salt
2 eggs
1 baking sheet (35 × 28-cm/14 × 11-in)

For the topping:
150 g/5 oz butter
225 g/8 oz caster sugar
1 tablespoon honey
3 tablespoons single cream
150 g/5 oz flaked almonds

For the filling:
150 g/5 oz caster sugar
40 g/1½ oz cornflour
4 egg yolks
600 ml/1 pint milk
1 vanilla pod
15 g/½ oz powdered gelatine
600 ml/1 pint double cream

Make a yeast dough as shown in the basic recipe on page 46. Cover and leave to rise for 1½ hours. Roll out and line the baking sheet then leave to rise for a further 45 minutes. Prick all over with a fork. Melt the butter with the sugar, honey and cream, remove from heat and stir in the almonds. Cool then spread over the dough. Bake in a moderately hot oven (200 C, 400 F, gas 6) for 25 to 30 minutes or until brown and crisp.

Make a vanilla custard with the sugar, cornflour, egg yolks, milk and vanilla pod (see page 50). Sprinkle the gelatine over the hot custard and stir until thoroughly dissolved. Strain and cool. Whip the cream and fold into the custard. Cut the dough into two layers and cut the top layer into 20 slices. Spread the cream on the dough base. Chill for an hour, replace the cut top layer and then cut right through into slices.

Dresden Slices

For the dough:
450 g/1 lb strong plain flour
25 g/1 oz fresh yeast or 15 g/½ oz
dried yeast
8 tablespoons lukewarm milk
100 g/4 oz butter, melted
100 g/4 oz caster sugar
½ teaspoon salt
grated rind of ½ lemon
2 eggs
1 roasting tin (36 × 28-cm/14 × 11-in),
lined and greased

For the filling:
2 eggs
100 g/4 oz caster sugar
¼ teaspoon salt
grated rind of 1 lemon
450 g/1 lb curd cheese, softened

For the butter-egg mixture:
175 g/6 oz butter
150 g/5 oz caster sugar
½ teaspoon vanilla essence
4 eggs
50 g/2 oz plain flour
50 g/2 oz flaked almonds

Make a yeast dough as in the basic recipe (see page 46). To make the curd filling, first whisk the eggs and sugar until pale and thick. Add the salt, grated lemon rind and then the curd cheese and beat until light and frothy. When the yeast dough has risen roll it evenly to fit the base of the roasting tin. Turn up the edges and prick all over with a fork, cover with oiled cling film and leave to rise for a further 45 minutes. Spread with the curd mixture. Cream the butter and sugar until pale and fluffy, add the vanilla essence and gradually beat in the eggs. Fold in the sifted flour. Spread this mixture over the curd layer and sprinkle with the flaked almonds. Bake in a moderately hot oven (200C, 400F, gas 6) for 25 to 30 minutes. Leave to cool and cut into 24 slices.

Butter Cake

For the dough:
450 g/1 lb strong plain flour
25 g/1 oz fresh yeast or 15 g/½ oz
dried yeast
8 tablespoons lukewarm milk
75 g/3 oz butter, melted
25 g/1 oz caster sugar
½ teaspoon salt
2 eggs
1 baking sheet (36 × 28-cm/14 × 11-in)

For the topping:
275 g/10 oz butter
¼ teaspoon salt

1 **The evenly rolled dough** should have been left to rise on the baking sheet. Using the tips of two fingers make indentations all over the dough. Press right through to the base to prevent the holes reclosing as the dough rises further.

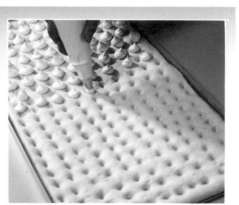

2 **Cream the butter** until light and fluffy. Add the salt. Spoon into a piping bag with a plain nozzle and pipe small whirls of butter all over the cake – they need not be directly over the holes for the butter will run into them as it melts.

100 g/4 oz flaked almonds
100 g/4 oz caster sugar
¼ teaspoon ground cinnamon

Make a yeast dough as in the basic recipe (see page 46). Knead for about 10 minutes. Cover and allow to rise for 1–1½ hours, then knead for a further 2–3 minutes. Roll out evenly to fit the baking sheet. Place on the baking sheet, cover with oiled cling film and leave to rise for a further 45 minutes. Continue as in the photographs alongside.

When the cake has risen completely bake in a moderately hot oven (200 C, 400 F, gas 6) for about 20 minutes. The cake should be brown and crispy on top but still nice and soft inside. Cut into 24 slices.

3 **Spread the flaked almonds** evenly over the cake, then mix the sugar with the cinnamon and sprinkle over the cake. This is easiest with a sieve providing the mesh is coarse enough to allow the sugar through.

Nut or Poppy-Seed Crescents

For the dough:
675 g/1½ lb strong plain flour
100 g/4 oz icing sugar
3 egg yolks
50 g/2 oz fresh yeast or 25 g/1 oz
dried yeast
175 g/6 oz butter, melted
2 teaspoons salt
grated rind of 1 lemon
250 ml/8 fl oz lukewarm milk

For the nut filling:
100 g/4 oz walnuts, ground
100 g/4 oz biscuit or bread crumbs
50 g/2 oz raisins, chopped
grated rind of 1 lemon
150 g/¼ pint sugar syrup

For the poppy seed filling:
75 g/3 oz poppy seeds, ground
75 g/3 oz biscuit or bread crumbs
50 g/2 oz caster sugar
5 tablespoons milk
1 tablespoon rum
50 g/2 oz raisins, chopped
2 egg yolks to glaze

Either make the dough by working all the ingredients together in a well in the flour and then working in the flour from the outside inwards (see photographs on the right). If using dried yeast dissolve this first in the milk and leave for 10 minutes or until frothy, then place in the flour well. Shape into a ball, place in a bowl, cover with oiled cling film and leave in the refrigerator for an hour or until doubled in volume. Alternatively make the yeast dough as in the basic recipe (see page 46).

To make the nut filling mix together the ground walnuts, crumbs, raisins and grated lemon rind. Add the syrup and stir in. The filling should be firm but malleable. To make the poppy filling, mix together the poppy seeds, crumbs and sugar. Bring the milk to the boil and stir in to the poppy seed mixture. Work in the rum and then the raisins. Halve the dough and shape each piece into a long roll of about 3.5-cm/1½-in. in diameter and then cut each into 2.5-cm/1-in lengths. Shape each of these into a ball. Shape each of the fillings into an even roll and cut similarly into 2.5-cm/1-in lengths. Roll three balls of dough at a time into small ovals (see photographs), rolling them slightly thinner at the tapering ends. Shape the fillings you are going to use into small rolls, place on the pastry and roll up carefully. Squeeze the dough firmly together at the edges to prevent any filling escaping during baking. Roll the dough between your hands until quite thick at the centre but tapering at either end. Fold the nut-filled dough into a V shape around your finger. Place them on a lightly greased baking sheet, opening the ends out slightly. Shape the poppy filled dough into crescents. Place on the baking sheet. Brush all the crescents thoroughly with the beaten egg yolks. Leave in a cool place to dry. After 30 minutes recoat with egg yolk and leave to dry until the yolk begins to set. The quantities given make 50 crescents. Baking time: about 15 to 20 minutes in a moderately hot oven (200C, 400F, gas 6).

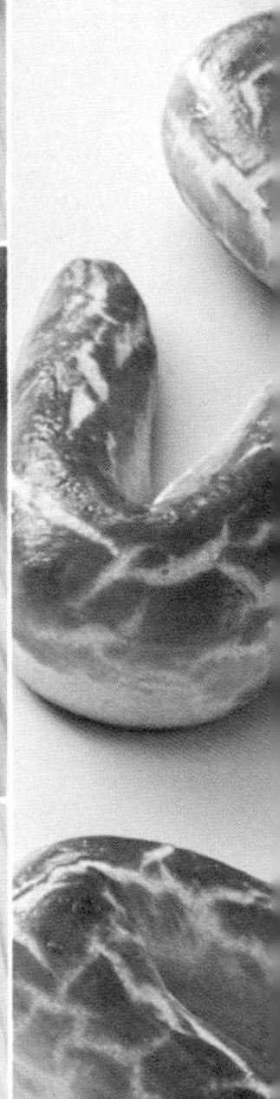

into the cheese mixture. Mix the poppy seeds with the remaining sugar and breadcrumbs. Bring the milk to the boil and stir in the poppy seed mixture, continue to cook until most of the liquid has evaporated. Place 4 teaspoons of cheese and poppy-seed mixtures alternately in small heaps on the cakes. Place a spoon of plum purée in the centre. Leave the cakes to rise for 45 minutes and then bake in a moderately hot oven (200 C, 400 F, gas 6) for 20 to 25 minutes.

Bohemian Plum Rounds

For the dough:
450 g/1 lb strong plain flour
25 g/1 oz fresh yeast or 15 g/½ oz dried yeast
300 ml/½ pint lukewarm milk
75 g/3 oz caster sugar
½ teaspoon salt
grated rind of 1 lemon
1 egg
75 g/3 oz butter, melted

For the topping:
350 g/12 oz curd or cream cheese
50 g/2 oz butter, softened
225 g/8 oz caster sugar
2 eggs, separated
25 g/1 oz cornflour
1 tablespoon rum
225 g/8 oz poppy seeds, ground
2 tablespoons breadcrumbs
300 ml/½ pint milk
225 g/8 oz plum purée
1 egg yolk to glaze
225 g/8 oz Apricot Glaze (see page 60)
50 g/2 oz flaked almonds, toasted

Sift the flour into a bowl and make a well in the centre. Crumble in the fresh yeast and dissolve in the lukewarm milk. Alternatively dissolve the dried yeast in the milk and leave for 10 minutes or until frothy. Cover the bowl with oiled cling film and leave to stand for 15 minutes. Beat the sugar, flavourings and egg into the melted butter. Stir into the yeast mixture and then work in the flour and knead to give a firm but light yeast dough. Cover the bowl with oiled cling film and leave to rise for 1–1½ hours. Then divide the dough into 50 g/2 oz pieces. Shape each into a ball and then press into flat cakes with a raised rim, about 10-cm/4-in. in diameter. Prick with a fork to prevent the dough rising during baking. Place on a lightly greased baking sheet and brush the rims with beaten egg yolk.

Stir the curd cheese with the soft butter and 75 g/3 oz of the sugar until smooth. Beat in the egg yolks, cornflour and rum. Whisk the egg whites until stiff but not dry then whisk in 75 g/3 oz of sugar and fold

These cakes are especially good straight from the oven, but they will stay fresh for several hours if you brush them with apricot glaze and then sprinkle them with flaked almonds.

This same recipe can be used for Bohemian Plum Slices. Here the baking sheet is covered with dough and topped with spoonfuls of curds, poppy-seed filling and plum purée. After baking cut into rectangular slices.

Almond Bows

For the dough:
25 g/1 oz fresh yeast or 15 g/½ oz dried yeast
300 ml/½ pint lukewarm milk
500 g/18 oz strong plain flour
275 g/10 oz butter, softened
50 g/2 oz caster sugar
½ teaspoon salt
2 egg yolks
1 egg yolk to glaze

For the filling:
225 g/8 oz marzipan
225 g/8 oz almonds, toasted and ground
½ teaspoon cinnamon
grated rind of 2 oranges
1 tablespoon rum
4 egg whites
1 egg yolk to glaze
1 quantity of Apricot Glaze (see page 60)
rum fondant icing

Blend the fresh yeast with 3 to 4 tablespoons milk, then add the remaining milk. Alternatively dissolve the dried yeast in the milk and leave for 10 minutes or until frothy. Sift 450 g/1 lb of the flour into a bowl and rub in 50 g/2 oz butter. Add the milk yeast liquid then stir in the sugar, salt and egg yolks and work together to give a smooth, medium-firm dough. Knead for 10 minutes or until pliable. Put in a bowl, cover with oiled cling film and leave overnight in the refrigerator.

Work the remaining flour into the rest of the butter. Spread this on to a large piece of greaseproof paper and shape into a neat rectangle of 15 × 20-cm/6 × 8-in. Chill well. Roll the dough into a rectangle of 20 × 64-cm/8 × 24-in. Place the butter in the centre of the dough, brush the edges with egg yolk and fold over the top then the

bottom of the dough. Press the edges firmly together then give the dough three single turns (see puff pastry, page 42) allow it to rest in the refrigerator for about 20 minutes between each turn.

Blend together the marzipan, ground almonds, cinnamon, orange rind, rum and egg whites into a spreadable filling. Roll out the dough to a rectangle 76 × 36-cm/30 × 14-in. Spread the filling down the centre of the dough, leaving a 12-cm/4½-in strip free down one side and a 1-cm/½-in strip free down the opposite side. Brush these free strips with egg yolk. Fold the widest side without the filling over to cover half the filling and then fold over the remaining dough which is covered with filling. Seal the edges then cut the filled roll of dough into 2.5-cm/1-in strips. Cut lengthways along the centre of each with a pastry wheel but do not cut right through. Fold the ends over into this slit. Place the bows on a baking sheet leaving plenty of space between them, cover with cling film and leave to rise for 45 minutes or until doubled in size. Glaze with egg yolk and bake in a hot oven (220 C, 425 F, gas 7) for 15 to 18 minutes. Brush with apricot glaze and ice with rum fondant. The quantities given will make 30 bows.

Hazelnut Snails

dough as for Almond Bows

For the filling:
450 g/1 lb hazelnuts, toasted and ground
¼ teaspoon ground allspice
pinch of salt
225 g/8 oz caster sugar
5 egg whites
1 quantity of Apricot Glaze (see page 60)
lemon fondant icing

Mix the filling ingredients together to make a mixture of spreading consistency. Roll out the croissant dough to a rectangle 76 × 36-cm/30 × 14-in. Spread the filling over the dough, leaving a narrow border along the long sides. Then roll from both long sides in towards the centre and cut into 2-cm/¾-in slices. Place on a lightly greased baking sheet, cover with oiled cling film and leave to rise for 45 minutes or until doubled in size. Bake in a hot oven (220 C, 425 F, gas 7) for 15 to 18 minutes until golden brown. Brush with apricot glaze while still warm and cover with lemon fondant icing. These quantities make 40 snails.

Croissants

and *Pains au chocolat*

Croissants and chocolate-filled rolls are two specialities eaten with coffee in France, particularly at breakfast time. Croissants are quite heavily salted and the portion of salt to sugar also contributes to their individual taste. You could use salted butter for the recipe, but you would then have to reduce the quantity of salt.

1 kg/2 lb strong plain flour
40 g/1½ oz fresh yeast or 20 g/¾ oz dried yeast
600 ml/1 pint lukewarm milk
25 g/1 oz salt
100 g/4 oz caster sugar
450 g/1 lb unsalted butter
flour for rolling
egg yolk to glaze

Sift the flour and salt on to the worktop, make a well in the centre and crumble in the yeast. Dilute the fresh yeast with the lukewarm milk, mixing in a little of the flour at the same time. Alternatively dissolve the dried yeast in the milk and leave for 10 minutes or until frothy then mix in a little flour. Add the salt and sugar. Work all the ingredients together to give a light, smooth dough. Cover with oiled cling film and allow to rise for 1 to 1½ hours or until doubled in volume. Then knead the dough for a further 2 to 3 minutes, put in a bowl, cover with oiled cling film and leave in the refrigerator for 1 to 2 hours. Meanwhile soften the butter at room temperature and cream until smooth and of similar consistency to the dough.

Take the dough out of the refrigerator and roll into a 40-cm/16-in square. Press the butter into a 20-cm/8-in square slab, place on the centre of the dough and fold the ends over so that the butter is completely wrapped in the dough. Roll again into a sheet of 25 × 50-cm/10 × 20-in and then make three single turns (see classic puff pastry, page 42). Leave the dough to rest for 10 minutes in the refrigerator after each turn. Finally roll the dough to a rectangle of 30 × 60-cm/12 × 24-in. Take care to roll the pastry alternately in different directions. Leave the dough to rest for a few minutes and then cut in half lengthways to give two strips 15-cm/6-in wide. When you have made up the croissants cover them with a cloth and leave them to rise at room temperature. Brush with egg yolk and bake in a hot oven (220 C, 425 F, gas 7) for 20 minutes until crisp and golden brown. Quantities given will make 36 croissants.

1 **Cut the dough into triangles.** From two 15 × 60-cm/6 × 24-in strips cut triangles 10-cm/4-in wide. It is best to use a sharp knife or good pastry wheel, for it is essential that the pastry should be cut cleanly rather than pulled.

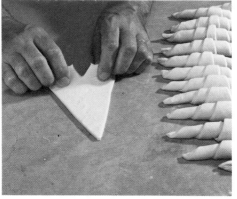

2 **Hold the narrow side** of the triangle (10-cm/4-in) in both hands and make a 2.5-cm/1-in slit along the centre to allow you to pull the pastry into the required shape. You can do this rather more exactly if you cut into all the triangles with a sharp knife before you begin shaping them.

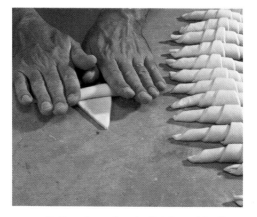

3 **Roll up the croissants.** It takes a bit of practice to get them all the same shape. When rolling them up pull the pastry outwards and if necessary roll them between your hands to get them to taper at the edges.

4 **Hold the end of the dough** on the worktop with your thumb. Roll the croissant with your other hand pulling gently at the same time so that the point you are holding becomes longer and thinner. This method of rolling makes the croissants much thinner at the ends.

5 **Place the croissants** well apart on a baking sheet. It is not necessary to grease the baking sheet. Place each croissant with the end of the pastry underneath so that they cannot unroll. Cover with oiled cling film and allow to rise for 45 minutes or until doubled in size.

6 **Beat the egg yolk** with a little milk and use to brush the croissants. If you want a very brown finish stir in 1 teaspoon icing sugar. Do not glaze the croissants until they are fully risen.

They taste best fresh from the oven. Both the dough and the finished croissants freeze well.

Roll out the croissant dough to 2.5-mm/1-in thick and cut into 7.5 × 10-cm/3 × 4-in rectangles. Place a strip of chocolate along one end. Brush the end of the dough with egg yolk and roll up. Leave to rise and then brush the outside with egg yolk. Bake in a hot oven (220 C, 425 F, gas 7) for 15 to 17 minutes.

Pains au chocolat, French chocolate rolls, have a wonderful combination of flavours. The chocolate goes well with the quite salty pastry and the flavour of fresh butter. If you cannot get the sticks of chocolate with which they are usually made, use a few pieces from a bar of chocolate or a little melted chocolate. Warm the chocolate and flavour with a few drops of rum (or dilute with a few drops of water) to give a thick cream. Spoon the chocolate into a piping bag with a plain nozzle and pipe a strip of chocolate on each piece of dough.

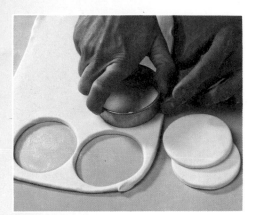

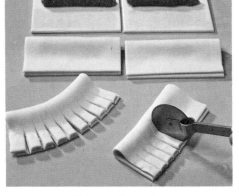

Shoe Soles

Roll puff pastry (see page 42) to 5-cm/¼-in thick and cut into 7-cm/3-in rounds with a pastry cutter. Sprinkle the worktop with caster sugar and roll the rounds of pastry on the sugar until they resemble long 'sole' shapes. Roll alternately on both sides so that each is coated in sugar. Arrange on a moistened baking sheet and bake in a hot oven (220 C, 425 F, gas 7) for 15 minutes or until brown and crisp. You can turn the soles over half way through the baking time so that they caramelise on both sides.

Nut Combs

Roll the puff pastry to 3-mm/⅛-in thick and cut into 10-cm/4-in squares. Stir 150 g/5 oz ground hazelnuts with 1 egg white, 75 g/3 oz caster sugar and 1 tablespoon rum. Spoon the mixture into a piping bag with a plain nozzle. Pipe a strip of nut mixture on each square of pastry. The quantities of filling given are enough for 12 cakes. Brush the pastry with egg yolk, fold over in half and, using a pastry wheel or sharp knife, cut teeth along one edge of the comb as illustrated above. Brush with egg yolk, leave to stand for 30 minutes and then bake in a hot oven (220 C, 425 F, gas 7) for 12 to 15 minutes. Brush with apricot glaze and then ice.

Cherry Puffs

Roll the puff pastry to 5-mm/¼-in thick and cut into 7.5-cm/3-in squares. For 12 cakes: into 100 g/4 oz finely chopped marzipan work 75 g/3 oz chopped glacé cherries, 50 g/2 oz chopped walnuts and a tablespoon Kirsch. Brush the squares of pastry with egg yolk and place a small pile of filling in the centre of each. Roll the left-over puff pastry out until thin and using a fluted pastry wheel cut 5-mm/¼-in strips of pastry and arrange in a cross over the filling on each cake. Brush the crosses with egg yolk. Leave the pastry to rest for a few minutes and then bake in a hot oven (220 C, 425 F, gas 7) for 15 to 18 minutes until golden brown. Brush with apricot glaze and then ice with Kirsch flavoured fondant icing.

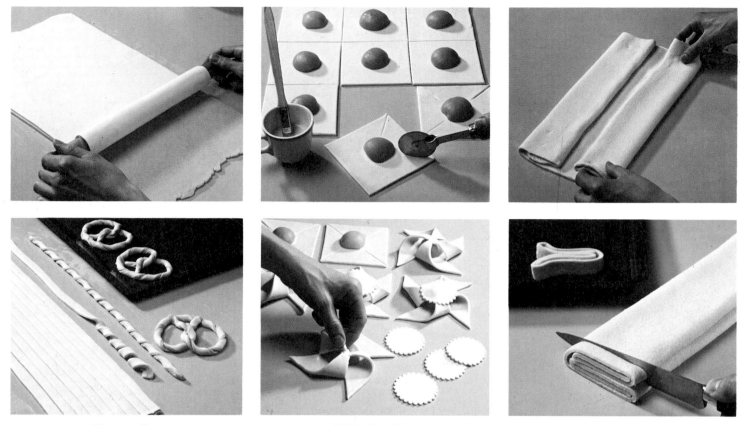

Pretzels

Roll out 450 g/1 lb puff pastry into a sheet of about 50 × 30-cm/20 × 12-in. Roll 450 g/1 lb sweet shortcrust pastry (see page 38) to the same size and brush with egg yolk. Using a rolling pin to help you, place the puff pastry over the shortcrust. Cut into strips 1.5-cm/$\frac{3}{4}$-in wide and twist into spirals. Shape into pretzels, brush with egg yolk and bake in a hot oven (220 C, 425 F, gas 7). Brush with apricot glaze and ice.

Windmills

Roll out the puff pastry to 5-mm/$\frac{1}{4}$-in thick and cut into 10-cm/$\frac{1}{4}$-in squares. Brush with egg yolk and place a canned apricot half in the centre of each square. Using a pastry wheel or sharp knife cut from each corner in to the centre. Fold alternate points over and squeeze together in the centre. Brush with egg yolk. Roll out the left-over pastry until very thin and cut into 5-cm/2-in rounds. Place one round over each cake. Leave the pastry to rest for 30 minutes and then bake in a hot oven (220 C, 425 F, gas 7) for about 15 minutes. Brush with apricot glaze and ice.

Pigs' Ears

Sprinkle the worktop with sugar and roll 675 g/1$\frac{1}{2}$ lb puff pastry into a rectangle of 45 × 30-cm/18 × 12-in. Turn the pastry over quite often as you roll so that it is evenly covered with sugar. For this quantity of pastry you should use about 225 g/8 oz caster sugar. Fold each narrow side over twice to meet at the centre and then fold over a third time. Cut the 30-cm/12-in length of pastry into 20 slices 15-mm/$\frac{3}{4}$-in wide and arrange on the baking sheet. Leave to rest for 15 minutes and then bake in a hot oven (220 C, 425 F, gas 7) for about 10 minutes, then turn the cakes over with a spatula and continue baking until caramelised on both sides.

Doughnuts

450 g/1 lb strong plain flour
25 g/1 oz fresh yeast or 15 g/½ oz
dried yeast
150 ml/¼ pint of lukewarm milk
50 g/2 oz butter, melted
75 g/3 oz caster sugar
1 teaspoon salt
3 eggs
plum purée or jam for the filling
vegetable oil for frying

1 **Divide up the dough.** Weigh 50 g/2 oz pieces of dough and roll them into balls between the palms of your hands. Then roll these with a small rolling pin into flat cakes of about 10-cm/4-in. in diameter. Place 1 teaspoon jam in the centre of each, taking care not to get any jam around the edges.

2 **Close up the doughnuts.** Hold each doughnut in turn on the palm of your left hand and using the fingers of your right hand bring the edges up and pinch together. The edges will seal better if they are first brushed with water. Roll the balls between your palms once more and place on a floured cloth.

Make a yeast dough with the ingredients above as shown on page 46. The dough is very light and must therefore be kneaded thoroughly until smooth and elastic. Cover with oiled cling film and leave the dough to rise for 1–1½ hours and then knead again for a few minutes. Divide the dough into 50 g/2 oz pieces and shape into balls then roll flat. Place a spoon of jam in the centre of each and using your fingers squeeze the dough together to enclose the jam. Roll the doughnuts between your hands until they are nice and round. Flatten slightly on a floured cloth, then cover with a second cloth or oiled cling film and leave to rise for a further 45 minutes or until they have doubled in volume.

Heat the vegetable oil in a large, deep saucepan. Lift the doughnuts carefully from the cloth and place a few at a time upside down in the fat (180 C, 350 F). After about 2 minutes turn the doughnuts over and fry for a further 2 minutes. Lift from the fat with a slotted spoon and drain quickly on a wire rack, then dust both sides with caster sugar. Rolling the doughnuts around the filling, as shown in the photographs on the left, gives a good rounded shape, but there are alternative methods. Roll the dough until 1-cm/½-in thick and cut into rounds with a 7.5-cm/3-in pastry cutter. Sandwich two rounds together at a time with the filling between them, moistening the edges with water and squeezing them together to seal the edges. There is also a third method which is very easy to do: in this case the filling is piped into the doughnuts after they are cooked. Although this is the quickest method the result is not as good as when the filling is cooked with the doughnuts.

The narrow strip of white around the centre is a sign that the doughnuts have been fried correctly. Clean oil is important for successful frying, otherwise it bubbles too much and you lose the white rim around the centre. Make sure that there is no flour sticking to the doughnuts when you put them into the fat.

Fried Choux Rings

250 ml/8 fl oz milk
100 g/4 oz butter
pinch of salt
1 teaspoon sugar
225 g/8 oz plain flour
5 eggs
greaseproof paper, greased
vegetable oil for frying
icing sugar for dusting, or apricot glaze
and Arrak fondant

Heat the milk gently in a saucepan with the butter, salt and sugar until the butter has melted, then bring to the boil. Sift the flour then add it all at once to the liquid. Remove from the heat and beat vigorously using a wooden spoon until the mixture forms a ball and comes away from the sides of the pan. Transfer the mixture into a bowl and cool slightly. Beat the eggs together then stir into the mixture gradually waiting till each portion is fully incorporated before adding more. Choux pastry for piping should be soft but firm enough to hold its shape after piping. The number of eggs required can vary according to size and the degree to which the pastry dried out on the heat, so if the mixture is very dry add more beaten egg carefully.

Transfer the choux pastry into a piping bag with a large star nozzle and pipe the mixture onto the greased paper. The rings should not be too large. Where possible fry immediately before a skin has chance to form, because this might prevent the cakes swelling and also might make them crack open. The rings are fried by holding the greaseproof paper in both hands, turning it upside down so that the choux rings appear underneath, lowering the paper on to the surface of the fat and slowly peeling back the paper as illustrated on the right. The fat's heat should melt the butter on the greaseproof paper so that the choux rings fall easily into the fat. A good quality vegetable fat is essential.

The rings are fried in the same way as doughnuts and should be turned after about 2 minutes and then fried for a further 2 minutes until golden and firm. Lift the rings out of the fat with a slotted spoon, drain on a wire rack and leave to cool before dusting with icing sugar.

These cakes are really delicious iced with Arrak-flavoured fondant. Brush the tops of the warm rings with a thin layer of apricot glaze. Leave to cool and then dip in fondant flavoured with a little Arrak.

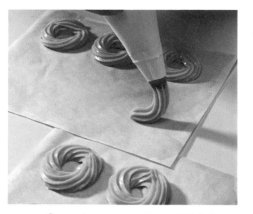

1 **Grease the greaseproof paper lightly** but evenly with soft fat and place in the refrigerator for a few minutes to harden. Using a piping bag with a star nozzle pipe equal rings onto the paper. Leave plenty of room between them.

2 **Hold the paper in both hands** and turn it upside down so that the cakes are clinging to the underside. Lower the paper onto the fat and slowly peel back the paper. The heat from the fat will melt the butter on the paper so that the cakes fall easily into the fat.

Good fat is essential for success. Use a fat that can be heated to a temperature of between 170 and 180 C/330 and 350 F without smoking or burning. Pure vegetable fat answers these requirements and is also neutral in taste, if you want a neutral taste. Butter fat is a useful alternative and gives a typical buttery flavour, but it needs much more careful handling and must on no account be allowed to overheat.

Famous Cakes and Pies

All over the world cakes and pastries have been made for symbolic reasons or for festive occasions such as a birthday, wedding or for Christmas. Cakes baked for symbolic purposes have a tradition that dates back centuries: disc-shaped cakes were baked in northern Europe for the festival of midsummer. Their shape was derived from that of the sun whose image was worshipped as the symbol of life and fertility. After the advent of Christianity cakes were made which celebrated great events in the Christian calendar. In monasteries, for example, cakes and pies were created to mark the most important religious festivals. A Twelfth-Night Cake is still made in some parts of Europe, especially in predominantly Catholic countries such as France or Italy, to symbolise the great feast of Epiphany on 6 January.

It was from these ancient traditions of a celebratory cake that the modern gâteau was born. The gâteau is based on the basic sponge or pastry mixtures which are then combined with creams and custards or butter cream, marzipan, chocolate, fondant or royal icing. This delectable confection is often further enhanced by being sprinkled with almonds, pistachios or other nuts which have been flaked, grated, toasted or made into praline; or decorated with caramel, chocolate shapes, marzipan flowers or candied fruit.

The choice of what to do is enormous and it is left for the individual to decide what combination best suits their need and taste. There is almost no limit as to what can be achieved with a little patience, creativity and imagination. In order to stir the imagination this chapter contains a good variety of different combinations that are tested and proved to be very popular and it is worth making a few of these up first before embarking on your own experiments.

The choice can be between a heavier cake or a lighter one such as the French Gâteau Saint-Honore or Millefeuille which are truly melt-in-the-mouth concoctions and should be eaten as soon as possible after being made and filled – a requirement which should not pose too many probems as they look and taste so good! Each country produces its own specialities but Germany and Austria are particularly renowned for the variety of gâteau that they have invented. One of the most famous of these must surely be the Black Forest Gâteau which is traditionally eaten with morning or afternoon coffee (not tea on the Continent!) in German *Konditorei*. This is a rich but light confection of chocolate sponge soaked in Kirsch and layered with cherries and cream. The equally famous Austrian speciality the Sachertorte is discussed in detail at the conclusion of this chapter because its history is so interesting.

Almond Chocolate Gâteau

1 25-cm/10-in round of shortcrust pastry
(see page 37)
75 g/3 oz redcurrant jelly
225 g/8 oz marzipan
8 egg yolks
½ teaspoon vanilla essence
100 g/4 oz caster sugar
4 egg whites
75 g/3 oz plain flour
40 g/1½ oz cocoa powder
50 g/2 oz ground almonds
1 quantity of Vanilla Butter Cream (see
page 54)
2 tablespoons almond liqueur (Amaretto)
125 g/4½ oz plain chocolate, melted
16 small macaroons to decorate

Beat 50 g/2 oz marzipan with 2 egg yolks until creamy, then add the remaining yolks with the vanilla essence and a third of the sugar. Beat until light and frothy. Whisk the egg whites until stiff but not dry then whisk the remaining sugar. Sift together the flour and cocoa powder and mix with the ground almonds. Beat a third of the egg whites into the egg yolk mixture and then fold in the rest. Gently fold in the flour mixture. Spread mixture on a sheet of greaseproof paper (see page 31) and bake in a hot oven (230C, 450F, gas 8) for about 10 minutes.

Take half the Vanilla Butter Cream for the filling and mix with 75 g/3 oz marzipan and the almond liqueur. Make up the cake as illustrated and cover with half the remaining butter cream. Make the remaining marzipan into a 25-cm/10-in round. Cover this with the melted chocolate and mark a lattice pattern. Cut the top into portions, place on the cake and decorate with whirls of butter cream and macaroons.

1 **Roll the pastry** and cut to the size of the cake. Place the pastry on a baking sheet and prick at regular intervals with a fork to prevent air bubbles forming underneath during baking. Bake until golden brown, leave to cool and then spread with the jelly.

2 **Cover a** 43 × 33-cm/13 × 17-in baking sheet with greaseproof paper and spread with the sponge mixture. When the cake is cooked turn it out on to a damp cloth and remove the paper. Spread evenly with half the butter cream.

3 **Using a ruler** to measure with, mark the cream at 4-cm/1½-in intervals and then cut into strips, keeping them as even in width as possible. Make sure you do not waste too much at the edges for the sponge quantities given do not allow for any wastage.

4 **Roll up the first strip.** Place the roll over the centre of the pastry base and then wind the other strips around it. Push the ends as close together as possible to give an even striped effect when the cake is cut.

5 **Place a sponge ring round the cake.** This gives the cake a nice even shape. Use a ring 5-cm/2-in deep as this will also act as a guide when you come to cover the top. Using a palette knife simply spread half the remaining butter cream over the top to the inside edge of the ring.

Pistachio Nut Gâteau

3 tablespoons maraschino liqueur
1 quantity of Butter Cream with eggs
(see page 54)
50 g/2 oz plain chocolate, melted
2 tablespoons finely chopped stem ginger
75 g/3 oz pistachio nuts, ground
40 g/1½ oz marzipan
1 Genoese sponge of 25-cm/10-in
(see page 28)
1 shortcrust base of 25-cm/10-in
(see page 37)
75 g/3 oz raspberry jam
1 tablespoon sugar syrup
1 tablespoon lemon juice
flaked almonds, toasted
16 chocolate flowers

Stir 2 tablespoons maraschino liqueur into the butter cream and divide it into four portions. Mix a quarter with the chocolate and ginger. Mix another quarter with the pistachio nuts (keeping the larger pieces for decoration) and marzipan. The remaining two quarters will be used for covering and decorating the cake.

Cut the Genoese sponge into three layers. Place the first layer on the pastry which you have first spread with raspberry jam. Stir together the sugar syrup, lemon juice and 1 tablespoon maraschino and use to moisten this base. Spread with the chocolate cream. Cover with the second layer of sponge, spread with the pistachio cream and then add the final layer which should also be moistened. Cover the cake with a very thin layer of cream and chill before finally covering it as shown in the photographs. Divide the cake into 16 portions, decorate with butter cream, ground pistachio nuts and chocolate flowers.

1 **The cake is first covered** over the top and sides with a very thin layer of butter cream and chilled to form a base for the top layer of butter cream. Place some of the butter cream on the top of the cake and spread as evenly as possible with a palette knife.

2 **Once the top is covered** cover the sides a little at a time using a palette knife. When the sides are evenly covered smooth the cream by turning the cake with your left hand and smoothing with the palette knife in your right hand.

3 **Using a pastry scraper** thickly cover the sides with butter cream as in the palette knife method. Pull the cake over the edge of the table so that you can turn it with one hand. Using the other hand hold the scraper vertical and smooth the side, avoiding lifting the scraper away from the cake if possible.

4 **Smooth the join.** This looks harder than it is. Using a broad clean knife or palette knife smooth any excess butter cream towards the middle of the cake. It is important to wipe the blade after each stroke or you will merely deposit the cream back on the edge.

5 **Sprinkle the edge** with flaked almonds. Using a palette knife to help slide the cake partly off the table. Hold the cake off the table in one hand and press on the almonds with the other. Work all round the cake in the same way..

Spanish Vanilla Cake

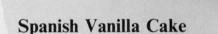

For the sponge:
100 g/4 oz plain chocolate
50 g/2 oz chopped mixed peel
50 g/2 oz blanched almonds, chopped
100 g/4 oz plain flour
50 g/2 oz butter, softened
100 g/4 oz marzipan
175 g/6 oz caster sugar
½ teaspoon vanilla essence
6 egg yolks
5 egg whites
25-cm/10-in tin with sloping sides or
straight-sided cake tin

For the decoration:
1 quantity of Apricot Glaze
(see page 60)
225 g/8 oz marzipan

350 g/12 oz plain chocolate, melted
12 marzipan flowers

Regardless of whether you are using a straight-sided cake tin or one with sloping sides, cover the base with greaseproof paper. Grease the sides of the tin and sprinkle with sifted flour. Cut the chocolate into fairly small pieces, but not too small or the mixture will go brown when you bake it. Mix the chocolate chips with the mixed peel, chopped almonds and sifted flour. In a mixing bowl work the butter into the marzipan. Add 50 g/2 oz sugar, the vanilla essence and 1 egg yolk and beat with a hand or electric whisk until light and creamy. Then beat in the remaining egg yolks one at a time. Whisk the egg whites until stiff but not dry then whisk in the remaining sugar. Fold the egg whites into the marzipan and butter mixture with a metal spoon. Finally

fold in the mixture of flour, chocolate, mixed peel and almonds extremely carefully so that the whisked whites do not collapse. Pour the mixture into the prepared tin and smooth the top. Bake in a moderate oven (180 C, 350 F, gas 4) for 50–60 minutes.

Leave the cake to stand for about 10 minutes after it comes out of the oven before turning it out of the tin. When cold remove the greaseproof paper and brush the sides and top sparingly with apricot glaze. Roll out the marzipan very thinly and cover the top and sides of the cake, trying to avoid any folds where possible. Place the cake on a wire rack and cover with a thin layer of melted chocolate. When the chocolate has set slightly divide the top into 12 portions with a warm knife and decorate each portion with a marzipan flower.

Here is an alternative method of covering or icing a cake which is especially good for smaller cakes of between around 18 and 25-cm/7 and 10-in. in diameter. Place the cake on a base, the same size or slightly smaller than the cake. The base of the tin in which you baked the cake is ideal.

With a little practice you can get results just as good as with the method described on page 133. There is no problem even with fairly runny icings for any drips can be easily removed. Drips of chocolate can simply be cut off with a warm knife.

1 The sides are covered first. The base should not be larger than the cake itself. Hold the cake in one hand while with the other you spread the butter cream with long continuous strokes over the sides. Put down the cake and then cover the top.

2 Cover the cake with chocolate. Using a small base avoids having to use a wire rack. Place the cake on its base on top of a smaller sponge ring. This makes it easy to remove any drips of icing once the cake is covered.

Marzipan Tart

For the pastry:
150 g/5 oz butter, softened
25 g/1 oz icing sugar
½ teaspoon vanilla essence
pinch of salt
1 egg yolk
225 g/8 oz plain flour

For the filling:
150 g/5 oz butter, softened
150 g/5 oz icing sugar
grated rind of 1 lemon
2 eggs
150 g/5 oz ground almonds
25 g/1 oz plain flour
1 flan tin of 25-cm/10-in diameter and
2.5-cm/1-in deep or similar-sized cake tin

Make the pastry by creaming the butter with the icing sugar, flavourings and egg yolk and then quickly work in the sifted flour. Do not handle the pastry more than necessary or it will become crumbly. Leave the pastry in the refrigerator for at least 2 hours, and preferably overnight.

Roll the pastry into a round and line the flan tin. Prick the base all over with a fork, cover with greaseproof paper and fill with baking beans. Lightly bake blind in a moderate oven (180 C, 350 F, gas 4) for about 20 minutes. Then remove the beans and paper.

Make the filling by creaming the butter with the icing sugar and grated lemon rind until light and fluffy then gradually beat in the eggs. Then quickly fold in the ground almonds followed by the sifted flour. Spoon the mixture into the baked tart case and smooth the top.

Bake in a moderate oven (180 C, 350 F, gas 4) for 40 to 45 minutes until the top is golden brown. You can either dust the tart with icing sugar or cover it with rum fondant icing.

Macaroon Cake

For the sponge:
8 eggs, separated
175 g/6 oz caster sugar
50 g/2 oz ground almonds
½ teaspoon vanilla essence
75 g/3 oz butter, melted
75 g/3 oz plain flour
75 g/3 oz fine biscuit crumbs
(e.g. digestive)

For the filling and decoration:
350 g/12 oz seedless raspberry jam
1 tablespoon raspberry liqueur
1 tablespoon sugar syrup
4 egg yolks
450 g/1 lb marzipan
sugar syrup to dilute
75 g/3 oz flaked almonds, toasted

Make a sponge using the method for the Chocolate Mixture on pages 30–1. Leave the sponge to stand overnight or longer and then cut into three layers. Sandwich the layers together with 225 g/8 oz raspberry jam and moisten the two top layers with a mixture of raspberry liqueur and sugar syrup. Beat the egg yolks into the marzipan one at a time until the mixture is of piping consistency. Spoon about two-thirds of the mixture into a piping bag with a star nozzle. Dilute the remaining mixture with sugar syrup until it is of spreading consistency. Use this mixture to cover the whole cake and then sprinkle the sides with flaked almonds. Divide the top into 14 portions and decorate each portion by piping along the edges with the marzipan mixture. Brown under a hot grill. Warm the remaining jam, spoon into a paper piping tube and fill the centres of the portions.

Apricot glaze will give the marzipan mixture a nice sheen if you brush it over while the mixture is still hot from the grill.

Nut Sandwich Cake

For the pastry:
225 g/8 oz butter, softened
225 g/8 oz icing sugar
1 teaspoon vanilla essence
pinch of salt
100 g/4 oz plain chocolate, grated
2 eggs
225 g/8 oz hazelnuts, toasted and ground
450 g/1 lb plain flour

For the filling:
100 g/4 oz Apricot Glaze
(see page 60)
150 g/5 oz fondant icing
1 tablespoon Kirsch
350 g/12 oz pineapple jam
6 glacé cherries
1 ring candied pineapple

Cream the butter with the sugar and flavourings and then fold in the chocolate followed by the eggs. Mix together the ground hazelnuts and sifted flour then incorporate quickly into the pastry. Leave the pastry in the refrigerator for about 2 hours.

Roll out the pastry and cut into four 25-cm/10-in rounds of even thickness. Bake these on a baking sheet in a moderate oven (180 C, 350 F, gas 4) for 15 to 20 minutes. Watch the pastry for the last few minutes since the chocolate makes it brown very quickly.

Choose the best shaped round for the top of the cake and spread thinly with hot apricot glaze. Melt the fondant icing in a bowl over a saucepan of hot water and add the Kirsch. If the icing is still too thick, thin with a little egg white. Spread the fondant evenly over the top of the cake, leave to cool slightly and then cut the top into 12 portions. Sandwich the rounds of pastry together with the pineapple jam and then slide the prepared top off its baking sheet and onto the cake. Decorate with glacé cherry halves and candied pineapple.

Millefeuille

with vanilla custard filling

This French cream slice is best eaten fresh because the cream soon makes the puff pastry a bit soft.

575 g/1¼ lb puff pastry (see page 42)
500 g/18 oz Simple Vanilla Cream (see page 50)
150 g/5 oz Apricot Glaze (see page 60)
175 g/6 oz fondant icing
1 tablespoon Kirsch
150 g/5 oz blanched almonds, toasted and chopped
sugar mimosa flowers to decorate

Divide the pastry into three and roll to make three 25-cm/10-in rounds. Make sure that each round is rolled in both directions otherwise it will not rise evenly. Leave the pastry rounds in the refrigerator for at least an hour. Place them on a baking sheet and prick all over with a fork. When you have assembled the cake cover the top with hot apricot glaze and leave it to cool slightly. Warm the fondant icing, flavour with Kirsch and if still too thick, thin with a little sugar syrup. Cover the top with the icing and when almost dry decorate with the sugar mimosa flowers.

Baking time for the pastry: 12 minutes in a hot oven (220C, 425F, gas 7).

Pithiviers

Despite the rather straightforward ingredients this pie needs to be made carefully if it is to be successful. The combination of almond cream filling with the buttery flavour of the puff pastry is really quite delicious.

1 kg/2 lb puff pastry (see page 42)
⅓ quantity of Almond Cream (see page 50)
1 egg yolk to glaze
icing sugar for dusting

It is important to allow the puff pastry enough resting time after each stage of preparation if it is to keep its form well during baking. When you have made up the pie leave it to stand again in the refrigerator for a few minutes before baking in a hot oven (220C, 425F, gas 7) for 30 minutes.

1 **Sandwich together two of the pastry bases** with the vanilla custard. Assemble the cake and press down slightly. Spread the custard that comes out of the sides evenly around the sides.

2 **Cover the top** of the remaining pastry round with apricot glaze and then with a thin covering of fondant icing flavoured with a little Kirsch. When almost dry cover the sides of the cake with chopped almonds and decorate the top with the sugar mimosa flowers.

1 **The puff pastry** must be rolled perfectly evenly so that the pie remains flat during baking. Cut out two 25-cm/10-in rounds using a ring and a very sharp knife and place one of the rounds on a baking sheet.

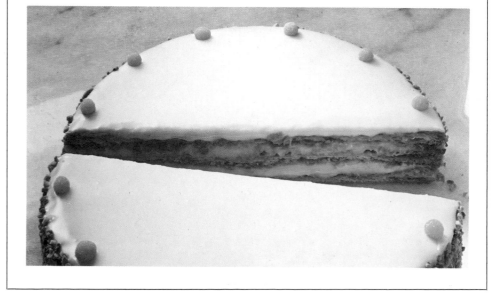

3 **Cover with the second round.** Lay the pastry on carefully to avoid disturbing the filling. Seal firmly around the edge by pressing all round with your finger tips. Leave the pie in the refrigerator for about 30 minutes.

The top of the Pithiviers should have a nice shine and be golden brown and crisp. A good finish can be obtained by dusting the top with icing sugar 5 minutes before the end of the baking time. The sugar will caramelise very quickly, so keep an eye on the pie during these last few minutes. The caramel coating improves the flavour considerably for without it the pie is not very sweet.

2 **Spread with the Almond Cream,** leaving an even 2.5-cm/1-in strip free of filling around the edge. Brush this strip with egg yolk taking care not to allow it to run over the edge for this would prevent the pastry rising at this spot.

4 **Decorate the edge.** This looks more difficult than it is. You can get a decorative effect simply with your fingers and a pointed knife. Press the edge down using your middle and ring finger and press the pastry in with the slanting blunt edge of the knife.

5 **A second way** of obtaining a decorative finish using only your fingers and a knife; this is attractive even after baking. Again hold the pastry firmly beneath your middle and ring fingers and holding the knife vertical bring the pastry in between your fingers.

6 **Score the top.** First brush it very carefully with egg yolk. Using a sharp pointed knife cut curved lines from the centre to the edge. Do not cut too deep for if you go right through the pastry the filling will run out.

Rich Poppy-Seed Cake

A popular cake in Austria and one with several different recipes.

150 g/5 oz butter, softened
225 g/8 oz icing sugar
grated rind of ½ lemon
1 tablespoon brown rum
pinch of salt
6 eggs, separated
225 g/8 oz poppy seeds, ground
50 g/2 oz plain flour
50 g/2 oz raisins, finely chopped
25-cm/10-in cake tin, greased and floured
350 g/12 oz marzipan
100 g/4 oz Apricot Glaze (see page 60)
350 g/12 oz plain chocolate, melted

Cream the butter with a third of the sugar. Add the grated lemon rind, rum and salt and beat in one egg yolk at a time. Whisk the egg whites until stiff but not dry then whisk in the remaining sugar. Mix the ground poppy seeds with the sifted flour and finely chopped raisins. Stir about a third of the egg white into the mixture then fold in the rest. Sprinkle on the poppy-seed mixture and fold in carefully to give a smooth mixture and pour into the prepared cake tin. Bake in a moderately hot oven (190 C, 375 F, gas 5) for 45 to 50 minutes.

When the cake is cooked leave it to cool in the tin for 30 minutes and then cut round the edge and turn onto a wire rack. Wrap the cake in cling film and leave overnight if possible. Roll out the marzipan very thinly. Brush the cake with a thin layer of apricot glaze and then cover in marzipan. Finally cover with the melted chocolate. While the chocolate is still quite soft divide the top into 14 portions with a warm knife to prevent the chocolate breaking when the cake is cut. This unfilled cake can be served with Italian Zabaglione. The distinctive flavour of the poppy seeds goes excellently with the Marsala in this Italian wine cream.

Carrot Cake

This Swiss cake was originally a feature of home baking only but can now be found in many patisseries. The finely grated carrots give the almond sponge a distinctive flavour as well as making it nice and moist.

225 g/8 oz baby carrots
225 g/8 oz caster sugar
pinch of salt
grated rind of 1 lemon
6 eggs, separated
350 g/12 oz unpeeled almonds, ground
100 g/4 oz plain flour
150 g/5 oz Apricot Glaze (see page 60)
150 g/5 oz fondant or royal icing
60 g/2 oz flaked almonds, toasted
25-cm/10-in flan or cake tin,
greased and floured

Wash the carrots and grate very finely. If they are coarsely grated or in long threads the cake will be difficult to cut. In a bowl beat a third of the sugar, the salt and grated lemon rind with the egg yolks. Whisk the egg whites until stiff but not dry then whisk in the remaining sugar. Mix together the ground almonds, sifted flour and grated carrot. Beat about a third of the egg whites into the yolk mixture. Carefully fold in the remaining whites and then the flour mixture. Pour the mixture into the prepared tin and bake in a moderately hot oven (190 C, 375 F, gas 5) for 40–60 minutes.

Leave the baked cake overnight before turning it upside-down out of the tin so that the flat base is now on top. Spread the top and sides with hot apricot glaze and then cover the top with fondant or royal icing. Leave for 1 to 2 hours until dry. Sprinkle the sides with flaked almonds and decorate the top with small marzipan carrots.

Engadine Nut Pie

'Tuorta da nusch a la veglia', as this pie is known in the Romance language, is an excellent example of the baking of the Engadine region of Switzerland, an area whose bakers have a good reputation.

175 g/6 oz butter, softened
100 g/4 oz icing sugar
pinch of salt
1 egg
350 g/12 oz plain flour
450 g/1 lb caster sugar
50 g/2 oz glucose syrup
2 tablespoons lemon juice
150 ml/¼ pint double cream
25 g/1 oz butter
50 g/2 oz clear honey
350 g/12 oz walnuts, coarsely chopped
1 egg yolk to glaze
23-cm/9-in tin with sloping sides

This pie can also be made in a normal straight-sided, loose-based cake tin and is then easier to remove from the tin.

Baking time: 30 minutes in a moderately hot oven (200 C, 400 F, gas 6).

Make a rich shortcrust pastry with the butter, icing sugar, salt, egg and flour. Leave the pastry to stand in the refrigerator for an hour to make it easier to roll. To make the filling, dissolve 225 g/8 oz sugar with the glucose and lemon juice then boil steadily to make a light caramel. In a separate saucepan bring the cream, the remaining sugar, butter and honey to the boil and stir into the caramel. Bring the mixture back to the boil and then stir in the coarsely chopped walnuts. Roll the pastry to 3-mm/⅛-in thick and line the tart tin cutting the pastry slightly above the edge of the tin. When cool add the nut filling and fold the edge of the pastry in over the edge of the filling. Brush this border of pastry with egg yolk. Roll out the remaining pastry to make a lid and place over the pie. Press down around the edges and cut off the excess pastry. Brush the top with egg yolk and mark a pattern using a fork. Bake as instructed and leave to cool. Serve either warm or cold. This nut pie keeps excellently and can be stored for a couple of weeks in a cool place. This is one reason why it is often given as a present.

Gâteau Saint-Honoré

This French speciality is internationally known. The filling is *crème patissière*, a vanilla custard, which is mixed hot with Italian meringue to make Chiboust Cream. Alternatively the meringue can be mixed with cold custard and set with gelatine. It is this method which is illustrated here.

The type of pastry used for the base can also vary. It can be made either of *pâte brisée* (a lightly sweetened shortcrust), quick puff pastry or left over puff pastry which after being rolled several times will not rise too much. If you want to use freshly-made puff pastry cut it into pieces, work it back into a ball and then leave it to stand for 15 minutes.

1 Using a piping bag and a 1-cm/½-in plain nozzle, pipe the choux pastry as evenly as possible around the edge of the pastry base. Pipe an additional spiral in the centre to hold the cream in place later.

2 Dissolve the sugar in the water then boil steadily to make a light caramel (160 C/320 F). Dip the top half of each choux bun into the caramel. You can also push the nozzle of the piping bag into the underside and fill them with cream if you want to.

3 Mix the vanilla custard with the meringue. Stir the dissolved gelatine into the whipped and slightly warmed custard and then fold in the Italian meringue with a metal spoon. You will need to do this very carefully to prevent the custard falling.

4 Using a spatula fill the cake with cream to the top of the choux pastry ring and smooth the top. The rest of the cream is piped into the cake. In France a special round nozzle with a triangle cut-out is used for this.

Recipe for a 25-cm/10-in cake:
225 g/8 oz shortcrust or 150 g/5 oz
puff pastry (see pages 37 and 42)
½ quantity of choux pastry (see page 36)
1 egg yolk to glaze
225 g/8 oz caster sugar
6 tablespoons water
400 g/14 oz Simple Vanilla Cream
(see page 50)
2 leaves gelatine or 1 teaspoon powdered
gelatine
3 egg whites
175 g/6 oz caster sugar
6 tablespoons water

Roll the pastry and cut 25-cm/10-in round (26-cm/10½-in for puff pastry as it shrinks slightly) and prick with a fork. Pipe the choux pastry on to this using a plain nozzle. Use the remaining choux pastry to pipe small balls onto a separate baking sheet for these cook more quickly. Brush with egg yolk using a soft brush. Bake in a hot oven (220 C, 425 F, gas 7) for 20 minutes or until golden brown. Dissolve the sugar in the water over a low heat then boil steadily to make a light caramel. Dip the choux balls in the caramel and stick to the ring of choux pastry with a little of the caramel.

Soften the leaf gelatine in cold water, squeeze out after 10 minutes and dissolve in a little hot water. Alternatively dissolve the powdered gelatine in a little hot water in a bowl over a saucepan of hot water. Stir the diluted gelatine into the smooth vanilla custard. Whisk the egg whites until stiff. Meanwhile boil the sugar and water to feather consistency (112 C/234 F) and pour in a slow trickle into the egg whites to make an Italian meringue. Continue whisking until cool and stir into the custard. Fill the cake and chill.

Zug Cherry Cake

This Swiss speciality has a combination of flavours which simply cannot be bettered. It is essential to use a good quality Kirsch, even though opinions differ widely over the quantity of brandy to be used. The quantity recommended here offers a good solution.

For the sponge:
4 eggs
2 egg yolks
100 g/4 oz caster sugar
75 g/3 oz plain flour
40 g/1½ oz cornflour
75 g/3 oz butter, melted

350 g/12 oz French Butter Cream
(see page 55)
6 tablespoons Kirsch
6 tablespoons sugar syrup
two 25-cm/10-in Japonais bases
(see page 36)
icing sugar for dusting
12 glacé cherry halves

The sponge is made in the same way as a Genoese sponge (see pages 28–9). The sponge base should be left at least overnight before it is used. Flavour the butter cream with the Kirsch. Mix the sugar syrup and Kirsch to make a syrup to moisten the cake.

Spread one of the Japonais bases with the Kirsch butter cream. Cut the top crust off the sponge so that the syrup will soak in evenly and then place it on top of the Japonais base. Brush the syrup on to the sponge, then spread with a thin layer of butter cream and top with the second Japonais base. Cover the cake with the remaining butter cream and sprinkle the sides with the toasted almonds. Chill the cake. Sprinkle with sifted icing sugar and using the back of a knife mark with the traditional lattice pattern. Decorate with glacé cherry halves.

Dobostorte

225 g/8 oz butter, softened
600 ml/1 pint milk
3 egg yolks
50 g/2 oz cornflour
400 g/14 oz caster sugar
1 teaspoon vanilla essence
50 g/2 oz cocoa powder
100 g/4 oz chocolate, melted
8 Dobos bases (see page 29)
1 teaspoon butter
few drops lemon juice

Cream the butter until light and fluffy. Blend 2 tablespoons of the milk with the egg yolks and cornflour. Bring the remaining milk to the boil with 225 g/8 oz sugar and the vanilla essence. Stir into the cornflour mixture return to the saucepan and bring to the boil stirring continuously. Continue to simmer for 2 minutes. Leave the vanilla cream to cool, then strain in a sieve and gradually beat into the butter. Finally stir in the cocoa powder and the melted chocolate.

Sandwich the bases together with the cream and then cover the whole stack with the butter cream as shown in the photographs on the right. To make the caramel topping, melt the teaspoon of butter in a saucepan and add the remaining sugar and lemon juice. Boil steadily, stirring continuously, to make a light caramel and spread immediately over the top layer of the cake.

Prince Regent Cake

7 eggs, separated
100 g/4 oz caster sugar
100 g/4 oz plain flour
50 g/2 oz cornflour
50 g/2 oz butter, melted
½ quantity of chocolate butter cream as for the Dobostorte, above
350 g/12 oz plain chocolate, melted

Make a Genoese sponge as instructed on pages 28–9 then spread the mixture on greaseproof paper as for the Dobos bases (see page 29) and bake. These bases are crisper than those made with Dobos mixture which is mixed cold and are therefore quite fragile. Sandwich the layers together with the chocolate butter cream then when you have made up the cake cover it with chocolate. When this has set cut through the chocolate with a warm knife to divide the cake into portions. This will prevent it breaking when you cut the cake.

1 **Place the first sponge** on a cake base with the side that was covered with paper underneath. Spread with the first layer of chocolate butter cream, making sure that it does not go over the edge, and cover with the next Dobos base.

2 **Place the second round of sponge** on top of the first, paper-side uppermost, and with the edges following those of the first base as closely as possible. Press the base down by hand or by using a second cake base.

6 **Trim the edges** of the last remaining Dobos base and cover with the caramel. The cake base underneath should be lightly greased so that any caramel which runs over the edge can be easily removed. Grease the palette knife too.

7 **While the caramel** is still warm cut the lid into portions. Use a long knife and grease the blade before making each cut to prevent the caramel sticking. You will have to work quickly as the caramel sets very quickly.

3 **Hold one corner** of the greaseproof paper in one hand and peel it back while you hold the base with the other hand to prevent it coming away from the butter cream layer. Spread the next layer of butter cream on top of the sponge and repeat using the next five Dobos bases.

4 **Even up the edges** using a 25-cm/10-in sponge ring as a guide. Cut around the inside of the ring with a long, sharp knife to remove any excess sponge.

5 **Cover the cake completely** with a thin layer of butter cream. Place the cake in the refrigerator for this layer to set and then repeat the process. The sides in particular should be smooth and even.

8 **Place the pieces of the lid** separately on the cake. Alternatively loosen the lid from the cake base with a knife and then slide the whole lid at once on to the cake.

Layer Cake

with Lemon Cream

3 lemons
50 g/2 oz sugar cubes
350 g/12 oz unsalted butter
175 g/6 oz caster sugar
4 egg yolks
6 Dobos bases (see page 29)
350 g/12 oz plain chocolate, melted
16 marzipan flowers
lemon curd to fill the flowers

Scrub the lemons under hot water and carefully extract the zest by rubbing with the sugar cubes. Heat a third of the butter with the lemon zest and sugar cubes, the juice of the lemons, the sugar and egg yolks in a saucepan stirring continuously until just below boiling point and then leave to cool. Cream the remaining butter until light and fluffy and fold in the almost cold mixture. Sandwich the Dobos bases together with this butter cream. Chill the cake in the refrigerator for a short time so that the cream sets a little then cover with the melted chocolate. If the cake is too cold the chocolate will set too quickly and go on too thickly. When the cake is covered in chocolate divide it into 16 portions with a warm knife. The flowers are made by rolling marzipan to 3-mm/$\frac{1}{8}$-in thick and then cutting them out with a 2.5-cm/1-in star cutter. Shape the flowers, stick them to the cake with a little melted chocolate and fill the centres with lemon curd.

Coffee Gâteau

with Morello Cherries

2 tablespoons instant coffee
1 tablespoon icing sugar
2 tablespoons hot water
1 quantity of Vanilla Butter Cream
(see page 54)
1 Genoese sponge (see pages 28–9)
225 g/8 oz morello cherries, drained
3 tablespoons sugar syrup
1 tablespoon Kirsch
225 g/8 oz marzipan
100 g/4 oz plain chocolate, melted

Completely dissolve the instant coffee and icing sugar in the hot water and leave to cool. Stir into the butter cream. Cut the Genoese sponge into three layers, spread the first sponge with butter cream and cover evenly with the cherries. Cover with the second sponge and press down firmly using a cake base, so that the cherries are pressed into the butter cream. Stir the Kirsch into the sugar syrup and use to moisten the top of the second sponge. Spread the second sponge with the coffee butter cream and top with the third sponge. Cover the cake with a thin layer of butter cream, chill the cake and then re-cover with a smooth layer of butter cream. Divide the cake into 16 portions and using a piping bag and a plain nozzle pipe a spiral of cream along each portion tapering towards the centre.

Roll out the marzipan thinly. Dust a cake base lightly with sifted icing sugar and place the marzipan on it. Cover the marzipan with the melted chocolate and while it is still warm mark it using an icing comb. Cut the marzipan to size using a 25-cm/10-in cake ring as a guide and cut into 16 portions. When the chocolate is completely set, place the wedges of chocolate marzipan at an angle on each portion of cake.

Prince Puckler Gâteau

1 sponge base ($\frac{1}{2}$ quantity of Genoese sponge, see pages 28–9)
1 chocolate sponge ($\frac{1}{2}$ quantity of Classic Chocolate Mixture, see page 30)
1 quantity of French Butter Cream
(see page 55)
400 g/14 oz plain chocolate, melted
50 g/2 oz sweetened strawberry purée
2 tablespoons syrup
2 teaspoons lemon juice
1 tablespoon brown rum
1 teaspoon chopped pistachio nuts
1 tablespoon sweetened strawberry purée

Split each sponge base in half to give two rounds about 1-cm/$\frac{1}{2}$-in thick. These rounds can either be sandwiched together alternately or made into a checkerboard cake as illustrated. To do this cut each round into five rings, using stencils as a guide and reassemble the rounds with rings of alternating colour.

Divide the butter cream into four portions. To cover the first layer of sponge flavour the butter cream with 40 g/1$\frac{1}{2}$ oz melted chocolate. Cover with the second chocolate-and-plain-sponge and moisten this with a mixture of rum and sugar syrup. Spread this with plain butter cream. Cover with the third sponge, moisten and cover with strawberry butter cream made by stirring the strawberry purée into the butter cream. Top with the last sponge, cover the cake with butter cream and chill briefly. Cover with the remaining melted chocolate. Divide the cake into portions using a warm knife. Pipe the remaining cream onto the cake in whirls (using a 1-cm/$\frac{1}{2}$-in nozzle) and decorate each whirl with a spot of strawberry purée and chopped pistachio nuts.

Hunyadi Gâteau

6 eggs, separated
225 g/8 oz icing sugar
225 g/8 oz hazelnuts, ground
100 g/4 oz chocolate, finely chopped
1 quantity of Simple Vanilla Cream
(see page 50)
4 leaves gelatine or 1½ teaspoons
powdered gelatine
300 ml/½ pint double cream
100 g/4 oz Apricot Glaze (see page 60)
450 g/1 lb melted chocolate for covering
and decoration
100 g/4 oz chocolate butter cream to
decorate (see page 56)

Draw three 25-cm/10-in circles on grease-proof or non-stick baking paper. Whisk the egg whites until stiff but not dry then gradually whisk in the sugar. Gently beat the egg yolks and lightly fold into the whisked whites. Mix the ground hazelnuts and chopped chocolate, and fold into the mixture. Spread the mixture over the drawn circles. Bake in a moderately hot oven (200 C, 400 F, gas 6) for 20 to 25 minutes. Leave to cool. Strain the cold vanilla custard. Soak the leaf gelatine in cold water for 10 minutes, squeeze out and dissolve in a little hot water. Alternatively dissolve the powdered gelatine in a little hot water in a bowl over a saucepan of hot water. Whisk the cream and fold in the dissolved gelatine. Fold the cream into the custard. Spread the first sponge thickly with the custard cream, cover with the second sponge and again spread thickly with the cream. Cover with the third sponge. Press down lightly on the top of the cake and even out any cream that squeezes out of the sides. Chill for an hour. Brush with the apricot glaze, cover with the melted chocolate and leave to set. To make the decorations: cover a baking sheet with greaseproof paper and pipe 16 blobs of chocolate onto the paper. Bang the sheet lightly on the worktop so that the blobs of chocolate spread to make chocolate buttons. Divide the cake into 16 portions. Pipe a whirl of butter cream on each portion and top with a chocolate button.

Hazelnut and Nougat Gâteau

7 egg whites
350 g/12 oz icing sugar
175 g/6 oz hazelnuts, ground
100 g/4 oz plain flour
pinch of cinnamon
½ teaspoon vanilla essence
50 g/2 oz nut nougat
3 tablespoons brandy
½ quantity of French Butter Cream
(see page 55)
225 g/8 oz raspberry jam
about 100 g/4 oz chocolate, melted
50 g/2 oz flaked almonds, toasted

Draw three circles (25-cm/10-in) on non-stick paper. Whisk the egg whites until stiff but not dry then gradually whisk in the sifted icing sugar. Add the hazelnuts, sifted flour, cinnamon and vanilla essence and fold in gently so that the egg whites do not fall. Transfer the mixture to a piping bag with a star nozzle and pipe spirals to fill two of the circles on the paper. Using the third circle for the top layer pipe a circle around the edge then fill the centre with a lattice pattern. Bake in a moderately hot oven (200 C, 400 F, gas 6) for about 15 minutes. The cake should still be moist.

Stir the nougat and brandy in a basin over a saucepan of hot water until the nougat melts, then carefully stir into the butter cream. Sieve the raspberry jam, heat and brush half of it thinly over the top layer of cake. Allow to set and cool. Cover this thinly with the melted chocolate so that the contours of the lattice remain visible. Sprinkle with half the almonds. Spread the bottom sponge with the remaining raspberry jam, cover with the second sponge and spread with half the butter cream and nougat mixture. Top with the decorated sponge lattice. Spread the sides with butter cream and sprinkle with the remaining almonds. Divide the cake into 16 portions.

Marron Gâteau

1 (439 g/15½ oz) can chestnut purée
8 egg yolks
1 teaspoon vanilla essence
1 teaspoon cinnamon
350 g/12 oz icing sugar
6 egg whites
100 g/4 oz plain flour
1 tablespoon rum
300 ml/½ pint double cream
3 leaves gelatine or 1 teaspoon powdered
gelatine
100 g/4 oz Apricot Glaze
(see page 60)
450 g/1 lb plain chocolate, melted, for
covering and decorating
100 g/4 oz marzipan
2 tablespoon pistachio nuts, chopped

Sieve the chestnut purée and stir until smooth. Divide into two. Blend one half with the egg yolks, vanilla essence, cinnamon and 50 g/2 oz of the sifted icing sugar. Whisk the egg whites until stiff but not dry then gradually whisk in 175 g/6 oz icing sugar. Fold in the yolks mixture. Sift the flour into the mixture and fold in gently. Pour the mixture into a 25-cm/10-in sponge ring and bake in a moderate oven (180 C, 350 F, gas 4) for about 45 minutes. Wrap the cake and leave overnight.

To make the chestnut cream mix the remaining chestnut purée with the rest of the icing sugar and rum. Whip the cream until stiff and fold into the chestnut purée. Soak the leaf gelatine in cold water for 10 minutes, squeeze out and dissolve in a little hot water. Alternatively dissolve the powdered gelatine in a little hot water in a bowl over a saucepan of hot water. Stir the dissolved gelatine into the purée mixture. Split the sponge into three layers and sandwich them together with the chestnut cream. Press lightly on the cake and smooth the edges. Chill for 30 minutes. Brush the apricot glaze over the top and sides of the cake. Shape the marzipan into 16 chestnuts. Dip the wider end in the chocolate and then in the pistachio nuts. Spread the remainder of the melted chocolate over the cake and leave to set. Divide the cake into 16 portions and decorate with the marzipan chestnuts.

Coconut Cake

2 fresh coconuts or 675 g/1½ lb
dessicated coconut
225 g/8 oz caster sugar
2 tablespoons brown rum
one 25-cm/10-in Genoese sponge
(see pages 28–9)
50 g/2 oz cornflour
600 ml/1 pint milk
1 vanilla pod
3 eggs, separated
16 glacé cherries to decorate

Bore through the 'eyes' of each coconut and pour off the liquid and reserve. Break the nuts open, remove the fresh coconut and finely grate. Bring 2 tablespoons of the coconut liquid to the boil with 50 g/2 oz of the sugar until the sugar dissolves, then add the rum. Alternatively soak 450 g/1 lb of the dessicated coconut in the rum and 50 g/2 oz of the sugar while preparing the custard. Cut the Genoese sponge into three layers.

Blend the cornflour with 2 tablespoons milk then add the egg yolks. Bring the remaining milk to boil with the vanilla pod and 2 tablespoons of the remaining sugar. Pour on to the cornflour mixture return to the heat and bring to the boil, stirring continuously. Meanwhile whisk the egg whites until stiff but not dry then whisk in the remaining sugar and carefully fold into the hot liquid. As soon as the whites are fully incorporated, remove the saucepan from the heat. You will have to work quickly now to fill and cover the cake with cream since it sets very quickly.

Spread the first layer of sponge with the cream, cover with the second and moisten with the coconut liquid mixture. Cover with cream and the last layer and again moisten. Cover the cake with the remaining cream, chill for a short time and then cover thickly with the grated fresh or remaining dessicated coconut. Divide the cake into 16 portions and decorate each with a glazé cherry.

Coffee Meringue Gâteau

8 egg whites
450 g/1 lb caster sugar
225 g/8 oz icing sugar
25 g/1 oz cornflour
350 g/12 oz butter
4 eggs
2 egg yolks
5 tablespoons boiling water
25 g/1 oz ground coffee
50 g/2 oz flaked almonds, toasted
14 mocha beans

Make a meringue mixture following the method shown on page 34. Using a piping bag and a 1-cm/½-in plain nozzle pipe four 25-cm/10-in meringue bases onto greaseproof or baking paper. Dry out the meringues in a very cool oven (110 C, 225 F, gas ¼) for 1½ hours and then peel off the paper.

Prepare the butter cream (as instructed for the Butter Cream with eggs on page 54). Pour the boiling water over the ground coffee. Leave to stand for about 10 minutes until the coffee is very strong, then strain and slowly stir into the butter cream. Sandwich the meringue bases together with a quarter of the butter cream and cover the cake with another quarter of the butter cream. Chill and then cover with a third quarter. Tip the flaked almonds into a sieve and sift the almond dust onto the top of the cake. Sprinkle the sides of the cake with the flaked almonds. Divide the cake into 14 portions and decorate each with a whirl of the remaining coffee butter cream and an edible mocha or coffee bean.

Black Forest Gâteau

450 g/1 lb morello cherries, poached
300 ml/½ pint cherry juice
100 g/4 oz caster sugar
1 stick cinnamon
2 heaped teaspoons cornflour
one 25-cm/10-in chocolate sponge (from Classic Chocolate Mixture, see page 30)
600 ml/1 pint double cream
2½ tablespoons sugar syrup
4 tablespoons Kirsch
chocolate flakes or rolls and icing sugar to decorate

Drain the cherries well in a sieve and bring 300 ml/½ pint of the juice to the boil in a saucepan with half the sugar and the cinnamon stick. Remove the cinnamon stick, dissolve the cornflour in a little of the cold juice and use to bind the hot juice. Simmer gently. Add the cherries and stir gently into the juice with a wooden spoon to avoid breaking the cherries. Continue simmering for a few minutes then remove the saucepan from the heat and leave to cool. Keep 16 cherries to one side to decorate. Cut the sponge into three layers. Sweeten the cream with the remaining sugar and whip until stiff. Spread the first sponge thinly with cream and then using a 2.5-cm/1-in plain nozzle pipe four rings of cream onto this sponge. Fill the spaces between the rings with the cold cherries. Press on the second sponge and moisten it with a mixture of the sugar syrup and Kirsch. Spread with cream, add the top sponge and moisten. Cover the cake with cream and decorate with whirls of cream topped with a cherry. Cover the centre of the cake with chocolate flakes and dust with icing sugar.

Frankfurt Ring

This is a cake which, in Germany at least, is almost as popular as the Black Forest Gâteau, although there are many different opinions on the way it should be made. The only common factor in the many different recipes seems to be the shape. The mixture can be either an ordinary sponge or a Genoese; the filling can be vanilla, coffee or even maraschino butter cream. The cake can be covered with either chopped almonds, hazelnuts or crushed praline.

It is, of course, impossible to say which of these is best, but praline does seem to be a favourite. These crisp bits of caramelised almond complement the soft sponge and cream extremely well. In the following recipe a coffee butter cream filling and a sponge flavoured with Kirsch is chosen.

The sponge is made in the same way as the Genoese Mixture on pages 28–9.

3 eggs
1 egg yolk
75 g/3 oz caster sugar
pinch of salt
75 g/3 oz plain flour
25 g/1 oz cornflour
50 g/2 oz butter, melted
1 quantity of Vanilla Butter Cream
(see page 54)
25 g/1 oz icing sugar
2 tablespoons diluted instant coffee
2½ tablespoons Kirsch
2½ tablespoons sugar syrup
praline, recipe on the left
16 glacé cherry halves
3 pint ring mould, greased and floured

To make the praline, heat 150 g/5 oz caster sugar in a saucepan until the caramel is pale brown. Stir in 150 g/5 oz coarsely chopped toasted almonds. Remove the saucepan from the heat and pour the hot, malleable praline onto an oiled marble slab or baking sheet. Grease the rolling pin with oil also to prevent the praline sticking. Roll the hot praline out to about 1-cm/½-in thick and leave to cool. Crush with a heavy weight or meat hammer. Work inside a sponge ring to prevent the breaking praline going all over the worktop.

Grease the tin thoroughly and sprinkle with sifted flour. Fill with the sponge mixture and bake in a moderately hot oven (190 C, 375 F, gas 5) for 35 to 40 minutes. Leave the cake for a few minutes before turning it out of the tin and leave overnight. The cake will stay moist if you cover it with a large basin or wrap it in cling film once it is completely cool. The next day cut the cake into four layers. Keep a third of the butter cream to one side and flavour the rest with the icing sugar and coffee. Fill the cake as shown in the photographs on the left, soaking each layer of sponge (except for the first) with a mixture of the Kirsch and sugar syrup.

Cut the sponge into four layers. Spread the first ring with coffee butter cream. Cover with the second ring and moisten with the Kirsch-sugar syrup mixture. Repeat for the next two rings to give the cake a full, rich flavour. Chill the cake, cover with butter cream and smooth out with a strip of greaseproof paper. Cover with the crushed praline, pressing it on to the sides with your hand. Using the rest of the butter cream pipe 16 whirls around the top and top each with a glacé cherry half.

Apricot Cream Gâteau

For the sponge:
5 egg yolks
100 g/4 oz marzipan
75 g/3 oz caster sugar
1 teaspoon vanilla essence
3 egg whites
50 g/3 oz plain flour
25 g/1 oz cornflour
50 g/2 oz plain chocolate, grated

For the filling:
75 g/3 oz caster sugar
300 ml/½ pint milk
3 egg yolks
6 leaves gelatine or 20 g/¾ oz
powdered gelatine

50 g/2 oz marzipan, broken into small
pieces
2½ tablespoons Amaretto (almond liqueur)
300 ml/½ pint double cream, whipped
675 g/1½ lb stewed apricots

For the decoration:
175 g/6 oz meringue shells
450 ml/¾ pint cream
1 tablespoon sugar

Draw two circles of 25-cm/10-in diameter on greaseproof paper. Beat 1 egg yolk into the marzipan then gradually beat in the remaining egg yolks, 25 g/1 oz of the sugar and the vanilla essence until pale and thick. Whisk the egg whites until stiff but not dry then whisk in the remaining sugar. Sift together the flour and cornflour and mix in the grated chocolate. Stir a third of the egg whites into the yolk mixture and then gently fold in the remaining whisked whites and the flour mixture. Spread the cake mixture evenly over the circles, place the paper on a baking sheet and bake in a hot oven (220 C,

425 F, gas 7) for 10 to 12 minutes. Trim the edges of the sponges using a cake ring and then place the ring over one of the sponges.

Gently heat the sugar, milk and egg yolks in a saucepan until thick enough to coat the back of a spoon (see page 53). Be careful not to boil or overheat the mixture or the egg yolks will curdle. Stir in the leaf gelatine, which you have previously dissolved in hot water or the powdered gelatine which has been dissolved in a little water in a bowl over hot water. Strain the mixture. Stir in the chopped marzipan while the liquid is still hot, then stir in the almond liqueur. When the mixture is cool but still runny fold in the whipped cream. Spread about half of the cream filling on the sponge. Cover with the drained apricot halves (keeping four or five to one side for the decoration) and cover with the rest of the cream. Leave in the refrigerator to set.

Loosen the ring by cutting round with a knife, then lift off the ring. Chop the meringue cases into even pieces. Spread the cake with a thin layer of the remaining whipped cream and sprinkle all over with the meringue. Divide the cake into 16 portions, pipe a whirl of cream on each using a 1-cm/½-in star nozzle and top with a slice of apricot.

Flaky Choux Gâteau

with Alpine strawberry cream filling

This is a light cream cake made with crisp choux pastry. It should be eaten within 2 to 3 hours or the choux pastry will become soft.

100 g/4 oz butter
pinch of salt
1 teaspoon sugar
250 ml/½ pint water
150 g/5 oz plain flour
4 eggs, lightly beaten
350 g/12 oz Alpine strawberries or small strawberries quartered
50 g/2 oz icing sugar
1 tablespoon rum
1 litre/2 pints double cream
75 g/3 oz caster sugar
icing sugar for dusting

Sprinkle a large baking sheet lightly with flour. Using a 25-cm/10-in sponge ring mark the size of five choux bases on the baking sheet. Make the choux pastry with the butter, salt, sugar, water and flour as described on page 36. Add the eggs gradually to make a soft choux pastry of spreading consistency. If the 5 eggs prove too little you can thin the pastry with a little egg white or another whole egg. Spread five thin bases (3-mm/⅛-in thick at the most) in the circles. Bake in a hot oven (230 C, 450 F, gas 8) for 10 minutes or until crisp and golden, then turn the bases and cook for a further 10 minutes.

Choose the three best bases for the cake and trim the edges if necessary. Cut or break the remaining rounds into small pieces.

Pick out the best strawberries to use for decoration (48 in all) and then sprinkle the rest with icing sugar and rum. Coarsely crush with a fork and leave to set for 30 minutes. Sweeten the cream with the icing sugar and whip until stiff. Stir about two-thirds of the cream into the crushed strawberries and sandwich together the three choux rounds. Cover the cake with the remaining strawberry cream and sprinkle thickly with the flakes of choux pastry. Pipe 16 whirls of plain whipped cream on to the top and decorate each with three strawberries. Dust the top with a little icing sugar.

Pischinger Cake

250 g/9 oz butter, softened
100 g/4 oz hazelnuts, toasted and chopped
150 g/5 oz caster sugar
½ teaspoon vanilla essence
½ teaspoon instant coffee
2 egg yolks
1 packet Karlsbad baking wafers
225 g/8 oz chocolate, melted

Melt a teaspoon of the butter in a saucepan, add the coarsely chopped, lightly toasted hazelnuts with 100 g/4 oz sugar, and caramelise stirring continuously. Pour the mixture onto an oiled marble slab, leave to cool slightly and then finely crush. You can use the method shown for praline on page 147.

Cream the remaining butter with the remaining sugar, vanilla essence and instant coffee until light and fluffy. Then stir in the egg yolks and crushed nut caramel. Use the mixture to sandwich together five baking wafers, cover the cake with half the remaining filling, and chill. Cover the cake with a second, more even layer of filming and chill again. Then cover with the melted chocolate.

Pischinger Cake is another Austrian speciality which now has little in common with the nut cake as originally invented by the Viennese pastry chef Oskar Pischinger. His fellow-bakers have since invented more practical ways of using his idea as the present cakes show. It is essential to use best quality baking wafers (obtainable from delicatessens) for these play a large part in the success of the cake. If baking wafers are unobtainable try using the Pompidour fan wafers which are used for ice cream.

The story of one Viennese cake

How is it that a cake as modest as the modern Sachertorte has become so world-famous and has retained all its fascination over the decades? Austrian bakers should consider themselves lucky to have such a cake – a cake which has hit the headlines many times over the years. It is thanks to two organisations, the Hotel Sacher and the great Viennese bakery Demel that the cake's image has been brought to the public's attention. They simply could not agree which of them was entitled to the original recipe and in the end it was left to the law courts to decide. At the Sacher Hotel the cake is filled with apricot jam while at the Demel bakery it is simply covered in chocolate. In any other situation a disagreement of this kind would soon be forgotten, but not so in the traditional Sacher and Demel organisations. Tradition is no joking matter in the city of Vienna.

At the Demel bakery (where there is no jam in the cake) one can feast – amidst the aroma of cake and coffee – from cakes which complement perfectly the chandeliers, mirrors and ornate decor. Dressed in black with white collars, Demel's attractive young ladies (it would almost be an insult to refer to them as waitresses) avoid the personal pronoun – 'Has the gentleman already ordered?' or 'Does madam require cream?' – adopting a manner of speech which gives the whole proceeding something of the atmosphere of a Viennese stage set from the turn of the century. But this is the real world, even though there is a director in the background who knows something about both show business and art. This is Udo Proksch, alias Serge Kirchhofer. He preserves the traditions passionately and anyone who is doubtful about this will soon be won over by the quality of the cakes. No modern influences are tolerated and nowadays there can be no other confectioner that can claim to have resisted modern technology as consistently as Demel's have done. For Master Leschanz, who runs the bakery, there can be no compromises: only the freshest and the best is good enough.

This is something which these traditionalists share curiously enough with the proponents of nouvelle cuisine, although their recipes could never be adapted to fit the new trend towards low-fat foods. They make their own jams and stewed fruits, they have their own mills producing unbleached flour, while in the basement there are old-fashioned machines producing nougat, marzipan and even their own Demel chocolate. A little further along quick-fingered girls make a variety of pralines by hand.

The following recipe for Sachertorte is so to speak 'neutral', and any similarity to the original is purely accidental!

100 g/4 oz plain chocolate
100 g/4 oz butter, softened
100 g/4 oz icing sugar
5 egg yolks
1 teaspoon vanilla essence
4 egg whites
50 g/2 oz plain flour
100 g/4 oz ground almonds
23-cm/9-in sponge ring or tin, greased and floured
1 quantity of Apricot Glaze (see page 60)
1 quantity of Boiled Chocolate Icing (see page 64)

Melt the chocolate in a bowl over a saucepan of hot water and keep warm. Beat the butter with a third of the icing sugar and the egg yolks until creamy. Stir in the vanilla essence and the lukewarm chocolate. Whisk the egg whites until stiff but not dry then whisk in the remaining sugar. Fold gently into the yolk mixture with the sifted flour and almonds. Pour into the prepared tin and bake in a moderate oven (180 C, 350 F, gas 4) for 40 to 50 minutes. When cool cover the cake with a thin layer of apricot glaze and then with the chocolate icing.

All the traditions of Viennese baking are encapsulated in the Sachertorte. The Hotel Sacher's version is filled with apricot jam and claims to be the 'original Viennese Sachertorte'. In the modern hotel kitchens the cakes are covered one after the other with delicious chocolate. Those of the Demel bakery are made without jam. Their Anna Cake has also become quite famous, probably because of its unusual shape which looks like a turban. One of Demel's waitresses, dressed in the customary black with white collar, presides over the cake stands of the restaurant.

Small Cakes

Small cakes are a fairly recent innovation. In the past big was beautiful in baking. The larger and more sumptuous the better, and in keeping with the spirit of the times cakes were often made as large as wagon wheels.

It was not until Victorian times, with its emphasis upon the individual, that small cakes began to form the centrepoint of the window display of a food patisserie. These delicate little cakes were entirely in keeping with an age in which hard physical labour was becoming a thing of the past and where it was becoming less necessary for food merely to satisfy hunger. It is hardly surprising that in modern times these small pastries make up an increasing proportion of patisserie's sales.

This new concept placed a different emphasis on the external appearance of the baker's creations, an emphasis which was even more important here than with the larger gâteaux. This explains why the products were sold both in the form of large cakes and in a miniaturised version as small cakes or slices. For the baker these slices were easier to divide into individual portions than the larger gâteaux. In home baking quantities for large cakes could be halved to provide suitable sizes for the smaller family. Almost all 'large recipes' could be reduced in this way, even the well-known Linzertorte, Sachertorte or Baumkuchen. A more unusual example of the small cake is provided by the Swiss roll, in which a flat sponge is rolled with a lemon or chocolate cream, nut, fruit or truffle filling. The roll is then cut into individual slices before serving to provide an attractive display.

Small, rum-soaked savarins with a variety of delicious fillings make excellent desserts while, despite the adverse effects of mass production, home-made Chocolate Sponge Drops have remained a favourite with children for 150 years. These were invented in Vienna in 1822 when a magician called Kutom Bulchia Titescan was enjoying great popularity. A clever confectioner honoured the Indian magician by creating a dessert whose chocolate coating and cream filling were meant to represent the brown complexion and dazzling white teeth of the conjuror. Even today these cakes are known as 'Indians' in Vienna.

Small cakes are, of course, always a favourite with children as well as adults. Both like the idea of an individual portion, which are served up in the form of éclairs or cream horns. Small cakes are usually especially attractive visually – for example the Alpine Strawberry Tartlets or the Raspberry Meringues in this chapter. A combination of two or three different varieties of small cake on the table would suit the older child's tea party equally well as a morning coffee party for adults. Care should be taken to display the cakes as attractively as possible on pretty china with napkins as this will enhance their appeal.

Chocolate Sponge Drops

The following recipe can serve as a basic recipe for small sponges which retain their shape during baking. Chocolate Sponge Drops are the most familiar and popular of these small cakes. They are usually filled with ordinary whipped cream, but you can use a light custard (*crème patissière*).

5 egg yolks
75 g/3 oz caster sugar
7 egg whites
75 g/3 oz cornflour
50 g/2 oz plain flour

1 quantity of Apricot Glaze
(see page 60)
1 quantity of Boiled Chocolate Icing
(see page 64)
600 ml/1 pint double cream
50 g/2 oz caster sugar

Prepare the cake mixture as shown in the photographs on the right. The technique differs from the usual sponge mixture in that the cornflour is mixed with the egg whites and then the beaten yolks folded into the whites – not in reverse order as is usual.

Brush the cooked sponges with apricot glaze, cover with chocolate and sandwich together with whipped cream (using a piping bag and a 2.5-cm/1-in star nozzle). If you prefer to fill the Chocolate Sponge Drops with custard, first soak the sponges in a mixture of 1 tablespoon sugar syrup and 1 tablespoon rum. Prepare the custard using 600 ml/1 pint milk (see page 50) and sandwich together the sponges with the custard. Then glaze and cover with chocolate.

2 Whisk the egg whites until stiff but not dry then whisk in the remaining sugar. The whites should be glossy and firm enough to cut with a knife. Fold in the sifted cornflour using a metal spoon.

3 Pour about half the yolks onto the whites and fold in gently using a metal spoon. Then fold in the remaining yolks. Unlike the normal sponge mixture the yolks are here added to the whites and not the other way round.

1 Separate the eggs and tip 5 yolks into a mixing bowl. Beat the yolks until pale and thick with 1 tablespoon of the sugar. Do not overbeat the yolks, the mixture only needs to be the consistency of thick cream so that it will combine easily with the egg whites.

4 The last step is to fold in the sifted flour. Work very gently using a metal spoon for at this stage the mixture can easily lose some of its volume, and it needs to be firm for Chocolate drops.

5 Pipe the mixture. Cover a baking sheet with greaseproof or non-stick baking paper. Using a large piping bag with a 2.5-cm/1-in plain nozzle pipe half spheres of the mixture onto the paper. Hold the piping bag vertical and squeeze in one continuous stream for each cake. Leave room for the cakes to swell during baking.

6 Correctly baked drops should rise evenly and have a fairly smooth surface. It helps to give them a light sprinkling of sifted flour before baking. Bake in a moderately hot oven (200 C, 400 F, gas 6) for the first 5 minutes, then reduce the temperature to moderate (180 C, 350 F, gas 4) for about 10 minutes.

7 Place the sponge drops on a wire rack to cool. Press a spoon into the base of each drop while still warm to make a hollow for the filling, if required.

8 **Brush the top with apricot glaze.** As in the other iced sponges the apricot glaze provides an insulating layer. The glaze must be hot so that it can be brushed on thinly. An alternative method is to dip the sponges quickly into the glaze and brush off the excess.

9 **Prepare the chocolate** as described on page 64. Dip the glazed sponges into the melted chocolate. Remove by spearing them on a small pointed knife or cocktail stick and place on a wire rack to drain.

10 **The finished Chocolate Sponge Drop.** The two halves are glazed and coated in chocolate. The sponges do not need a hollow in the base since the cream is piped between them. For moister chocolate drops dampen the sponges with a mixture of sugar syrup and rum or Arrak before glazing.

Marzipan Potatoes

A cake made with drop sponges (as for Chocolate Sponge Drops). You can use sponges either with or without the hollow in the base. The round potatoes are cut with a knife to look like jacket potatoes. To make the oval potatoes, pipe ovals onto the baking sheet and after baking make a hollow in the bases and fill with a mixture of .equal quantities of vanilla custard and whipped cream. Then wrap in marzipan and dip in cocoa powder.

12 sponge drops
1 tablespoon rum
1 tablespoon sugar syrup
1 quantity of Vanilla Butter Cream
(see page 54)
25 g/1 oz plain chocolate, melted
100 g/4 oz pineapple jam
350 g/12 oz marzipan
cocoa powder

Make a hollow in the bases of the sponge drops if they do not already have one, moisten with a mixture of the rum and syrup and leave to soak in. Stir a third of the butter cream with the melted chocolate and fill half the sponges. Fill the remaining sponges with pineapple jam and sandwich each with a butter cream sponge. Cover with the remaining butter cream. Roll out the marzipan until thin, cut into 10-cm/4-in rounds and cover the sponges, pinching the marzipan together and cutting off the excess with scissors. Dip in the cocoa powder and make three cuts in the top with a pointed knife, pressing back the marzipan so that the butter cream below becomes visible. Place the marzipan potatoes in paper cases.

Oval marzipan potatoes look very realistic. The oval sponges are filled and thinly coated with vanilla butter cream. They are wrapped in marzipan and the eyes made with a thin piece of wood or skewer.

Sponge Omelettes

These omelettes can be filled with any possible variety of light custard, with fruit, ice cream or whipped cream. They are an excellent cake for occasions when the time is short for the sponges can be made well in advance. They freeze well but will also stay fresh for a few days just wrapped in cling film.

5 egg yolks
75 g/3 oz caster sugar
pinch of salt
grated rind of ½ lemon
4 egg whites
40 g/1½ oz cornflour
40 g/1½ oz plain flour
40 g/1½ oz butter, melted

Beat the egg yolks with a quarter of the sugar until pale and thick and then add the salt and lemon rind. Whisk the egg whites until stiff but not dry then whisk in the remaining sugar. Fold in the egg yolk mixture then fold in the sifted cornflour and flour. Finally stir in the melted butter. Fold all the ingredients together very carefully to avoid the mixture falling. Pipe the mixture onto the baking sheet and bake in a hot oven (220C, 425F, gas 7) for about 10 minutes. Do not allow the sponges to become brown round the edges or they will break when folded over. Fill with cream, custard or fruit. The mixture makes about twenty 15-cm/6-in omelettes.

1 **Cover the baking sheet** with greaseproof paper and, using a pencil and a pastry cutter as a guide, draw circles of 15-cm/6-in diameter. Fill the circles with a spiral of mixture using a piping bag and a 1-cm/½-in plain nozzle. Leave 2.5-cm/1-in between each omelette.

2 **Peel off the paper.** Turn the greaseproof paper upside down onto a lightly floured surface, cover with a damp cloth and leave to cool. When cool, remove the paper.

Éclairs

250 ml/8 fl oz water
50 g/2 oz butter
pinch of salt
225 g/8 oz plain flour
5 to 6 eggs

1 quantity of Apricot Glaze
(see page 60)
225 g/8 oz fondant icing
4 teaspoons instant coffee diluted in
a little hot water
600 ml/1 pint double cream
100 g/4 oz caster sugar

Make a choux pastry by bringing the water to the boil with the butter and salt. Tip all the sifted flour into the saucepan in one go and stir over the heat until the mixture forms a ball and comes away from the sides of the pan. Transfer mixture to a bowl and leave to cool. Beat in the first egg and when fully incorporated beat in the next egg, continuing in this way until the mixture is of piping consistency. Spoon the choux pastry into a piping bag with a plain nozzle and pipe 20 lengths of pastry on to a lightly greased baking sheet. Bake in a hot oven (230 C, 450 F, gas 8) for 15 to 20 minutes, pouring a little water onto the base of the oven to create plenty of steam. While still warm brush the éclairs with apricot glaze, leave to cool and then cover with the fondant flavoured with half the coffee. When the icing is dry cut the éclairs in half lengthways. Whip the cream and sugar until stiff and stir the remaining coffee into the cream. Fill the éclairs with cream using a piping bag and a star nozzle.

Alpine Strawberry Tartlets

For the pastry:
150 g/5 oz butter
100 g/4 oz icing sugar
1 teaspoon vanilla sugar
pinch of salt
1 egg yolk
250 g/9 oz plain flour
10–12 tartlet tins

For the filling:
200 g/7 oz caster sugar
40 g/1½ oz cornflour
5 egg yolks
600 ml/1 pint milk
1 vanilla pod
4 egg whites
450 g/1 lb Alpine strawberries or small
strawberries quartered
600 ml/1 pint double cream

Mix the butter, icing sugar, flavourings, egg yolk and sifted flour to make a smooth shortcrust pastry. Chill, then roll out and use to line the tartlet cases. Press the sides well into the tin and prick several times with a fork. Bake in a moderately hot oven (200 C, 400 F, gas 6) for about 10 minutes until golden.

Make a vanilla custard with 75 g/3 oz of the sugar, the cornflour, egg yolks, milk and vanilla pod (see page 50). Whisk the egg whites until stiff but not dry then whisk in remaining sugar. Stir the whisked whites into the boiling custard. Keep 100 g/4 oz strawberries to decorate. Crush the rest with a fork and stir into the hot custard. Spoon into the tart cases, leave to cool and decorate with whipped cream and strawberries.

Chocolate Chimneys

275 g/10 oz marzipan
75 g/3 oz plain flour
4 egg whites
150 ml/¼ pint milk
plain chocolate, melted for coating
150 ml/¼ pint double cream

Work the marzipan with the sifted flour and a little egg white, then gradually work in the remaining egg white. Press through a sieve and leave overnight in the refrigerator in a covered bowl. Lightly grease two baking sheets with butter and sprinkle with sifted flour. Add the milk to the marzipan mixture and stir thoroughly. Using a palette knife spread a thin, even layer of marzipan on the baking sheets. Bake in a moderately hot oven (190 C, 375 F, gas 5) for 5 to 7 minutes until golden brown. Cut into 10-cm/4-in squares and return to the oven until brown and crisp, about 5 minutes. Remove one at a time from the baking sheet while still hot using a spatula and roll immediately round a thin rolling pin of 2.5-cm/1-in diameter, or the handle of a thick wooden spoon, pressing the ends together. Slide off the rolling pin and leave to cool. Cover the chimneys with the melted chocolate and fill with whipped cream.
Makes 24.

Dutch Slices

350 g/12 oz quick or left-over puff
pastry (see page 44)
350 g/12 oz jar morello cherries *or*
425 g/15 oz can red cherries
100 g/4 oz caster sugar
¼ teaspoon cinnamon
1 tablespoon cornflour
600 ml/1 pint double cream
75 g/3 oz redcurrant jam
100 g/4 oz fondant icing

On a lightly floured surface roll out the
pastry (rolling in opposite directions as
customary with puff pastry) to a rectangle
of about 25 × 45-cm/10 × 18-in as it
shrinks slightly during baking. Place on
greaseproof paper on a baking sheet and
prick all over with a fork. Leave to stand for
15 to 20 minutes and then bake in a hot oven
(220 C, 425 F, gas 7) for 10 to 15 minutes
until golden brown. Leave to cool and then
trim the edges. Drain the cherries in a sieve.

1 **Cut the puff pastry into two strips.** Use a
ruler as a guide and make sure the strips
are both 10-cm/4-in wide. Cover one strip
with hot redcurrant jam and fondant icing. Leave
to dry and then cut into 5-cm/2-in lengths.

2 **Place the other strip of pastry** between
two lengths of wood, which should be 5-
cm/2-in deep and 40-cm/16-in long.
Spread the cherries down the centre of the pastry.
Using a piping bag and large plain nozzle pipe a
line of cream down either side of the cherries.
Cover with the remaining cream.

Bring the juice to the boil with half the sugar
and cinnamon and bind with the cornflour.
Add the cherries and bring back to the boil.
When cool spread on the puff pastry. Whip
the cream with the remaining sugar until
stiff and then spread over the cherries. Boil
the redcurrant jam, spread on a second
piece of pastry and leave to set. Cover with
fondant icing and assemble the cake as
shown in the photographs.

Coffee Cherry Slices

These are made in almost exactly the same
way as the Dutch Slices. The only difference
is that the cream is flavoured with strong
ground coffee (or instant coffee) and a little
more sugar added to bring out the flavour of
the coffee. Flavour the fondant icing with
coffee and a dash of coffee liqueur.

3 **Smooth the top** of the cream using a
broad knife or palette knife. Then run a
small pointed knife along the inside of
each piece of wood and remove the wood.
Smooth the sides if necessary.

4 **The finished Dutch slices.** Lift the cut top
with a wide palette knife and place gently
on the cream. Then using a thin, sharp
knife cut through to make ten slices. Wipe the
knife after cutting each piece to avoid smearing
the cream on the next slice.

Raspberry Meringues

8 egg whites
225 g/8 oz caster sugar
225 g/8 oz icing sugar
50 g/2 oz melted plain chocolate for
decoration
6 tablespoons red wine
150 g/5 oz caster sugar
4 teaspoons cornflour
450 g/1 lb fresh raspberries
2 tablespoons raspberry liqueur
600 ml/1 pint double cream

Make the meringue mixture as shown in the photographs on page 34. Cover a baking sheet with greaseproof paper and with a pencil draw circles of 7.5-cm/3-in. in diameter. Using a piping bag and a 1-cm/½-in star nozzle pipe spirals of meringue to cover the circles. Bake in a very cool oven (110 C, 225 F, gas ¼) for 2 to 2½ hours. Peel off the paper and dip the meringues in shallow chocolate.

Boil the red wine and half the sugar and bind with the cornflour. Add two-thirds of the raspberries and bring back to the boil. Add the raspberry liqueur. Purée and strain the remaining raspberries. Whip the cream and remaining sugar until stiff and stir in the raspberry purée. Spoon the raspberry cream into a piping bag with a 1-cm/½-in nozzle and pipe a ring of cream onto half the meringues. Fill the centre of each ring with the raspberry mixture and top with a second meringue.

This recipe makes about 30 meringue bases – i.e. 15 complete cakes.

Cream Horns

These crisp puff pastry cases can either be made as horns or rolls and you can buy metal shapes to help make either. They are often filled with a light custard but they are especially good with lightly sweetened whipped cream. The cream can be flavoured with fruit purée, for example strawberry or raspberry.

To make 10 horns:
450 g/1 lb puff pastry (see page 42)
1 egg yolk diluted with a little milk
flaked almonds for sprinkling
(optional)
300 ml/½ pint double cream, whipped
50 g/2 oz caster sugar
icing sugar for dusting.

On a lightly floured surface roll the pastry into a rectangle of about 50 × 30-cm/20 × 12-in. When rolling change direction frequently, rolling first from left to right and then from

front to back. Cut the pastry into ten strips each 2.5-cm/1-in wide and brush with the diluted egg yolk. Make sure no egg gets onto the cut edges of the pastry or it will stick to the metal shapes. Twist the strips around the metal shapes in a spiral and stick the ends firmly together. Brush again with egg yolk and, if you want to use almonds, dip in the flaked almonds at this point. Place on the baking sheet with the end of the pastry underneath, leave to stand for about 15 minutes and then bake in a moderately hot oven (200 C, 400 F, gas 6) for 15 to 18 minutes until golden. Remove the metal shapes while still warm and when cool fill with the cream sweetened with the caster sugar and dust with icing sugar.

Strawberry Cream Roll

For the sponge:
6 egg yolks
75 g/3 oz caster sugar
pinch of salt
1 teaspoon vanilla essence
3 egg whites
100 g/4 oz plain flour
baking sheet (36 × 25-cm/14 × 10-in),
lined and greased

For the filling:
350 g/12 oz Alpine strawberries or
small strawberries quartered
5 leaves gelatine or 15 g/½ oz
powdered gelatine
4 tablespoons Sauterne wine
450 ml/¾ pint double cream
75 g/3 oz caster sugar (more if the
fruit is sour)
icing sugar for dusting

Beat the egg yolks with a quarter of the
sugar until pale and thick then stir in the salt
and vanilla essence. Whisk the egg whites
until stiff but not dry then whisk in the
remaining sugar. Pour the egg yolk mixture
into the whisked whites and fold in gently.
Finally fold in the sifted flour. Spread the

mixture onto the prepared baking sheet and
bake in a hot oven (230 C, 450 F, gas 8) for 8
to 10 minutes, keeping an eye on the cake
during the last few minutes to judge when
cooked. Turn out and leave to cool.

Purée the strawberries in a food processor
or blender. Soak the gelatine in cold water
for 10 minutes, squeeze out and then
dissolve in the hot wine. Alternatively
dissolve the powdered gelatine in a little hot
water in a bowl over a saucepan of hot water
than stir into the hot wine. Stir into the fruit
purée. Whip the cream and sugar until stiff
and stir in the strawberry purée. Peel the
paper off the sponge, spread with strawberry cream (see photographs on page 31)
and leave in the refrigerator for a few
minutes. Then roll up and dust with icing
sugar. Cut into 12 slices.

Hazelnut Cream Roll

For the sponge:
6 egg yolks
75 g/3 oz caster sugar
1 teaspoon vanilla essence
3 egg whites
50 g/2 oz plain flour
25 g/1 oz cornflour
50 g/2 oz hazelnuts, toasted and ground
baking sheet (36 × 25-cm/14 × 10-in),
lined and greased

For the filling:
600 ml/1 pint double cream
50 g/2 oz caster sugar
100 g/4 oz hazelnuts, toasted and ground

For the praline:
100 g/4 oz caster sugar
75 g/3 oz hazelnuts, chopped
18 whole toasted hazelnuts or chocolate
buttons

Beat the egg yolks with a quarter of the
sugar and the vanilla essence until creamy.
Whisk the egg whites until stiff but not dry
then whisk in the remaining sugar. Fold into
the egg yolk mixture. Sift together the flour
and cornflour and mix with the ground
hazelnuts. Fold into the mixture. Spread the
prepared baking sheet evenly with the
mixture. Bake in a hot oven (230 C, 450 F,
gas 8) for 8 to 10 minutes. Keep an eye on
the sponge after the first 6 minutes for if it
becomes too brown it will break when you
try to roll it. When cooked turn out onto a
cloth.

Whip the cream and sugar until stiff.
Spoon about a quarter of the cream into a
piping bag with a 1-cm/½-in star nozzle and
keep to decorate. Stir the ground hazelnuts
into the remaining cream. Peel off the paper
and spread the hazelnut cream evenly over
the sponge. Roll up and pipe two or three
lengths of cream along the top of the cake,
spread with a palette knife and then smooth
off with a strip of greaseproof paper (see
method for the Frankfurt Ring on page
167).

Make the praline by melting the sugar,
add the chopped hazelnuts and continue as
described on page 147. Finely crush the
praline and sprinkle over the roll. Cut into
12 slices and decorate each with a whirl of
cream topped with a whole hazelnut or a
chocolate button.

Lemon Roll

For the sponge:
6 egg yolks
75 g/3 oz caster sugar
pinch of salt
grated rind of 1 lemon
3 egg whites
75 g/3 oz plain flour
15 g/½ oz cornflour
baking sheet (36 × 25-cm/14 × 10-in),
lined and greased

For the filling:
3 egg yolks
150 ml/¼ pint white wine
100 g/4 oz caster sugar
juice of 2 lemons
grated rind of 1 lemon
6 leaves gelatine or 4 teaspoons
powdered gelatine
300 ml/½ pint double cream
icing sugar for dusting

Use the ingredients to make a sponge for a roll as described on pages 30–1.

Beat the egg yolks with the white wine, sugar, lemon juice and grated lemon rind. Soften the leaf gelatine in cold water for 10 minutes. Heat the egg yolk mixture to just below boiling point, stirring continuously. Squeeze out the leaf gelatine, dissolve in the hot mixture and leave to cool. Alternatively dissolve the powdered gelatine in a little hot water in a bowl over a saucepan of hot water and stir into the mixture. Whip the cream and fold into the cool but still runny mixture. Spread the sponge evenly with the lemon cream. Wait for a few minutes to give the gelatine a chance to work and for the cream to set and then roll up and dust with icing sugar. Cut into 12 slices.

Chocolate Roulade

For the roulade:
6 egg whites
175 g/6 oz caster sugar
1 teaspoon vanilla essence
75 g/3 oz plain chocolate, melted
50 g/2 oz plain flour
baking sheet (43 × 33-cm/17 × 13-in)
lined and greased

For the butter cream:
350 g/12 oz unsalted butter
175 g/6 oz caster sugar
50 g/2 oz cornflour
3 egg yolks
300 ml/½ pint milk
2 tablespoons Kirsch
cocoa powder for dusting
175 g/6 oz raspberry jam to decorate

Whisk the egg white until stiff then gradually whisk in the sugar. Add the vanilla essence and then fold in the melted chocolate with a metal spoon. The egg whites will fall considerably. Finally fold in the sifted flour and pipe the mixture onto the prepared baking sheet. Bake in a hot oven (220 C, 425 F, gas 7) for 10 to 12 minutes. Leave the roulade to cool on the baking sheet for 5 to 10 minutes so that it dries out slightly. This prevents it sweating and sticking to the paper when you try to turn it out of the tin. Prepare the Vanilla Butter Cream (see page 54) and flavour with the Kirsch. Spoon some of the butter cream into a piping bag with a star nozzle and keep to decorate. Spread the remaining cream on the roulade, roll up and dust lightly with the cocoa powder. Cut into 14 slices and decorate each slice with a whirl of butter cream and a dab of jam.

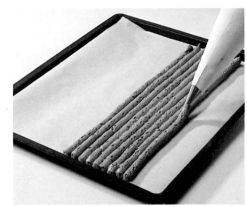

1 **Pipe the chocolate mixture.** The baking sheet should be covered with greaseproof paper. Spoon the mixture into a piping bag with a 1-cm/½-in plain nozzle and pipe lengths of mixture on to the paper. They should not be too close together but just touching with no gaps between.

2 **Bake the sponge as instructed** and leave to cool for a few minutes, then turn out onto a sheet of greaseproof paper. When cool, peel off the paper from the baking sheet. Spread the roulade with raspberry jam and then with an even layer of Kirsch butter cream.

Sponge roll with lemon cream. Using the same recipe for both the sponge and the filling you can vary this recipe by using orange or lime rather than lemon juice. If you use very sweet oranges add a little lemon juice.

3 **Roll up the roulade.** This is quite easy if you use the paper to help you. Lift the paper towards you in both hands so that the roulade automatically rolls up. Move your hands further down the paper and lift and pull again until the sponge is completely rolled.

4 **The finished cake.** Before slicing, dust the roulade with cocoa powder. This helps bring out the rather unusual flavour of this roll with its bitter chocolate sponge contrasting markedly with the raspberry jam and Kirsch butter cream.

Traditional Festive Baking

In Milan there lived an old confectioner who was very poor and whose only possession was a beautiful daughter who was the apple of his eye. His love for the beautiful Adalgisa was shared by a young nobleman with the picturesque name of Ughetto della Tella. If he was to win the daughter the young man had no choice but to go to the father's shop and offer his services as a baker, and he was able to win the old man's favour when he invented a cake which was to make the three of them rich and famous overnight. This was the world famous Milan Panettone.

This is a story which has been handed down through the generations, although at the time of its 'discovery' the Panettone already had a long history. It was one of many Christmas cakes baked in ages past in celebration of the winter solstice, which also include the North German 'Klaben' and the Christian 'Stollen' (adapted into Christian symbolism in the form of a swaddled baby), English fruit cake, Central European fruit loaves, the French Bûche de Noël (a richly decorated sponge roll), the Danish 'Kransekager' made of marzipan and the Epiphany Cake with its fascinating origins in the Roman Saturnalia. Throughout the Middle Ages it was customary to bake a pie for the feast of Epiphany. These contained a small object such as a bean or a small porcelain figure, and whoever found the bean in his portion became 'king for a day'. This is a custom which has recently been revived in Switzerland. These cakes also include the richly decorated 'Grittibänzen' baked in Switzerland for St Nicholas' Day and the New Year pretzels which are a good luck symbol.

Easter is the time for lambs and hares. Pagan spring fertility symbols were later adopted by the Christian world – the name Easter itself is derived from the name of a pagan god. A Russian speciality for Easter is the 'Kulitsh', a yeast-dough cake which is cylindrical in shape and the taller the better.

It is not only for the established festivals of the Christian calendar that cakes have been baked over the centuries. Weddings are equally important and in many areas special cakes are made to celebrate the occasion. The most famous of these is the English wedding cake which has now made its way to the Continent too. Photographs taken at the weddings of Queen Victoria's children in the nineteenth century show the intricacy of the decoration for such cakes: temples, castles, cupids, doves and flowers. And things have not changed greatly today: the modern wedding cake is usually of several tiers, covered in marzipan and then intricately decorated with sugar and icing. There is no other area of cooking so influenced by custom and tradition as the baking of cakes and pastries.

Kulitsch

a Russian Easter loaf

This is a traditional cake made in an unusual shape from an extremely fine and nutritious yeast dough. Like the Passha, a dish made from curds and fruit, it is eaten at Easter, and since the two are usually eaten together here are the recipes for both.

Traditionally the table on which it is served is decorated with brightly coloured eggs.

Kulitsch and Passha are both traditional features of Easter in Russia and the two should be eaten together. The cake which is extremely tall needs a tin or ring of 15-cm/6-in. in diameter and 15-cm/6-in deep. An empty fruit tin cut down to the right size would be ideal.

575 g/1¼ lb strong plain flour
40 g/1½ oz fresh yeast or 20 g/¾ oz dried yeast
300 ml/½ pint lukewarm milk
100 g/4 oz raisins
100 g/4 oz chopped mixed peel
50 g/2 oz blanched almonds, chopped
1 tablespoon rum
225 g/8 oz butter, softened
150 g/5 oz caster sugar
½ teaspoon salt
1 teaspoon vanilla essence
pinch of ground saffron
8 egg yolks
tin of 15-cm/6-in diameter and 15-cm/6-in deep

150 g/5 oz icing sugar
2 tablespoons water
1 tablespoon lemon juice
candied fruit to decorate

In a large bowl (which will later have to take all the ingredients) stir 2 tablespoons of the sifted flour with the crumbled fresh yeast and the lukewarm milk. Cover the bowl and leave in a warm place for about 10 minutes. Alternatively dissolve the dried yeast in the lukewarm milk and leave for 10 minutes or until frothy, then add 2 tablespoons of the sifted flour and leave for a further 10 minutes. In a small basin soak the raisins, chopped peel and almonds in the rum.

In a basin cream the butter with the remaining sugar until light and fluffy, add the flavourings and then beat in the egg yolks one at a time. Add this mixture and the remaining sifted flour to the yeast mixture and beat to give a soft, smooth dough. Cover the bowl with oiled cling film and leave to rise for 1 to 1½ hours or until doubled in size, then work in the fruit. Line the tin with greased greaseproof paper, fill with the mixture, cover with oiled cling film and leave to rise until it has once more almost doubled in volume.

Bake in a moderately hot oven (200 C, 400 F, gas 6) for the first 15 minutes, then reduce the oven to moderate (180 C, 350 F, gas 4) and bake for a further 60 minutes. Check with a wooden skewer to see if the cake is cooked right through. Leave the cake to cool in the tin for 30 minutes, then turn it out and leave until completely cool. Stir the water and lemon juice into the icing sugar to make a thick icing and cover the cake. Decorate with candied fruit.

Passha

an Easter curd dish

You can make a pyramid mould with plywood. To take the quantities given in this recipe the mould will have to be of the following dimensions: base 10 × 10-cm/4 × 4-in, top 7 × 7-cm/3 × 3-in, height 13-cm/5-in. You will need a piece of wood 11 × 11-cm/4½ × 4½-in to weight the curd mixture. A flower pot – even a round one – provides a useful alternative. Use one with a top diameter of about 15 cm/6 in.

150 g/5 oz butter, softened
pinch of salt
5 eggs
300 ml/½ pint soured cream
1 kg/2 lb curd cheese
75 g/3 oz raisins
225 g/8 oz caster sugar
grated rind of 1 lemon
100 g/4 oz blanched almonds
75 g/3 oz chopped mixed peel

12 glacé cherries
candied orange and lemon peel
to decorate

Beat the butter until light and fluffy and then transfer to a saucepan with the salt, eggs, soured cream and curd cheese. Heat the mixture very gently, stirring continuously, but on no account allow it to boil. As soon as any bubbles appear, remove the saucepan from the heat and stir until cold. Stir the raisins into the mixture with the sugar, lemon rind, half the almonds chopped up and the mixed peel.

Line the mould or plant pot with muslin, fill with the curd mixture and press down firmly. Cover with a plate weighted with the wood and chill for 12 hours. Before serving turn the curd out of the mould and remove the muslin. Decorate with glacé cherries, the remaining almonds and candied peel.

Easter Lamb

75 g/3 oz butter, softened
75 g/3 oz caster sugar
2 eggs, separated
grated rind of ½ lemon
100 g/4 oz plain flour
50 g/2 oz cornflour
1 lamb-shaped cake tin, greased and
floured
icing sugar for dusting

Cream the butter with half the sugar, the
egg yolks and lemon rind. Whisk the egg
whites until stiff but not dry then whisk in
the remaining sugar. Fold the whites into
the creamed mixture and then fold in the
sifted flour and cornflour. Pour the mixture
into the prepared tin and bake in a moderate
oven (180 C, 350 F, gas 4) for 25 to 30
minutes. Leave the cake to cool for 5 to 10
minutes before opening the tin. When cold
dust with icing sugar.

Easter Bread

575 g/1¼ lb strong plain flour
40 g/1½ oz fresh yeast or 20 g/¾ oz
dried yeast
300 ml/½ pint lukewarm milk
100 g/4 oz butter
75 g/3 oz caster sugar
1 teaspoon salt
grated rind of 1 lemon
3 egg yolks
100 g/4 oz raisins
1 egg yolk to glaze

Sift the flour into a bowl, make a well in the
centre and in the well stir the fresh yeast into
the lukewarm milk. Cover the bowl and
leave for 15 minutes. Alternatively dissolve
the dried yeast in the lukewarm milk for 10
minutes or until frothy then pour into the
flour well. Melt the butter, add the sugar,
flavourings and egg yolks. Pour this mixture
into the well and then knead all the
ingredients to give a smooth, elastic dough.
Cover with oiled cling film and leave to rise
for 1 to 1½ hours or until doubled in size.
Knead in the raisins. Divide the dough into
two halves, shape each into a ball, place on
the baking sheet and flatten slightly. Brush
with egg yolk, cut a cross on the top and
leave to rise for 15 minutes. Bake in a hot
oven (220 C, 425 F, gas 7) for the first 5
minutes, and then in a moderately hot oven
(190 C, 375 F, gas 5) for 25 to 30
minutes until cooked.

A cross, the symbol of Easter, is cut in the top of
each loaf. First leave the loaves to rise for about
1–1½ hours, then brush with egg yolk and cut a
cross with a sharp knife before leaving the loaves
to rise for a further 15 minutes. The bread should
visibly increase in volume.

Sift the flour into a bowl and make a well in the centre. Crumble the fresh yeast into the well and stir with the lukewarm milk. Alternatively dissolve the dried yeast in the lukewarm milk and leave for 10 minutes or until frothy, then pour into the flour well. Sprinkle this mixture with flour, cover the bowl and leave to stand for 15 minutes. When the flour shows definite cracks pour in the mixture of the melted butter, sugar and salt and work all the ingredients together into the dough. Transfer the dough to the worktop and knead to give a smooth, elastic dough. Return the dough to the bowl, cover with oiled cling film and leave to rise for 1 to 1½ hours or until doubled in size.

Easter Basket

To make the basket you can use a round, oval or – as here – an egg-shaped mould. You can use a special half-egg-shaped mould as used for chocolate eggs, or a cardboard egg can serve the same purpose, but this will have to be covered with two or three layers of foil. It is also a good idea to cover a metal mould with foil for this makes it much easier to remove the basket from the mould after baking.

1 kg/2 lb strong plain flour
40 g/1½ oz fresh yeast or 20 g/¾ oz dried yeast
450 ml/¾ pint lukewarm milk
100 g/4 oz butter, melted
150 g/5 oz caster sugar
1 teaspoon salt
egg yolk to glaze
1 tablespoon preserving sugar
half-egg mould, 28-cm/11-in long
royal icing

1 **Shape about two-thirds** of the dough into thin, even rolls. To cover a mould of the size recommended you will need 15 rolls of about 35-cm/14-in. in length and 18 rolls of about 30-cm/12-in. Begin by placing two lengths at right-angles on the worktop and working from the centre out, weave the lengths under and over.

2 **Make a lattice of dough.** Place a second roll parallel to the first. Place the next length at right-angles and take it under the first length. Place alternate rolls from left to right and top to bottom, weaving them under and over to make an even lattice.

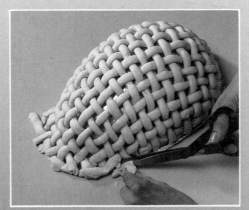

3 **Place over the mould.** First draw the shape of the mould on to greaseproof paper as a guide when you make the rim of the basket and grease with butter. Cover the mould with aluminium foil. Place the lattice of dough over the mould and press it onto the mould lightly. Cut off any excess dough.

4 **To make the foot of** the basket, roll two thin strands of dough of 40-cm/16-in. in length and twist together. Shape into a ring and stick to the base with egg yolk, pressing firmly together. Cover with oiled cling film and leave the dough to rise for 30 minutes then brush lightly with egg yolk before baking.

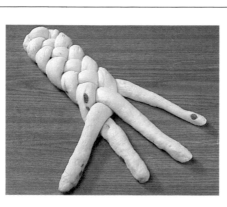

5 Use the remaining dough to make three rolls 110-cm/44-in. in length and weave into a plait 90-cm/36-in long. Place the greaseproof paper on a baking sheet. Place the plait around the shape you drew on the paper and seal the ends. Cover with oiled cling film, leave to rise for 30 to 40 minutes, brush with egg yolk and sprinkle with sugar.

6 Bake the basket in a moderately hot oven (200 C, 400 F, gas 6) for 25 to 30 minutes and the rim for about 20 minutes at the same temperature. When the basket is almost cold turn it over and remove the mould. Then carefully peel away the foil and leave the basket until cold.

7 Assemble the basket. Both the basket and the rim must be completely cold. Spoon the royal icing into a greaseproof piping bag and pipe around the edge of the basket. Carefully slide the rim onto the edge of the basket and press gently into place.

Austrian Plaited Loaf

575 g/1¼ lb strong plain flour
40 g/1½ oz fresh yeast or 20 g/¾ oz dried yeast
300 ml/½ pint lukewarm milk
100 g/4 oz butter, melted
100 g/4 oz caster sugar
1 teaspoon salt
grated rind of 1 lemon
1 egg
75 g/3 oz raisins
75 g/3 oz chopped mixed peel
1 egg yolk to glaze
1 quantity of Apricot Glaze (see page 60)
rum fondant icing

Make a preliminary yeast mixture with 50 g/2 oz flour, the fresh or dried yeast and lukewarm milk, cover the bowl and leave to stand for 15 minutes (see page 46).

Beat the melted butter with the sugar, salt, lemon rind and egg. Add this to the yeast mixture with the remaining flour and work together to give a smooth, elastic dough. Cover and leave to rise for 1 to 1½ hours. Knead in the raisins and mixed peel and then leave

to rise once more. Divide up the dough. Weigh 675 g/1½ lb dough for the four-strand plait, 350 g/12 oz for the three-strand plait and the rest is for the twist. Flatten the bottom plait with the edge of your hand, brush with egg yolk and cover with the next plait. Repeat with the top plait. Cover and leave to rise for a further 45 minutes then brush with egg yolk. Bake in a moderately hot oven (200 C, 400 F, gas 6) for 30 to 40 minutes. Brush with apricot glaze and ice while still warm.

Tirolean Fruit Loaf

'Genuine' fruit loaf is often made with soured bread dough which combines with the fruit to give the loaf an excellent flavour.

225 g/8 oz dried stoned prunes
275 g/10 oz dried pears
225 g/8 oz dried figs
1 litre/2 pints lukewarm water
100 g/4 oz hazelnuts
100 g/4 oz walnuts
100 g/4 oz chopped mixed peel
100 g/4 oz raisins
100 g/4 oz currants
150 g/5 oz caster sugar
1 teaspoon ground cinnamon
½ teaspoon each of allspice, aniseed and salt
1 tablespoon rum
2 tablespoons lemon juice
575 g/1¼ lb bread dough (see page 46)
225 g/8 oz strong plain flour
halved blanched almonds and 1 glacé cherry to decorate

In a covered bowl steep the prunes, pears and figs in the lukewarm water overnight. The next day drain off the water and finely dice the fruit. Coarsely chop the hazelnuts and walnuts and add the chopped peel. Place the fruit, nuts and peel in a bowl with the raisins and currants. Stir in the sugar, flavourings, rum and lemon juice, cover the bowl and steep for at least an hour. Add 150 g/5 oz of the bread dough together with the flour and knead vigorously with the fruit.

Shape the mixture into two longish loaves and smooth the top using wetted hands. Divide the remaining dough into two halves and roll out on a floured worktop as thinly as possible. Wrap each fruit loaf in a sheet of dough, brush the edges with water and squeeze together under the loaf. Place the loaves on a lightly greased baking sheet, cover with a cloth and leave to rise at room temperature for 30 minutes. Then brush the tops with water and decorate with the almonds and glacé cherry. Bake in a hot oven (220 C, 425 F, gas 7) for the first 10 minutes and then in a moderately hot oven (180 C, 350 F, gas 4) for a further 60 to 70 minutes until cooked.

Pear Loaf

This loaf, as it originated in the farmhouse kitchen, was an everyday fruit loaf which used dried pears as the main ingredient. Nowadays recipes include so much dried fruit and nuts that the flavour of the dried pears is much less pronounced. In Germany it is now usual to flavour the fruit with plenty of Kirsch.

350 g/12 oz dried pears
100 g/4 oz dried figs
100 g/4 oz dried prunes, stoned
½ litre/1 pint lukewarm water
450 g/1 lb wholemeal flour
25 g/1 oz fresh yeast or 15 g/½ oz dried yeast
175 g/6 oz caster sugar
½ teaspoon salt
2 teaspoon cinnamon
½ teaspoon ground cloves
grated rind of 1 lemon
50 g/2 oz blanched almonds, chopped
75 g/3 oz blanched hazelnuts

Steep the pears, figs and plums overnight in the water then drain, reserving the liquid, and coarsely chop. Sift the flour into a basin, crumble the fresh yeast into a well in the centre and stir with 150 ml/¼ pint of the lukewarm water in which you soaked the fruit. Leave to stand for about 10 minutes. Alternatively dissolve the dried yeast in the lukewarm water leave for 10 minutes or until frothy then pour into the flour well. Add the sugar and flavourings and knead to make a light dough. Leave to rise for 10 to 15 minutes before working in the fruit, almonds and whole hazelnuts. Shape into a longish loaf, place on a lightly greased baking sheet, cover and leave to rise for about an hour. Bake in a moderate oven (180 C, 350 F, gas 4) for about 1½ hours.

Grittibänz

This is the Swiss version of the 'Saint Nicholas loaf', a figurative loaf that is baked in many areas to celebrate Saint Nicholas' Day. These are simple figures whose only form of decoration are two currants pressed into the dough for eyes. The body is made with a ball of dough which is rolled into a long oval before the legs are made by cutting from the base up to the centre with a knife. The sides are then cut to make the arms.

The Swiss Grittibänz, which were known as 'Chriddibenz' when they first appeared in 1850, are quite intricate fabrications, regardless of whether they come from the confectioner's shop or household kitchen.

1 kg/2 lb strong plain flour
40 g/1½ oz fresh yeast of 20 g/¾ oz dried yeast
450 ml/¾ pint lukewarm milk
100 g/4 oz butter, melted
100 g/4 oz caster sugar
1 teaspoon salt
grated rind of 1 lemon
2 eggs
2 egg yolks and water to glaze

Sift the flour into a bowl, make a well in the centre and in the well stir the crumbled fresh yeast with the luke-warm milk. Alternatively dissolve the dried yeast in the lukewarm milk and leave for 10 minutes or until frothy, then pour into the flour well. Sprinkle this mixture with flour, cover the bowl and leave to stand until the flour shows distinct cracks. Meanwhile melt the butter and beat with the sugar, salt, lemon rind and eggs. Add this mixture to the yeast mixture and work all the ingredients together to make a uniform dough. The dough should be neither too firm nor too soft so that it can be shaped easily. Cover with oiled cling film and leave to rise for 1 to 1½ hours. The figures (two to four from the quantities given) are formed basically from a flattened ball of dough. Then the head is made. The arms, legs and hat are shaped from the ball and stuck with egg yolk then other elements such as beard, nose, eyes, are shaped separately and stuck on with egg yolk. The finished figure is left to rise for at least 20 to 25 minutes and then baked in a moderately hot oven (190C, 375F, gas 5) for 20 to 35 minutes (depending on size).

Panettone

This is one of the best traditional Christmas cakes and, like the Christmas Stollen, is now widely mass-produced, although the conveyor-belt Panettones usually bear little relationship to the handmade or home-made cakes of Milan. The most difficult thing is to achieve the typical Panettone shape (for non-Italian cooks in any case), for it is difficult to get hold of the right tin. These cakes are just as good, however, made in a sponge ring or cake tin, or try using a metal saucepan of the correct size.

675 g/1½ lb strong plain flour
40 g/1½ oz fresh yeast or 20 g/¾ oz dried yeast
300 ml/½ pint lukewarm milk
225 g/8 oz butter
150 g/5 oz caster sugar
1 teaspoon salt
grated rind of 1 lemon
pinch of nutmeg
6 egg yolks
175 g/6 oz chopped mixed peel
150 g/5 oz raisins
75 g/3 oz blanched almonds, chopped

Sift the flour into a bowl, make a well in the centre, crumble the fresh yeast into the well and mix the yeast with the lukewarm milk. Alternatively dissolve the dried yeast in the lukewarm milk and leave for 10 minutes or until frothy then pour into the flour well. Cover this mixture with a layer of flour and leave to stand for 15 to 20 minutes. When the top shows distinct cracks, melt the butter and beat with the sugar, flavourings and egg yolks. Add this mixture to the ingredients in the bowl and stir them all together to give a smooth, light dough. Knead well until the dough is smooth and elastic. Cover the bowl and leave to rise for 20 minutes. Mix the chopped peel with the raisins and almonds, then work into the dough. Cover the bowl with a cloth and leave the dough to rise for a further 15 to 20 minutes.

Cover a baking sheet with greaseproof paper and place a sponge ring on it. Line the sides with lightly greased paper and pour the dough into the ring. Leave to rise for 20 to 25 minutes before baking in a moderately hot oven (190 C, 375 F, gas 5) for 1 hour 20 minutes to 1½ hours. Check with a skewer to see if the cake is cooked right through. Panettone does not keep well and should be eaten within a couple of days. It can be kept longer if it is covered with apricot glaze and fondant icing.

Christmas Stollen

Illustrated on page 162

575 g/1¼ lb strong plain flour
25 g/1 oz fresh yeast or 15 g/½ oz
dried yeast
300 ml/½ pint lukewarm milk
50 g/2 oz caster sugar
1 egg
1 teaspoon vanilla essence
grated rind of ½ lemon
½ teaspoon salt
200 g/7 oz butter
175 g/6 oz raisins
50 g/2 oz blanched almonds, chopped
75 g/3 oz chopped mixed peel
1 tablespoon rum
65 g/2½ oz melted butter for coating
100 g/4 oz icing sugar for sprinkling

Sift 450 g/1 lb of the flour into a bowl, make a well and in the well stir the crumbled fresh yeast with the lukewarm milk. Alternatively dissolve the dried yeast in the lukewarm milk for 10 minutes or until frothy, then pour into the flour well. Sprinkle the mixture with flour, cover the bowl and leave for 20 minutes. Add the sugar, eggs, vanilla essence, lemon rind and salt to the yeast mixture and knead to give a dry, firm dough. Leave the dough to rise for 30 minutes. Work the butter with the remaining flour, work into the yeast dough and then leave the dough to rise for a further 30 minutes. Mix together the raisins, almonds and peel and steep in the rum. Then work the fruit mixture quickly into the dough and leave to rise for a further 30 minutes. Knead gently on a lightly floured board.

Shape the dough into two balls initially and roll these into long loaves of about 30-cm/12-in. Roll the centres of the loaves with the rolling pin so that they are thicker down both sides. Round off the ends and then fold over lengthways into the familiar Stollen shape. Cover a baking sheet with greased paper, place the Stollen on the baking sheet, cover with oiled cling film and leave to rise for 20 to 30 minutes or until it has visibly increased in volume. Bake in a moderately hot oven (200 C, 400 F, gas 6) for about an hour and test with a skewer to make sure that it is cooked through. While still warm brush all over with the melted butter and sprinkle with the icing sugar. This coating of butter and sugar will keep the Stollen moist.

Almond Stollen

450 g/1 lb strong plain flour
25 g/1 oz fresh yeast or 15 g/½ oz
dried yeast
300 ml/½ pint lukewarm milk
1 egg
50 g/2 oz caster sugar
½ teaspoon salt
grated rind of ½ lemon
pinch of nutmeg
150 g/5 oz chopped mixed peel
175 g/6 oz blanched almonds, chopped
75 g/3 oz melted butter for coating
100 g/4 oz icing sugar for sprinkling

Sift the flour into a bowl and crumble the fresh yeast into a well in the centre. Stir with the lukewarm milk, sprinkle with flour and leave to stand until the flour shows distinct cracks. Alternatively dissolve the dried yeast in the lukewarm milk and leave for 10 minutes or until frothy then pour into the flour well and sprinkle with flour. Beat the egg with the sugar and flavourings and add to the yeast mixture. Beat all the ingredients together to give a firm dough and leave to rise for 30 minutes. Mix the chopped peel with the almonds. Work into the dough and then leave to rise for a further 30 minutes.

Make the dough into two loaves as for the Christmas Stollen and place on greased paper on a baking sheet. Cover with oiled cling film and leave to rise for a further 20 to 25 minutes until they have increased visibly in volume. Bake in a moderately hot oven (200 C, 400 F, gas 6) for an hour and then test with a skewer. While still warm brush the loaves with the melted butter and sprinkle with the icing sugar.

Pistachio Nut Stollen

575 g/1¼ lb strong plain flour
25 g/1 oz fresh yeast or 15 g/½ oz
dried yeast
300 ml/½ pint lukewarm milk
1 egg
75 g/3 oz caster sugar
½ teaspoon salt
grated rind of ½ lemon
1 teaspoon vanilla essence
175 g/6 oz butter
175 g/6 oz chopped mixed peel
100 g/4 oz pistachio nuts, finely
chopped
50 g/2 oz icing sugar
1 tablespoon maraschino liqueur
100 g/4 oz marzipan
65 g/2½ oz melted butter for coating
100 g/4 oz icing sugar for sprinkling

Make a smooth, firm dough, using the method described for the Christmas Stollen, with 450 g/1 lb of the flour, the yeast, milk, eggs, sugar and flavourings. Cover the bowl and leave to rise for 10 minutes. Meanwhile work the butter with the remaining flour and peel. Work this mixture into the dough and leave to rise for a further 30 minutes. Work the pistachio nuts, icing sugar and maraschino into the marzipan. Roll this marzipan to about 1-cm/½-in thick and cut into 1-cm/½-in cubes. Work these quickly into the yeast dough so that they remain whole.

Shape the dough to make two Stollen and place on baking paper on a baking sheet. Cover with oiled cling film and leave to rise for 20 to 25 minutes. Bake in a moderately hot oven (200 C, 400 F, gas 6) for 50 to 60 minutes. Brush the melted butter all over the warm Stollen and then sprinkle with the icing sugar.

Chocolate Christmas Cake

450 g/1 lb plain chocolate, finely
chopped
300 ml/½ pint double cream
75 g/3 oz butter
2 tablespoons rum
1 chocolate sponge (see pages 30–1)
1 tablespoon rum
1 tablespoon Cointreau
1 tablespoon sugar syrup (see page 60)

To decorate:
chocolate fans
chocolate leaves
marzipan Santa Claus

Prepare a Canache cream using the chocolate, cream, butter and rum, as described on pages 56–7. Divide the sponge into three layers. Spread the first layer with Canache cream and top with the second. Mix the rum, Cointreau and sugar syrup together and use half to moisten this sponge. Cover with a second layer of cream and then add the top layer and moisten once more with the remaining liquid. Spread the remaining cream over the cake and sprinkle the bottom edge with small chocolate leaves.

To decorate the top make fans from block chocolate (see page 66) and, working from the outside in, arrange in three overlapping rings on the top of the cake. Place the marzipan Santa Claus in the centre.

Bûche de noël

This chocolate log is a traditional French Christmas cake which can be decorated in a variety of ways. The basic cake is always a plain sponge, usually filled with chocolate butter cream, but occasionally with coffee or nut butter cream. It is frequently decorated with green marzipan palm leaves, sometimes with chocolate flowers or, as illustrated, with meringue mushrooms.

For the sponge:
8 egg yolks
100 g/4 oz caster sugar
pinch of salt
grated rind of 1 lemon
5 egg whites
100 g/4 oz plain flour
25 g/1 oz cornflour

For the cream:
350 g/12 oz caster sugar
8 tablespoons water
7 egg yolks
400 g/14 oz butter, softened
50 g/2 oz cocoa powder
75 g/3 oz plain chocolate

For the decoration:
marzipan leaves
meringue mushrooms

Make a sponge roll as described on pages 30–1. Prepare the cream as for French Butter Cream (see page 55). Cream the butter with the cocoa powder and chocolate, then beat in the egg yolks. Spread the sponge with half the butter cream, roll up and cover with a thin layer of cream. Using a piping bag and small fluted nozzle cover the cake with thin strips of cream. The rest is up to you and your imagination. The cake in the photograph is decorated with marzipan leaves and meringue mushrooms.

Galette des rois

This flat puff-pastry pie has long been the traditional dish for Twelfth Night in France north of the Loire and its popularity is spreading to southern France too in recent times.

To serve 12:
1 kg/2 lb puff pastry (see page 32)
450 g/1 lb Almond Cream (see page 56)
1 egg yolk to glaze
50 g/2 oz caster sugar
3 tablespoons water
1 tablespoon rum

The cake is made in the same way as the Pithiviers (see pages 136–7). Halve the chilled puff pastry and roll each half to 3-mm/$\frac{1}{8}$-in thick. Leave the pastry to stand for 10 minutes. Spread one round of pastry with the Almond Cream leaving a 2.5-cm/1-in border. Brush the border with egg yolk, cover with the second round of pastry and seal the edges. Pattern the edges with the back of a slanting knife. Chill for about 30 minutes.

Place the pie on a moistened baking sheet and brush carefully with egg yolk. Using a sharp, pointed knife cut leaf designs into the top layer of pastry, taking care not to cut right through. Leave to stand for a further 15 minutes. Bake in a hot oven (230 C, 450 F, gas 8) for the first 15 minutes and then lower the temperature to moderately hot (200 C, 400 F, gas 6) and bake for a further 20 minutes.

Boil the sugar and water to make a syrup and flavour with the rum. Brush the syrup over the pie as soon as it comes out of the oven.

Epiphany Cake

The baking of special cakes to celebrate Epiphany or Twelfth Night on 6 January is an old custom which has its origins in the Roman Saturnalia (the feast in honour of the god Saturn). This festival of gluttony, in which everyone could take part, was carried over into early Christian Europe. One ingredient of the feast was the choosing of a king. A bean was hidden in a cake and whoever found it became king for a day. The custom of including a bean in a cake – or a coin – still survives today. In Switzerland the custom of the Epiphany cake was revived after the Second World War and has remained popular.

450 g/1 lb strong plain flour
25 g/1 oz fresh yeast or 15 g/$\frac{1}{2}$ oz dried yeast
300 ml/$\frac{1}{2}$ pint lukewarm milk
100 g/4 oz butter
75 g/3 oz caster sugar
1 teaspoon salt
grated rind of 1 lemon
pinch of grated nutmeg
2 eggs
100 g/4 oz raisins
50 g/2 oz blanched almonds, chopped
1 tablespoon rum
1 egg yolk to glaze

Sift the flour into a bowl and make a well in the centre. In the well dissolve the crumbled fresh yeast in the lukewarm milk. Alternatively dissolve the dried yeast in the lukewarm milk, leave for 10 minutes or until frothy then pour into the flour well. Sprinkle the mixture with flour, cover the bowl with a cloth and leave for 15 minutes. Melt the butter and beat with the sugar, flavourings and eggs. Add to the bowl while still warm and work all the ingredients together to make a smooth dough. Knead for 10 minutes or until the dough is smooth and elastic. Cover the bowl and leave to rise for 1 to 1$\frac{1}{2}$ hours. Meanwhile sprinkle the raisins and almonds with the rum and leave to soak. Knead quickly into the risen dough. Divide the dough into two and shape one half into a flattened ball. Place the dough on a lightly greased baking sheet. Divide the remaining dough into seven pieces and shape these into balls. Dilute the egg yolk with a little water. First glaze the large piece of dough, place the smaller ones around it and similarly glaze. Cover with oiled cling film and leave to rise for 45 minutes or until doubled in size, brush once more with egg yolk and then bake in a moderately hot oven (200C, 400F, gas 6) for 35 minutes or until cooked. You can make the Epiphany cake more attractive by dusting with icing sugar or sprinkling with almonds or sugar crystals before baking.

Wedding Cake

A basic rich fruit cake is the starting point for wedding, Christmas and special birthday or occasion cakes. This kind of cake will keep for months, even years, and it is solid enough to allow two or three smaller cakes to be arranged in tiers on it. In Britain it is customary with a wedding cake for the top tier to be kept for the christening of the first child.

Here is the recipe for a 30-cm/12-in round (or 28-cm/11-in square) cake. The quantities can be halved to make a smaller cake which will fit on top.

225 g/8 oz raisins
675 g/1½ lb currants
450 g/1 lb sultanas
175 g/6 oz mixed chopped peel
100 g/4 oz blanched almonds, chopped
5 tablespoons brandy
375 g/13 oz butter, softened
400 g/14 oz soft brown sugar
8 eggs
grated rind of 3 lemons
1 teaspoon nutmeg
2 teaspoons cinnamon
2 tablespoons black treacle
450 g/1 lb plain flour
2 quantities of Apricot Glaze
(see page 60)
1.25 g/2½ lb marzipan
5 egg whites
1.5 kg/2¾ lb icing sugar
juice of ½ lemon

Steep the raisins, currants, sultanas, peel and almonds in the brandy overnight in a covered bowl. Cream the butter and sugar together until light and fluffy, then beat in the eggs one at a time. Stir in the lemon rind, nutmeg and cinnamon then add the treacle. Fold in the sifted flour and finally stir in the steeped fruit, peel and almonds. Place the mixture into a greased and lined tin and bake in a cool oven (140C, 275F, gas 1) for 3 hours. Check the cake at this time by testing with a metal skewer. If it comes out clean the cake is ready. If it is not and the top is becoming too brown cover with a double thickness of greaseproof paper and place back in the oven.

After baking wait at least an hour for the cake to cool slightly before turning out on to a wire rack. When it is cold you can prick the base with a skewer and pour on a little brandy to keep the cake moist. Wrap the cake well in greaseproof paper and store in an airtight tin. Keep for at least a month, preferably longer, before proceeding to the next stage.

Brush about half of the apricot glaze over

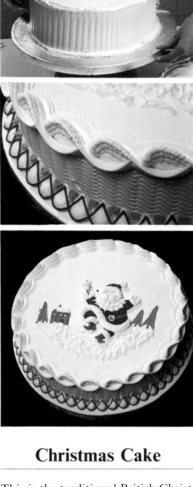

Christmas Cake

This is the traditional British Christmas cake and, like the wedding cake, is made of a dark, heavy fruit cake but is usually more highly spiced. Like the wedding cake it is covered in marzipan and then iced.

The Christmas cake can be made into a real work of art as we see in the photograph of one decorated by Susan Greenway. After the second layer of icing the sides have been given a rippled effect with an icing comb. The decorative edge is made in several stages allowing the icing to harden between each step. The Father Christmas is first outlined using a stencil and then filled in with white and coloured icing – or edible food colourings. Alternatively you can simply spread the second layer of icing roughly with a knife to give the effect of deep snow.

the top of the cake. Roll out about a third of the marzipan to 1-cm/1-in thick and cover the top of the cake. Brush the sides with the remaining glaze and use the rest of the marzipan rolled out into a long strip to cover the sides.

Wait a further couple of months before icing. Make a royal icing by whisking the egg whites until frothy then gradually beat in the icing sugar and lemon juice until the icing appears shiny and very white. Use to cover the cake as illustrated on the right. Leave the cake to dry then repeat the process until there are three or four layers of icing and the surface is very smooth. Patterns of decoration for the cake should be marked out first with greaseproof stencils and then printed on to the cake by sticking a pin through the greaseproof paper on to the icing of the cake. It is very helpful to have a rotating cake stand for this job and a selection of fine icing nozzles are essential.

It is possible for you to make the cake and have the icing done professionally if you are not confident about tackling the job yourself and this is an option worth considering.

Susan Greenway is the wedding cake specialist at the London Intercontinental Hotel. She has decorated this two-tier wedding cake with an admirable accuracy. She uses greaseproof piping bags and a selection of small piping nozzles together with a rotating cake stand which is a great help for both coating and decorating the cake.

Cakes for Special Occasions

Unlike Britain where there is the wedding and Christmas cake, other countries have no traditional recipes or forms of decoration for these cakes. In these countries cakes for special occasions are usually a light sponge filled with a custard cream or whipped cream. These are of fairly recent date and have no lengthy history behind them. There are no special recipes for specific occasions (with the exception of the French Bûche de noël), and no set style or method of decoration. Anything goes!

This lack of tradition has its advantages for there are no established traditions to restrict the choice of a cake for Christmas, Easter, weddings or birthdays. The only criteria is whether the cake is to be made several days in advance or whether time allows it to be made on the day. You can choose from a whole range of plain or filled cakes and you can take advantage of the wide choice either when choosing a cake from a confectioner's or making your own. When choosing a cake for a special occasion you should bear in mind that the prime consideration is that the cake or gâteau should taste good. This is often forgotten in the desire to have a cake that looks good and we tend to expect a birthday or christening cake to be something quite exceptional, as the cake tends to be the high-point of the occasion. You may want to decorate a christening cake with a smiling baby in pink marzipan or to make a Donald Duck for a child's birthday cake and this can be someting of a problem. Many housewives will set about the task with enthusiasm and often with some success, but the professional chef should assess his artistic capabilities more realistically and try to influence his customers in other directions. It is obviously better for a cake to be simple but perfect rather than attempting intricate decoration that does not really come off. In the final analysis it is the taste of the cake that always determines whether or not it has been a success.

Almond Butter Cream Cake

This butter cream cake has the simplest of decoration. The marzipan figures can be made well in advance and a supply of these amusing figures will quickly turn any ordinary butter cream or cream cake into something special. They can also be used on gâteau which you have already decorated in portions.

> 50 g/2 oz marzipan
> 6 eggs, separated
> 1 teaspoon vanilla essence
> pinch of salt
> 100 g/4 oz caster sugar
> 50 g/2 oz biscuit crumbs
> 75 g/3 oz ground almonds
> 50 g/2 oz plain flour
> 25-cm/10-in cake tin, greased and floured
>
> 350 g/12 oz butter
> 150 g/5 oz caster sugar
> 40 g/1½ oz cornflour
> 3 egg yolks
> 600 ml/1 pint milk
> 1 vanilla pod
> 25 g/1 oz plain chocolate, melted
>
> 1 tablespoon Amaretto (almond liqueur)
> 1 tablespoon sugar syrup
> flaked almonds, toasted and ground
> 3 glacé cherries, halved

First work 1 egg yolk into the marzipan until creamy. Transfer to a mixing bowl and beat with the remaining egg yolks, vanilla essence, salt and a third of the sugar. Whisk the egg whites until stiff but not dry then gradually whisk in the remaining sugar. Fold the whites into the yolk mixture and finally fold in a mixture of the crumbs, ground almonds and sifted flour. Pour the mixture into the prepared tin and bake in a moderately hot oven (190 C, 375 F, gas 5) for 35 to 40 minutes. Leave the cake overnight and then cut into three layers.

Prepare the butter cream as described on page 54. Stir the melted chocolate into a quarter of the cream and spread on the first sponge. Cover with the second sponge and moisten with a mixture of Amaretto and syrup. Spread this layer with vanilla butter cream, cover with the last sponge and moisten once more. Cover the cake with a thin layer of cream, chill and then re-cover. Cover the sides quite thickly and ripple with an icing comb. Sprinkle the top with the almonds and decorate with whirls of butter cream, glacé cherry halves and marzipan decorations.

Chocolate Hedgehogs

These jolly hedgehogs show that there are other ways of using sponge cake besides the usual round cake. You can cut up a round sponge base to make the hedgehogs or bake them individually in special tins. The following ingredients will make two hedgehogs.

> *For the sponge:*
> 5 eggs
> 2 egg yolks
> 150 g/5 oz caster sugar
> ½ teaspoon grated lemon rind
> 150 g/5 oz plain flour
> 25 g/1 oz cornflour
> 100 g/4 oz butter, melted
>
> *For the filling:*
> 350 g/12 oz butter
> 150 g/5 oz caster sugar
> 50 g/2 oz cornflour
> 3 egg yolks
> 300 ml/½ pint milk
> 1 vanilla pod
> 75 g/3 oz chocolate, melted
> 100 g/4 oz blanched almonds, cut into spikes
> 500 g/18 oz plain chocolate
> marzipan and icing to decorate

Prepare a Genoese sponge as shown on pages 28–9. Bake in oval sponge tins or in hedgehog tins, previously greased and floured. Leave the sponge overnight if possible and then cut into three layers.

Make a Vanilla Butter Cream as shown on page 54 and flavour with the melted chocolate. Sandwich the three layers together with two-thirds of the butter cream and spread the remainder over the hedgehogs. Stick the almond spikes all over the body but leave the heads free. Chill until the cream has set slightly. Place the hedgehogs on a wire rack and cover with the melted chocolate. Leave to set and then cut away the wire rack. Make a nose out of marzipan and fix it in place. Pipe the whites of the eyes with white icing and use a dab of chocolate for the pupils.

Glossary

A

Agar-Agar, jellying agent made from several types of East Asian seaweeds.

Agen prunes, semi-dried plums, a speciality of Agen, a French town on the Garonne.

Almond Cream, an almond confectioner's cream made with butter, ground almonds, icing sugar, eggs and cornflour. Used for cake fillings and also in flans either alone or with fruit, see page 56.

Almond essence, finely ground, sweet almonds are heated in milk or water and then drained through a muslin cloth. Used for almond milk, blancmange, etc.

Almond liqueur, an aromatic liqueur made by distilling pulped almonds.

Almond liqueur, an aromatic liqueur made by distilling pulped almonds.

Almond paste → Marzipan.

Almond sponge mixture, a sponge mixture made by beating the egg yolks and whites separately and adding ground almonds or marzipan with the flour.

Amaretto → Almond liqueur.

Angelica, a plant classed as a herb, the stalks of which are candied and used as a decoration for desserts.

Antilles rum, type of rum distilled in the Greater and Lesser Antilles.

Apostle cake → Brioches, see pages 116–17.

Apricot brandy, a brandy-based fruit liqueur made with fresh or dried apricots.

Apricot glaze, a glaze made with apricot jam, sugar, water and lemon juice. Used mainly as an insulating layer between the cake and the icing or other covering, see page 60.

Arancini, dried and candied orange peel cut into round slices.

Armagnac, famous brandy from south-west France with minimum alcohol content of 38 per cent proof. It matures in oak vats and its flavour is excellent for cake fillings.

Arrak, a brandy with three different methods of preparation. Usually made from rice, but occasionally from molasses and in South-East Asia from palm wine (made by tapping the sap of the coconut palm). Excellent for flavouring cream fillings.

B

Baba, ring-shaped yeast cake soaked in spirits or syrup.

Baiser, meringue mixture of egg whites and sugar, see page 34.

Baumé, Antoine, French chemist (1728–1804), inventor of the saccharometer. The scale is divided into units known as Bé, a shortened version of his name.

Bavarian cream, type of custard made with egg yolk, sugar, milk, vanilla, gelatine and whipped cream, see page 53.

Bavaroise → Bavarian cream.

Beef suet, once used in the baking of Christmas Stollen and mixed with butter to make puff pastry.

Bénédictine, strongly-flavoured, French herb liqueur.

Bergamot liqueur, pear liqueur.

Bienenstich, flat yeast cake spread with a mixture of butter, sugar, honey and flaked almonds before baking and filled with whipped cream once cold. See Honey and Almond Slices, page 119.

Binding agent, a substance which thickens a liquid and makes it smooth. Examples include: corn, rice and potato starch, Agar-Agar, gelatine, tragacanth, pectin and gum arabic.

Biscuits à la cuiller → Sponge fingers.

Biskotte, Austrian term for sponge fingers.

Black bun, Scottish fruit cake with extremely high currant content.

Bremen Klaben, a kind of Stollen made with yeast dough and containing almonds, raisins and currants. Baked for special occasions particularly at Christmas.

Bun cases, paper cases with pleated sides in various sizes for small cakes, petits fours or sweets.

Butter pastry, Austrian term for puff pastry.

C

Calvados, French apple brandy which matures for about six years in oak casks. Named after the area in which it originated.

Cannelle, cinnamon bark.

Cannelons, tubes of marzipan filled with whipped cream or light butter cream.

Caramel, brown, burnt sugar.

Chaudeau, a frothy wine sauce, served hot.

Chocolate, cooking, a substitute for eating chocolate, made basically from vegetable fat and with a low cocoa content.

Cherry brandy, sweet, brandy-based liqueur, made from cherry juice and crushed cherry stones.

Chestnut → Marron.

Chestnut purée → Marron purée.

Christmas log → Bûche de noël, see page 172.

Coffee essence, extremely strong extract of coffee beans.

Cognac, French brandy from the Charente region, which has to mature for several years in oak casks.
Cointreau, light French liqueur, flavoured with orange rind.
Confectioner's cream, *crème patissière*, made with sugar, egg yolk, flour or cornflour, milk and vanilla, see page 50.
Copra, dried kernel of the coconut which is rich in fat.
Cordial Médoc, French liqueur made from Cognac, peel of Curaçao oranges and dessert wine.
Cornflour, swells in liquid at 60–70 C/140–150 F. Used as a binding agent in the making of custards, sweet sauces, etc; binds at simmering point, see page 12.
Cream of tartar, sour potash of tartaric acid which during fermentation precipitates the production of alcohol.
Crème, term applied to a number of very sweet French liqueurs, made generally from fruit, for example:
Crème d'ananas – pineapple liqueur
Crème de cacao – chocolate liqueur
Crème de cassis – blackcurrant liqueur
Crème des fraises – strawberry liqueur
Crème de menthe – green mint liqueur
Crème de moka – coffee liqueur
Crème de prunelle – sloe liqueur.
Crème bavaroise – Bavarian cream, see page 53.
Crème Chantilly, sweet whipped cream, see page 51.
Crème de truffes, another name for Canache cream, see page 56.
Crème fouettée, whipped cream.
Crème patissière, confectioners cream, see page 50.
Crème Saint Honorè, Chiboust cream, a light cream for cake fillings, see page 51.
Crumbs, grated bread, sponge or biscuits.
Curaçao, orange liqueur, made originally with the rinds of curaçao oranges, cane sugar and brandy, made nowadays with a base of wine brandy, gin and other brandies.
Curds, the cheese-like substance produced when milk turns sour.
Custard sauce, eggs beaten with sugar and milk (flavoured with vanilla or lemon rind). Used with fruit pies, for example.

D

Diplomat cream, cold vanilla custard (confectioner's cream) flavoured with a liqueur and mixed with an equal quantity of whipped cream.
Doughnuts, balls of yeast dough which are deep-fried. English and American term.
Duchesses, small choux pastries.

E

Éclair, long French cakes of choux pastry, filled with custard or cream and then iced, see page 157.
Egg Canache, a Canache cream made with milk chocolate and egg yolks.
English cream → Vanilla sauce.
Essence, concentrated liquid used for flavouring.

F

Feuillantines, small cakes of puff pastry.
Fig cake, ground hazelnuts beaten with sugar, butter and egg yolks and then egg whites followed by flour, cinnamon, grated nutmeg, chopped dates, walnuts and figs and grated lemon rind folded into the mixture. The cake tin is lined with Linz pastry, filled with the mixture and baked.
Florentines, flat cakes which keep well, made with butter, sugar, honey, cream, almonds and candied orange peel. These round cakes are coated with chocolate after cooking and decorated with an icing comb.
Fondant, fondant icing. A thick white icing of boiled sugar, in contrast to royal icing which is made cold from egg whites and sugar. To use, fondant should be warmed to body temperature over a pan of hot water, see page 60.
Frangipane, cooked cake filling made with flour or cornflour, eggs, milk and vanilla mixed with finely crushed macaroons. A mixture of almond cream and confectioner's cream is also known as frangipane.

Fruit brandy, made from fermented fruit or fruit juice, either berries, core or stone fruits. Unfermented fruit distilled with alcohol produces a spirit, e.g. raspberry spirit.
Fruit purée, pulped and strained fruit.
Fruit syrup, fruit juice and sugar.

G

Galette, plain flat cake containing a lot of butter and cooked on a baking sheet.
Gâteau, French term for any type of large cake. They can vary in shape, be filled or unfilled, iced or un-iced, but are usually decorated in some way, although this is not essential.
Gaufres, French term for waffles.
Gelatine, pure, tasteless substance derived by prolonged boiling of animal or fish bones. A jellying agent in powder or leaf form. Its main use in baking is for custards and jellies. There is no difference in strength between leaf or powder gelatine. Leaf gelatine should be soaked in cold water for 10 minutes, squeezed out, then added to the hot liquid. Powdered gelatine should be dissolved in a little hot water in a bowl over a saucepan of hot water.
Genoese, fine sponge mixture, see pages 28–9.
Gingerbread glaze, edible starch heated and boiled with water. Used to give a shine to gingerbread, macaroons, etc.
Glacé fondante → Fondant.
Glacé icing, sugar stirred to a thick paste with hot water and flavoured.
Glacé royale → Royal icing.
Glucose, grape sugar or dextrose, together with fructose, a natural sugar found in fruit.
Grand Marnier. French Cognac-based liqueur, flavoured with bitter oranges.
Grappa. Italian grape brandy.
Grillage. Austrian term for melted sugar with coarsely chopped nuts.
Gum arabic (Senegal gum, acacia gum). Obtained from the sap of tropical acacia trees. Comes as a colourless powder to be diluted in twice the amount of water and used to glaze macaroons, etc.

H

Hazelnut cake, mixture of Genoese sponge with ground hazelnuts, baked in round or square tin. The cake is cut into four or five rounds, then sandwiched together and coated in hazelnut butter cream. Decorated with chopped, toasted hazelnuts and icing sugar.

Hutzelbrot, highly spiced fruit loaf of yeast dough with prunes and stewed pears. An Advent speciality.

I

Icing, sugar or chocolate coating for desserts, or small and large cakes.

Indians, Austrian name for Chocolate Sponge Drops, see pages 154–5.

Irish Mist, name of a liqueur which consists of Irish whiskey flavoured with herbs.

Italian meringue, whisked egg whites sweetened with sugar syrup, used in butter cream.

J

Jelly, jellified fruit juice, eaten plain or with a filling.

K

Kipferl, Austrian term for croissants.

Kirschröster, easy cherry cake, made with cherries, grated breadcrumbs and an egg custard.

Kirsch, brandy made with the fermented pulp of small black cherries. Made in the Black Forest and Vosges areas and in Switzerland.

Kithul palm (*Caryota urens*), type of sugar palm; sap is tapped from the trunk and flower buds to make sugar.

Klöben, crescent-shaped yeast cakes, filled with chopped almonds, currants and candied peel.

Königskuchen, a cake made by creaming butter with egg yolks, sugar and grated lemon peel before folding in flour, whisked egg white and dried fruit. Baked in greased, paper-lined loaf tin. See Rum and Raisin Cake, page 76.

Kransekager, Danish speciality. Rings of macaroon mixture decorated with piped royal icing and put together to form a tall, tower-like cake.

L

Lebkuchen, general term covering spice cake, gingerbread and honey cake.

Lemon sugar (orange sugar), cube or loaf sugar used to grate the rind of citrus fruit.

Liebesknochen, German name for éclairs.

Linz pastry, almond shortcrust, see pages 40–1.

M

Macaroons, small cakes made with ground almonds, sugar and egg whites.

Mandarinette, a liqueur flavoured with mandarin peel.

Maraschino, Italian liqueur made with a brandy of fermented Marasca cherries (Dalmatia) and spices.

Margarine, butter and fat substitute, originally usually made from beef suet but nowadays from vegetable fats.

Marille, Austrian name for apricots.

Marron, edible chestnut (*Castanea sativa* or *C. vesca*). Cultivated chiefly in the Mediterranean region. Available fresh in autumn and winter, but all the year round sweetened or unsweetened in tins or in purée form.

Marron purée, butter and sugar are heated and then used to caramelise peeled chestnuts before milk is added and cooked until the chestnuts are soft. It is then puréed in a blender and mixed with whipped cream.

Marsala, Italian dessert wine, sweet or dry. Excellent for flavouring a variety of custards.

Marzipan, preparation made with sweet almonds and sugar. Used to decorate and cover cakes, in almond cream and in a variety of cake mixtures.

Melon or pumpkin seeds, these dried seeds can be used instead of almonds, particularly to sprinkle on cakes.

Meringue, whisked egg white that contains no trace of yolk. Sugar is gradually added during whisking. Also small cakes of sweetened whisked egg whites which are dried out in the oven rather than baked, see page 34.

Mikado Gâteau, consists of three Genoese sponges and three meringue bases, sandwiched together and coated with rum butter cream, sprinkled with chopped, toasted almonds and dusted with icing sugar.

Mince Pie, filled with a mixture of raisins, sultanas, chopped almonds and apple, suet, sugar, spices and rum or brandy. Baked between two layers of puff pastry to make small tarts, eaten hot. British speciality particularly for Christmas.

Mirabell, a brandy made with mirabelle plums which can be produced either by the fermentation process or by distilling unfermented fruit.

Mirliton, small puff pastry tarts.

Mostacciole, small, rectangular, Italian cakes, flavoured with cloves and nutmeg and covered in chocolate.

Muffins, English yeast-dough cakes.

Muffkuchen, Cinnamon and almond sponge cake from Germany.

N

Napfkuchen, cakes, usually of yeast mixture, baked in a deep, round (Gugelhupf) tin.
Necci, Italian chestnut cake.
Negerküsse, small sponges or biscuits, sandwiched with meringue as whipped cream and coated in chocolate.
Nid de Pâques, French Easter basket. A sponge ring sandwiched with butter cream and piped all over with a spaghetti piping nozzle. Decorated with sugar eggs.
Nonpareilles, hundreds and thousands; tiny, coloured sugar sweets.

P

Palmier, small puff pastry cakes, also known as pigs' ears.
Paris-Brest cake, choux mixture piped in a thick ring onto a baking sheet and baked. Cut through horizontally and filled with Saint Honoré cream mixed with crushed praline. Dusted with icing sugar.
Paris cream, a chocolate cream, made by boiling 300 ml/½ pint double cream and stirring in 255 g/8 oz plain chocolate. When cold it is whisked (Canache, see page 56).
Pâte à choux, choux pastry, see page 36.
Pâte brisée, rub-in pastry, see page 37.
Pâte feuilletée, puff pastry, see pages 42–3.
Pâte levée, yeast pastry, see page 44.
Pâte sucrée, sweet shortcrust, see page 38.
Peach Brandy, a liqueur with brandy base, made with fresh or dried peaches.
Pectin, a soluble jellying agent obtained from plants, which combines with fruit acids and sugar to form a jelly. Extracted from unripe fruit such as apples, quinces, currants, lemons and sugar beet. Commercially prepared apple or beet pectin comes in liquid or powder form. Used in flan glazes and to make jellies and jams.
Persipan, marzipan substitute, made by heating the ground kernels of apricot or peach stones with sugar.

Petits fours, small biscuits served with after-dinner coffee, can be filled with cream or iced, or served plain.
Pie, a pastry dish, either savoury or sweet, made in a ceramic dish with a filling and lid of shortcrust, puff or rub-in pastry.
Pigs' ears, puff pastry rolled on sugar, folded twice into the centre and cut into thick slices. Caramelises during baking, see page 127.
Pinza, Italian yeast-dough Easter bread which has a deep cross cut into the top.
Piping icing, a very thick sugar icing applied with a piping bag to make delicate sugar decorations such as whirls, flowers, etc.
Pithiviers, thin round base of left-over puff pastry, with puff pastry rim and lid and filling of almond cream, see pages 136–7.
Platz, yeast cake from Thuringia.
Platzek, flat Polish cakes of various flavours.
Port, red or white Portuguese dessert wine. Matures for three years in oak casks. Maximum alcohol content 25 per cent. Dry to semi-sweet.
Potato flour, potato starch.
Praline, confection of almonds and burnt sugar, see page 147.
Profiteroles, small choux pastry cakes with cream or custard filling.
Prophet cake, large yeast dough cake (Brioche).
Purée, pulp of various kinds of fruit.
Putitz, type of Strudel cake made with yeast pastry.

Q

Quillets, small sponge cakes

R

Raffinade, refined sugar, see page 17.
Rahm, name for cream in southern Germany and Switzerland.

Regent Cake → Prince Regent Cake, see page 142.
Rehrücken, chocolate sponge cake baked in a long tin, spiked with almond sticks and covered in melted chocolate, see page 77.
Rodonkuchen, kind of Napfkuchen.
Roquille, preserved peel of Seville oranges.
Roulade, sponge roll, see pages 30–1.
Royal icing, white sugar icing made with icing sugar, egg white and lemon juice.
Royale, egg custard.
Rum, distilled spirit of which the best types are made from fresh sugar cane. Other types are made from molasses. As well as classifying rums by country of origin as in Jamaica or Cuba rum, there is also either white (colourless) or brown rum, coloured with sugar colouring.

S

Sabayon, frothy wine sauce made with egg yolks, sugar, spices and white wine which are whipped in a bain-marie. An accompanying sauce to desserts.
Saint-Honoré cake, Gâteau Saint-Honoré, named after the patron saint of French bakers, see page 140.
Salambos, short, wide cakes filled with vanilla confectioner's cream. The top is dipped in sugar and sprinkled with chopped pistachio nuts.
Sand cake, plain round sponge cake.
Sauce, mixture of milk, egg and sugar which is poured over a variety of cakes or puddings.
Savarin, ring-shaped yeast cake, baked in a special savarin tin, soaked in syrup and liqueur while still hot and with a variety of fillings.
Savoy sponge, a fine sponge cake baked in a sandwich tin which is eaten plain with fruit or chocolate sauce or stewed fruit.
Schlotfeger (Chocolate Chimneys), a marzipan mixture which is rolled into a tube around a rolling pin after cooking, before covering with chocolate and filling with whipped cream, see page 157.

Sherry, Spanish dessert wine from Jerez, available either dry or sweet.

Shoe Soles, rounds of thinly rolled puff pastry, rolled over granulated sugar into ovals. Caramelised during baking, see page 126.

Slivovitz, fine plum brandy, with crushed plum stones added during distillation.

Spanish wind, small half-spherical meringues.

Sponge, light cake made either with or without butter and baked in various shapes.

Sponge fingers, light biscuits used in the making of several cakes and puddings. An essential ingredient of making some desserts.

Spritzkuchen, balls of choux pastry formed by piping and then fried in hot oil, see Fried Choux Cakes, page 129.

Starch, edible, finely ground wheat, corn or potato flour. Used in cake mixtures, custards and for binding.

Strauben, sweets fried in fat.

Striezel, long plaited, yeast-dough cake, see page 167.

Strudel, a dessert made with pastry stretched extremely thin, covered with a filling, rolled up and baked in a flat pan.

Stuten, long cake-like loaf made with raisins and currants.

Sugar, boiling:

Short thread: 106 C/223 F, wet your index finger and thumb and pinch a little syrup between them. When you open and close your fingers quickly a short thread should be formed.

Long thread: 113 C/236 F, test as for short thread to give a longer thread. This highly concentrated syrup is used for stewed fruit and jam making.

Bubble: 112 C/237 F, dip a small wire ring in the syrup and blow gently. Small bubbles should form.

Large bubble: 114 C/238 F, test as for bubble but blow harder. Large bubbles should form. Used for fondant or Italian meringue.

Soft ball: 116 C/240 F, take a little syrup from a wooden spoon and dip immediately into iced water. The sugar should easily form a ball. Used for Italian meringue or butter cream.

Hard ball: 130 C/265 F, when a little syrup is poured into iced water it forms a ball,

sets immediately but remains slightly sticky.

Soft crack: 140 C/275 F, when dropped into iced water the syrup separates into threads which are hard but not brittle.

Hard crack: 150 C/300 F, the syrup separates into hard and brittle threads in iced water. Sugar, crystalised, white sugar in fairly large crystals used mainly to sprinkle on loaves and cakes.

Sugar, spun, sugar boiled with 3 per cent glucose to 145 C/288 F and then pulled to and fro with a whisk to make extremely fine threads of sugar.

Sugar colouring, dark-brown sugar syrup. Caramel is heated to over 180 C/350 F, i.e. burnt. Hot water is then added and the liquid brought to the boil. Used to colour cream fillings, fondant, etc.

Sugar syrup, made by boiling 450 g/1 lb sugar with 600 ml/1 pint water for 1 minutes to 102 C/220 F on the sugar thermometer. Can be made in advance and stored until needed. Used to moisten cakes, to stew fruit, as a glaze or to dilute fondant.

Süster, yeast-dough cake with almonds.

Syrup, thick concentrated sugar solution sometimes with fruit juices or extracts added. Also glucose syrup obtainable from chemists. Also home-made boiled sugar made by dissolving 450 g/1 lb sugar in 300 ml/½ pint water.

T

Tarte, French name for flat fruit flans (baking sheet flans), whereas gâteau refers to a taller cake.

Tartelette, French term for small shortcrust tart cases which are baked blind. Can be filled with custard, jelly, fruit and cream.

Tia Maria, coffee liqueur.

Tiered cake, cake made by combining two cakes of different size.

Thousand-leaf cake → Gâteau Millefeuille, see page 136.

Treacle, syrup made from the tapped sap of the sugar palm.

V

Vacherin Chantilly, filling of whipped cream and vanilla. Decorated with whipped cream, candied cherries and angelica.

Vacherin glacé, Vacherin with ice-cream filling, decorated with whipped cream.

Vanilla cream, whipped cream flavoured with vanilla: Chantilly cream, see page 51.

Vanilla sauce, custard; sauce made with milk, egg yolks, sugar and vanilla. Served separately with various desserts or as the basis for a range of flavoured custards.

Vanilla sugar, flavouring of sugar with at least 5 per cent vanilla pod pith.

Vanillin, flavouring which tastes and smells of vanilla. Forms naturally in vanilla pods through fermentation. Also manufactured synthetically, but of lower quality.

W

Wafers, thin, pale-coloured biscuits made by taking a mixture of flour and water. Used as a base for cakes made with delicate almond sponge. Sometimes used to form layers for cakes.

Wähe, Swiss flans, both sweet and savoury.

Weinbrand, brandy made in the same way as Cognac by distilling wine.

Whisky, spirit made by distilling fermented barley, rye, wheat and maize. Scottish whisky is made chiefly from barley malt and has a slightly smoky flavour. A similar grain spirit from Ireland is spelt 'Whiskey' as is that from America which is, however, made almost exclusively from maize. Minimum alcohol content 43 per cent.

Wiesbaden pineapple cake, waffles sandwiched together with nougat, marzipan and pineapple jam and covered with chocolate.

Windmasse, meringue mixture usually made with boiled sugar.

Z

Zabaglione, Italian wine dessert, usually made with Marsala.

Technical Terms Explained

A

au four, baked or browned in the oven.

B

bain-marie, a container partially filled with hot water over which custards or cake mixtures are beaten warm or foods kept warm.

batterie, a set of kitchen utensils, e.g. bowls or pans in assorted sizes.

batterie de pâtisserie, baking utensils.

beurre manié, a mixture of flour and butter.

binding, to make a liquid thicker by adding eggs, gelatine or starch.

blanching, to plunge almonds or pistachio nuts in boiling water and then to peel off the skins; to boil briefly; to plunge fruits (e.g. peaches) into boiling water to loosen the skin.

blind, bake, the baking of pastry cases unfilled or lined with greaseproof paper and weighted with dried beans which are removed after baking.

browning, to quickly colour a cake or mixture (meringue) in a hot oven.

C

candying, covering fruit or fruit rind with a thick sugar solution and then drying.

caramelise, coating or mixing (e.g. nuts) with sugar cookecd to a caramel.

chemise, outside coating.

clarifying, (of butter) to remove impurities by heating over a gentle heat and straining the clear fat into a separate bowl leaving the sediment behind.

coating, to cover cakes, flans, with butter cream, whipped cream, flaked almonds etc.

confectioner, baker of sweet cakes which are often sold on the premises with tea or coffee.

couleur, colouring, particularly brown sugar colouring.

creaming, beating butter or fat with some other ingredient or alone until light and fluffy.

D

decoration, embellishment of a cake or flan.

deep-frying, frying pieces of dough or fritters in plenty of hot fat until golden brown.

dough, general term for mixtures of ingredients made by the kneading process (unlike cake mixtures which are beaten).

drain, to remove liquid by pouring through a sieve.

dunking, dipping cakes or praline in melted chocolate

F

fashion, to give shape to, to form.

fermenting, the ripening process in a yeast mixture.

filter, to drain off liquid through a fine sieve or paper.

flaming, pouring alcohol over a dish (e.g. Christmas pudding) and then setting light to it, so that the alcohol is burnt off to leave only the flavour of the spirit.

flouring, dusting tins, moulds with flour after greasing with butter; sprinkling the worktop with flour.

fluted, with a ribbed or pleated edge, e.g. tins.

folding in, combining whisked mixtures such as egg whites with other ingredients so that the volume is not lost. Best achieved with a metal spoon.

frappé, chilled in ice.

friture, deep fat for frying doughnuts or fritters.

G

gimblettes, rings of choux pastry.

glazing, to cover a cake or pastry with a substance which gives it a shiny surface; used specifically of boiled, strained apricot jam or egg yolk.

gratinate, to brown the top of a dish.

greasing, to coat the inside of a tin with butter or oil to make it easier to remove the food from the tin after baking.

I

icing, sugar coating spread over cakes or pastries.

L

liaison, thickening.
lining, covering the insides of a tin or dish with thinly rolled pastry.

M

macerate, to soak chopped or whole fruits, pieces of sponge cake, etc., in a liqueur or spirit sweetened with icing sugar.
marinate, to season and make tender by soaking.
masking, to cover a mould or tin with a thin covering of jelly before adding the filling.
mixture, general term for sponge. meringue, etc., in uncooked state. A preparation made with eggs which is mixed by the beating process (unlike dough which is kneaded).
model, old-fashioned baking mould often of carved wood; to shape, form, e.g. marzipan.
moisten, to soak sponges and small cakes with sugar syrup (flavoured with fruit juice, liqueur or spirit).

O

oily, used to describe marzipan when it has been handled too much and the almond oil separates from the other ingredients.
oxidise, when raspberries, currants or black cherries turn blue or purple after stewing in pans that contain lead or are zinc-coated. Use only enamel or steel pans for cooking these fruits.

P

panaché, striped in various colours.
patisserie, section of a hotel kitchen in which fine cakes are made, or place where they are baked, sold or eaten.
patissier, pastry-cook, chef, responsible for the making of desserts.

perfuming, to give a dish a particular flavour and smell by adding an aromatic ingredient such as an essence, liqueur or spirit.
piping, shaping a mixture before cooking by using a piping bag and nozzle.
poaching, slow cooking in liquid without boiling.
praline, chopped almonds cooked in sugar to caramelise (see page 147).
pulp, fresh fruit mashed then passed through a sieve, liquidiser or blender.

R

ratafia, collective name for all sweet fruit liqueurs.
reduce, boiling a liquid to thicken it. Reduces the volume and increases the flavour.
refreshing, cooling hot food quickly by dipping in cold water.
renversé (e), upside-down, turned out of the tin.
rolling out, making pastry thin evenly by rolling to and fro with a wooden rolling pin.
royal (e), made with egg jelly.

S

sandwiching, joining together two cakes by means of cream, etc.
separating, dividing eggs into yolks and whites.
serving, preparing for presentation at the table.
setting, point at which a jelly, custard, mixture begins to thicken or become firm.
simmering, to boil very gently and slowly.
skimming, removing the scum which rises to the top of a liquid in order to clarify a sauce, for example.
strain, to pass through a sieve in order to reduce to a pulp or remove lumps.

T

temper, to warm chocolate slowly to 32 C/90 F before use, to produce an even texture and give a good flavour.
thickening, to partly bind a liquid with starches (e.g. fruit juice); to heat a custard to just below boiling point so that it coats the back of a spoon, or forms ripples when you blow on it.
turning out, removing food from the container in which it has been cooked or allowed to set.
turns, repeated rolling and folding of puff or croissant pastry.

V

vanilla, flavoured with vanilla.

W

whipping, beating cream, a sauce or custard with a whisk to make it lighter by working in air.
whisking, to beat until light and stiff.

Z

zest, thinly peeled rind of oranges, lemons or limes.
Zuckerbäcker, originally a tradesman who made refined cane sugar into loaf form. The term later came to be applied to any chef who made pastries with sugar decorations. Still used in Austria for a confectioner.

Dividing cakes into portions

Round cakes and gâteaux can be divided into equal portions simply and exactly by using a special cutter in plastic or tin (see overleaf). However most people do not have a cutter of this kind and have to rely on a long knife and judging by eye. The diagrams on the right should prove helpful in this case.

The basic rule is that the deeper and richer the cake, the more slices you can get from it. When deciding how many portions you are going to divide the cake into, you should also bear in mind that a fragile or soft cake cannot be cut into very small portions without breaking. Flat cakes such as fruit flans will usually cut into 12 portions. Cakes of medium depth (poppy-seed or lemon cake) will usually make 14 portions. Cream or butter cream gâteaux can be cut into 16 or 18 portions depending on size and depth. For 12 portions you need to make six diagonal cuts. The first cut divides the cake in half. The second and third cuts will divide the cake into sixths. These segments are then halved with three further cuts.

For 14 portions you need seven diagonal cuts. First cut the cake in half. The second cut makes two fourteenths. The third cut halves the two large segments. The next two cuts divide the two remaining large segments into thirds and the sixth and seventh cuts divide the remaining two large pieces in the same way.

For 16 portions you need eight diagonal cuts. The first two cuts divide the cake into quarters. The next two cuts halve each quater. The cake is now in eighths and four further cuts will divide each of these in half again.

For 18 portions you need nine diagonal cuts. Divide the cake in half. The second cut marks off two eighteenths. The next three cuts divide the large segments into quarters and then these are in turn halved with the remaining four cuts.

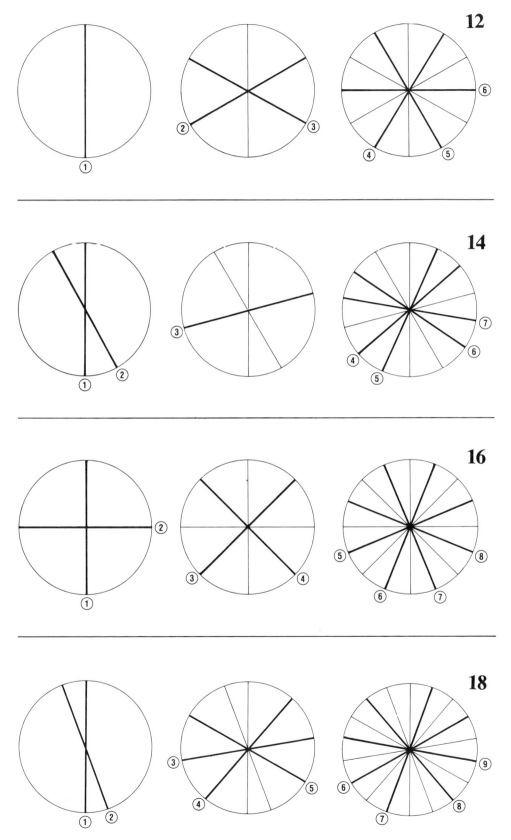

Utensils and equipment

Nowadays there is no limit to the amount of baking utensils and equipment that are available and every cook must decide for him or herself what utensils they themselves need. A lot of the manual processes, and even the complete process in some cases, can now be done mechanically of course.

The photographs on the right cover almost the complete range of equipment for a domestic kitchen, but are restricted to manual processes. Just as the step-by-step photographs at the beginning of the book deal mainly with manual preparation, the choice of utensils here has been limited by the same considerations. Most people will be familiar enough already with the mechanical and electrical appliances found in most modern household kitchens.

It is hoped that the photographs and descriptions of the utensils and tins will demonstrate the wide choice available and make the job of choosing what to buy easier. Baking requires special utensils and especially tins which do not form part of 'standard' kitchen equipment. But even with standard equipment one can make a start on baking and success does not depend entirely on having the right equipment.

If you begin on the path of home-baking by making the simplest recipes (the basic recipes which are explained by series of photographs in this book) you will only need a minimum of equipment. The main thing is to have a reliable oven which functions properly and a large worktop.

The choice of further equipment and utensils will depend on whether you want a kitchen on professional lines and on how often you intend to bake. If you are only going to make cakes occasionally there is no need to buy equipment which will only be required once, or at the most twice, a year.

It is possible to improvise in baking, but not at every stage. For the inexperienced success depends on following the recipe and method exactly, and here weighing and measuring correctly are very important and the relevant equipment is indispensable. You need scales which are accurate, a measuring jug to measure larger liquid measures while for small liquid measures you can use a graduated measuring cylinder. Very small quantities are given in the recipes in teaspoons and the smallest of all in pinches. This does not call for the fingertip sensitivity of the professional chef and should not worry the beginner unduly.

The experienced chef should not need detailed advice on equipment for most will have learnt all they need to know from past experience. They will no doubt have bought a marble slab already, having found that no other material is as good for working with chilled pastries or marzipan, and they will know where to use electrical appliances to save their muscle power without affecting quality. And only if this requirement can be met should the pastry-cook consider using mechanical aids.

Electrical equipment is not included in this section, since there are no appliances exclusive to baking which have not already been dealt with in the section on basic recipes.

Stainless steel saucepan, specially designed for an electric hob, stainless steel can be used to cook any ingredients. Copper saucepans with stainless steel lining. Ideal for cooking on gas. Conduct heat excellently. The best pans for working with sugar. Wood-framed sieve with metal or plastic mesh. For sifting flour or similar ingredients. Ideal for straining custard and fruit purée. Measuring cylinder, graduated glass tube for measuring small volumes of liquid.
Plastic measuring jug for larger liquid measures.
Stainless steel measuring jug, has the added advantage of being suitable for measuring hot liquids or for heating liquids.
Saccharometer, for measuring the density of sugar when making syrup.
Sugar thermometer, in degrees Celsius and Fahrenheit, with protective wire casing, for measuring temperature when boiling sugar.

Tartlet tins, plain or fluted, available in different diameters.
Fluted flan tins, 2.5-cm/1-in deep, 18–25 cm/8–10 in. in diameter. Tins with loose bases are ideal.
Aluminium sponge or flan rings, available in different depths and sizes. Stand on baking sheet and paper for baking or hold filled cake in shape.
Baking paper, excellent base for baking any type of cake.
Pie tins, for round tarts or pies with sloping edge.

Rolling pin with moving centre.
Available up to 10-cm/4-in. in diameter.
Pyrex rolling pin, comes with rings of various thickness which fit over the ends and allow easy rolling to a given thickness.
Plain rolling pin, helpful when lining tins with pastry; the most common rolling pin in France.
Patterned rolling pin. Used to produce a checked effect on marzipan or pastry. Also available to produce grooves.
Pastry wheel, plain or fluted.
Ruler, for marking rolled pastry.
Pastry stencils, domed tin shapes with a central hole through which they are held, are ideal for drawing circles.
Cake bases in aluminium or cardboard.
Sugar dredger for icing sugar, for kitchen use.
Cake cutter in plastic or tin.
Available for 12–18 portions.
Wire rack with tin. Used as base when covering large or small cakes with melted chocolate.

Balloon whisk with steel or wooden handle in various sizes. For beating sponge mixtures, egg whites and cream and stirring small quantities.
Wooden spoon, for stirring and binding custards.
Wooden spatula, for beating.
Wide-topped mixing bowl in copper, the ideal bowl for whisking meringue.
Stainless steel bowls, rounded shape with slightly flattened base makes whisking easier than in flat-bottomed basin.
Plastic mixing bowl set. These inexpensive bowls are ideal for beating and whisking providing they are kept away from direct heat.
Shallow plastic bowls, ideal for mixing small quantities and good for the refrigerator if covered in cling film or aluminium foil.

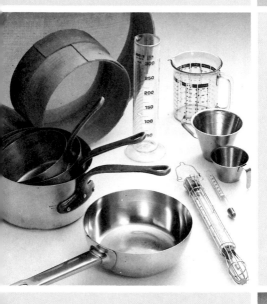

Piping bags in four sizes, in fabric or plastic.
Piping nozzles used with piping bag.
Most common are plain and fluted versions. There are also a range of more specialised nozzles for piping leaves, flowers etc.
Icing comb in plastic, for decorating cream and butter cream coatings.
Plain and fluted round cutters, basic baking equipment.
Special cutters, available in any shape imaginable.
Heart-shaped cutters can also be used as baking mould.
Cream-horn moulds, available as tubes or narrow cones.
Leaf-cutters for making pastry or marzipan decorations.
Kitchen scales, for precise weighing of ingredients.

Cake knife, straight blade for cutting and spreading all types of cake.
Palette knife in four sizes, for spreading custards and icing.
Angled palette knife, easier to use for spreading flat sheets of pastry particularly on baking sheet.
Fruit knife, pointed knife for all kinds of fruit.
Small pointed knife, used whenever intricate cutting is required.
Metal spatulas, for loosening cakes from baking sheet.
Brushes in various sizes. For thin application of glazes or icings.
Rubber spatula and plastic pastry scraper. Indispensable when making sponge mixtures or custards.
Grater, for finely grated citrus peel.
Citrus knife or zester, removes even strips of rind.

Spring Form cake tins, popular for domestic use. Available in several diameters. In tin, sheet-iron or non-stick finish. Smooth ring mould in various sizes and materials, e.g. aluminium, sheet-iron, tin and non-stick finish.
Loaf tins in non-stick finish, in 25 and 30-cm/10 and 12-in sizes.
Loaf tin in sheet-iron or tin, available in four different sizes. Adjustable loaf tin, adjusts in size from 23 to 38-cm/9 to 15-in aluminium.
Brioche tins, fluted tin moulds which can also be used for other types of cake.

The ceramic Gugelhupf mould, available in many sizes, bakes very evenly. Only disadvantage is that they are breakable.
Rehrücken or Balmoral tin in copper and also in other materials.
Marguerite tin, a copper mould with fluted top. Traditional tin for marguerite cake, but can of course be used for other cakes.
Ring mould in copper or tin; ideal for baking ring sponges, but also good for blancmanges and custards.
Old-fashioned German Gugelhupf mould in copper. Available in a variety of sizes and other materials, e.g. tin, enamel or ovenproof glass.